THE PUNISHMENT IMPERATIVE

The Punishment Imperative

The Rise and Failure of Mass Incarceration in America

Todd R. Clear and Natasha A. Frost

NEW YORK UNIVERSITY PRESS

New York and London

NEW YORK UNIVERSITY PRESS
New York and London
www.nyupress.org

References to Internet websites (URLs) were accurate at the time of writing.
Neither the author nor New York University Press is responsible for URLs that
may have expired or changed since the manuscript was prepared.

LIBRARY OF CONGRESS CATALOGING-IN-PUBLICATION DATA
Clear, Todd R.
The punishment imperative : the rise and failure of mass incarceration in America / Todd R.
Clear and Natasha A. Frost.
pages cm
Includes bibliographical references and index.
ISBN 978-0-8147-1719-6 (cl : alk. paper)
1. Imprisonment—United States. 2. Corrections—United States. 3. Criminal justice,
Administration of—United States. I. Frost, Natasha. II. Title.
HV9471.C574   2014
365'.973—dc23

New York University Press books are printed on acid-free paper, and their binding materials
are chosen for strength and durability. We strive to use environmentally responsible
suppliers and materials to the greatest extent possible in publishing our books.

Manufactured in the United States of America
c 10 9 8 7 6 5 4 3 2 1

Also available as an ebook

For Jaeli and Harlow Adrienne—that they might be part of the generation that brings about an end to mass incarceration.

CONTENTS

ACKNOWLEDGMENTS

In the academic world, much goes into the order of authorship, particularly for important works such as books. Although we have published this book with the authors listed alphabetically by last name, we emphasize here that we contributed equally to this book from conception through completion. Anyone who knows us knows that we work so well together because we each bring a different set of skills to every project, and so we each acknowledge the important contribution that the other made to seeing this book come to life. The gestation period was extended. We started writing this book before Natasha's daughter was even conceived . . . she will soon turn three. Clearly, some time has passed since we first proposed this book to NYU Press, and so we first and foremost thank our NYU Press editor, Ilene Kalish, for her endless patience and her unwavering support. Although we are sure that at times she thought she might never see the final manuscript, Ilene never once lost enthusiasm for the project.

That so much time passed was actually quite fortuitous because much changed between year-end 2008, when we first proposed the book and the overall incarceration rate was still increasing annually, and year-end 2012, when we have seen gradual, but steady, declines in prison populations for several years in a row. Subtle but persistent changes in incarceration-rate trends allowed us to rethink the core argument of this book in a way that would not have been possible had we met our initial publication schedule, or the one after that, or the one after that. We thank an anonymous but extremely helpful reviewer for his or her comments on the first complete version of the manuscript. Those comments allowed us to rethink the book's structure and ultimately to make the end the beginning.

As is often the case, the central ideas in this book reflect work that we have been doing together and separately for a number of years now. In many ways, this book represents a book-length expansion of an article that we first published several years ago (Natasha A. Frost and Todd R. Clear, "Understanding Mass Incarceration as a Grand Social Experiment," *Studies in Law, Politics, and Society,* 47 (2009), 159–91). The original argument made in our *Studies* article shows up throughout the book, but selected portions form the foundation of chapter 3 in particular. Similarly, chapter 7 unites revised versions of two recent articles arguing for reducing prison populations and pursuing justice reinvestment strategies, respectively (Todd R. Clear and Dennis R. Schrantz, "Strategies for Reducing Prison Populations," *The Prison Journal,* 91/3 (2011), 138S–59S; Todd R. Clear, "A Private-Sector, Incentives-Based Model for Justice Reinvestment," *Criminology & Public Policy,* 10/3 (2011), 585–608), and the reentry policy section of chapter 4 represents a revised version of a chapter written for a policy reader (Natasha A. Frost, "Reentry as a Process Rather Than a Moment," in K. Ismaili [ed.], *U.S. Criminal Justice Policy: A Contemporary Reader* [Boston: Jones and Bartlett, 2011], 159–82).

There are so many who have contributed in important ways over the years to the development of our thinking around the problem of mass incarceration—we could not possibly thank them all. A handful who certainly deserve mention include Michelle Alexander, Jim Austin, Katherine Beckett, Eric Cadora, David Garland, Michael Jacobson, Jim Lynch, Shadd Maruna, Marc Mauer, Debbie Mukamal, Joan Petersilia, Jonathan Simon, Michael Tonry, Jeremy Travis, Loic Wacquant, and Bruce Western.

Natasha would like to especially thank the members of the junior faculty writing group at Northeastern—Katya Botchkovar, Carlos Cuevas, Kevin Drakulich, Amy Farrell, Jake Stowell, and Greg Zimmerman—for their helpful comments on early versions of some of the chapters in this book (and for allowing her to regularly crash the junior faculty writing group sessions post-tenure). Special thanks also go to Nicole Rafter, who serves as the mentor for the writing group, and who helps us stay on track when sessions start to go scarily awry. Suffice it to say, criminology would be a much more exciting field if this group were responsible for titling manuscripts.

We close by acknowledging the love and support of our families and friends. The writing of a book is time-consuming and can be draining—not just for its authors but also for those who have to share time and space with them. For some reason, Dina and Bob put up with us through it all. When they grow tired of listening, we turn to others. In many ways, Todd has been trying to end mass incarceration since before it even really began, so he could not possibly acknowledge all those who have suffered through his explanations of concentrated disadvantage, coercive mobility, and the impacts of incarceration on individuals, families, and communities. He thanks them all for hearing him out even when they disagreed. Natasha is quite certain that her closest friend, Lisa McLaughlin, will be the first (and perhaps only) personal friend to read this book from beginning to end and looks forward to the spirited debates that will almost certainly follow. She thanks Lisa in particular for her love, support, and friendship over the past several years. She also remembers her brother-in-law, Andy Ellison, whose life ended far too soon while she was writing this book, and stands in awe of her sister Andrea and their kids, Austin, Tyler, and Isabel, for their strength and resolve in a time of overwhelming loss and grief.

Finally, our youngest kids, Jaeli and Harlow, to whom this book is dedicated, offered welcome distraction when the words just weren't coming. Our love for you knows no bounds.

1

The Beginning of the End of the Punishment Imperative

America's criminal justice system has deteriorated to the point that it is a national disgrace. Its irregularities and inequities cut against the notion that we are a society founded on fundamental fairness. Our failure to address this problem has caused the nation's prisons to burst their seams with massive overcrowding, even as our neighborhoods have become more dangerous. We are wasting billions of dollars and diminishing millions of lives.
—Senator Jim Webb, March 3, 2009[1]

In the early 1970s, the United States embarked on a subtle change in the way it punished people for crimes. The prison population, stable for half a century, shifted upward. At first, this was little noticed, so much so that even as the number of people behind bars was inching upward, prominent criminologists were hypothesizing that there was an underlying stability to the use of imprisonment across the United States.[2] By the end of that decade, the change was no longer subtle, and commentators began to describe a new harshness in the U.S. attitude toward crime and justice.

In the next chapter, we tell the story of the special character of American punitiveness. It is an extraordinary story of remarkable raw numbers that are all the more astonishing for the way we have gotten used to them. As we shall show, nowhere else in the democratic world, and at no other time in Western history, has there been the kind of relentless punitive spirit as has been ascendant in the United States for more than a generation. That relentless punitive spirit is the philosophy—the point of view—that we call "The Punishment Imperative." It has been the rationale for mass incarceration.

The short story is that this "new" attitude has become old; the punitiveness of the 1970s was nothing compared with the years to come. For the next forty years, virtually every aspect of the punishment system, from the way people were processed before trial to the way people were confined after conviction, grew harder. Like a drunk whose life descends increasingly into the abyss, U.S. penal policies grew steadily and inexorably toward an ever harder edge. Thresholds of punitiveness people never thought our democracy would ever have to confront became a part of official policy: life without parole and death penalties for young people; lengthy detention before trial; humiliation and long periods of extreme isolation during confinement; decades behind bars for minor thefts and possession of drugs. Such developments would have been unthinkable in the 1960s, but they would become the leading edge of penal reform in the years that followed.

We argue that it is useful to think of this period in U.S. penal history as a kind of grand social experiment that we call "the Punishment Imperative." As we will argue in more detail in chapter 3, the Punishment Imperative began with the co-alignment of an array of forces that came together to make the explosive growth in the penal system a social and political possibility.[3] A decade of rising crime rates fueled public alarm about basic safety, and crime also came to stand as a symbol for the disruption of standing patterns of entitlement and privilege. Media attention to victimizations by those who were formerly incarcerated fueled national sympathy for a victims' rights movement in the criminal justice system. A nonpartisan consensus developed that addressing crime and fear of crime was a high political priority. The emergence of a large pool of young black men who were unconnected to the labor market provided a group that could serve as a symbolic enemy around which to rally political forces and carry out a "war," but they were also a tangible target group that required some form of practical social control. The political economy made get-tough politics a successful strategy. Economic growth made penal-system investment possible, and working-/

middle-class job creation resulting from that growth provided further energy for an ever growing penal system.

Certainly, the story of the Punishment Imperative can be (and has been) told with different emphases and redirected nuances, but any version of the story will have to offer some aspect or another of the scenario above. The times came together to enable a great, though poorly articulated, social experiment in expanded social control. It has now been going on for almost forty years.

As we write, there are signs—strong signs—that the experiment is coming to an end. As we will argue, a combination of political shifts, accumulating empirical evidence, and fiscal pressures has replaced the commonsense idea that the system must be "tough" with a newly developing consensus that what has happened with the penal system can no longer be justified or sustained. Without fanfare, the results of the great punishment experiment have begun to come in, and they are in ever so many ways disappointing. The emotional and practical energy for punitive harshness, seemingly irresistible just a short time ago, now is oddly passé.

Indeed, the entire corrections system is, for the first time in more than a generation, shrinking. In the years 2009 and 2010, the number of people in both prisons and jails dropped—about 2 percent each year. In 2009, the number of people on probation and parole also dropped (about 1 percent), meaning that in 2010, for the first time in thirty-eight years, the number of people under correctional authority at the end of the year was smaller than the number at the beginning of that year.[4] This marks, we think, the unofficial "end" of the Punishment Imperative.

This book, then, is about the rise and fall of the Punishment Imperative. Volumes have been written about what the world has come to see as the special American punitiveness.[5] No other nation can tell quite the same story. What makes our retelling of this story useful, we hope, is that we offer it at a significant moment in the narrative of that story—its waning. Our plan is not just to document the character of the special American punishment era but also to show how its development, over time, produced the dynamics that inevitably fueled its conclusion.

This is not to say, of course, that the special American punitiveness has stopped in the same way one turns off an overhead light. The public sentiment for harsh treatment of people who break the law remains deeply seated in the political mind and social character of the nation. Moreover, the consequences of American punitiveness run far too deep and spread far too broadly to be easily discarded. Given these realities, the end of the grand experiment will feel less like a lightbulb being turned off and more like the slow cooling of a white-hot oven.

In fact, the waning of the punitive ethic has been going on for a while. At its height, in the 1980s, the correctional growth rate was typically as high as 8 percent per year or higher, but we have not seen that kind of growth rate for more than a decade. For the last ten years or so, the system has been more likely to grow at around 2 percent a year. This is the statistical evidence that suggests we have reached a watershed point in U.S. correctional history, when the steady rise in imprisonment shifts to a steady—if less steep—decline. The decline in the overall correctional population is but the current realization of a longer trend, in which the steam behind the Punishment Imperative has been declining for some time. Indeed, today's drop in correctional populations is consistent with a gradual decline in growth that has been going on since at least the beginning of the 2000s. The so-called fall, then, of the punishment agenda has been going on for some time, but its existence was masked by the fact that numbers continued to grow even as the energy for growth was dissipating.

In just the past couple of years, it seems we have reached a turning point in discourse around mass incarceration in particular. For many years, scholars of penology published books describing and seeking to better understand the impetus for the growth in punishment that resulted in mass incarceration. Scholarly attention then turned to documenting the deleterious effects of mass incarceration for individuals, families, and communities—with scholars documenting the ways in which mass incarceration had a tendency to exacerbate some of the most vexing social problems of our times. Today, though, we are increasingly seeing scholars write about reducing our reliance on incarceration and offering strategies for accomplishing meaningful reductions in prison populations without compromising public safety.[6]

And scholars are not the only ones with voices in this chorus. Journalists too have begun to publish feature stories profiling people and places that are trying to move away from incarceration and find new or innovative ways to deal with crime when and where it occurs.[7] Politicians are increasingly less concerned with coming across as "tough on crime" and more inclined to talk about ways to be "smart on crime." Federal legislation passed in recent years has a remarkably different character than legislation passed just one decade earlier.[8] Policymaking in the penal arena no longer consists solely of new ideas for increased punishments. Ideas in good currency today often emphasize lesser punishments as ways to improve public safety.[9]

The special American punitiveness, ascendant for more than a generation, ran so deeply in the political culture that it still resonates, and many (if not most) people would find it odd to suggest that it is a phenomenon in decline. But it is, in fact, the current political shifts that offer the most convincing evidence that something has changed. In the last three presidential elections, crime has scarcely been an issue. This pattern has been repeated in gubernatorial and other electoral campaigns. States such as Louisiana and Mississippi that reveled in their own homegrown, "get-tough" politics now lead the nation in prison downsizing.[10] Their governors announce prison reduction programs, including release programs that would have been unthinkable a decade ago. There was a time when even a hint of a policy that might have resulted in prison releases or reductions in sentencing would have spelled certain political death. Today, at least thirteen states are closing prisons after reducing prison populations.[11] That this kind of policy is no longer political anathema is a leading indicator of how much has changed.

What this brief discussion shows is that the Punishment Imperative was a *policy* experiment. Without question there were changes in the dynamics of crime, but they were tangential to the profound changes in crime policy described in chapter 4 that have dominated the American criminal justice scene for nearly forty years. What happened was

a deliberate, if haphazardly conceived, agenda of more and more punishment—a Punishment Imperative. Precisely because this was a policy
agenda, rather than some sort of social circumstance, we are able to ana-
lyze this time in American history using the grand social experiment
framework.

In the remainder of this chapter we describe what we think of as the
end of the great penal experiment that took place between 1970 and 2010
and outline the prospects for something new to emerge—something
with far less emphasis on prisons and much more emphasis on a con-
glomerate of correctional approaches. We argue that we have reached an
era in which a new milieu is fueling the prison populations and penal
system. Although we offer a fuller version of what we think that new
model might look like in our concluding chapter,[12] the short version
would probably read something like this:

*The worldwide economic crisis of 2008 has created pressure on U.S.
state and local governments to reduce their costs. One of the fastest-
growing costs is the prison system, and so there is impetus to control
prison costs—and that means reducing the number of prisoners. There is
bipartisan agreement that controlling prison costs is an important immediate objective. Because crime has been dropping nationally for more
than a decade, the get-tough movement has lost some of its salience with
the public (and therefore the politicians). There is a new bipartisan consensus that improving postrelease success for people who leave prison is
a high priority, and this has created public support for reentry programs.
A plethora of news media stories and social science studies about mass
incarceration and the plight of people who have been to prison has bal-
anced the national appetite for victims' rights with a sentiment that the
system has gotten out of control. There is growing belief that the "drug
war" has been, if not a complete failure, then at least a mistake. Increasingly, there is a call for correctional programs to be based on "evidence"
rather than ideology. One of the most popular new national programs is
"justice reinvestment," which seeks to control the rising costs of prisons
and invest the savings in projects that will enhance, rather than further
damage, communities.*

Justice reinvestment, the emerging model we advocate for in the concluding chapter, offers a new framework for the penal system to approach its work. To the extent that justice reinvestment—or something like it—becomes dominant, it signals a new era: the end, if slow and vacillating, to the grand penal experiment.

The End of an Era: Evidence from the Field

We do not have to look far to see strong evidence that a new conversation has taken hold in penal policy circles. As we write, evidence mounts daily that the experiment is grinding to a halt. As of August 2011, at least thirteen states—one-fourth of the states—have closed or plan to close a prison.[13] Michigan has already closed twenty-two prisons, and even the notoriously punitive state of Texas plans to close a 100-year-old prison. New York State, after a series of reforms that roll back the reach of the incredibly harsh Rockefeller Drug Laws, now plans to close seven prisons.[14] This is a trend that, in many ways, is stronger in traditionally very conservative states than in what most people think of as more liberal states.[15]

Great examples are provided by the states of Mississippi and Georgia.[16] Between 1997 and 1999, Mississippi opened seven new prisons. Soon after, the state's prisons and jails became so overcrowded that local sheriffs were in crisis. By 2008, the corrections budget had tripled to $348 million, and the state was facing an additional increase in population of at least 20 percent. Then the 2008 recession hit, and from the governor on down, people knew something needed to be done. Plans were developed to reduce the prison population immediately with a goal of one-fifth reduction by 2013. The dominant driver is, of course, the current fiscal crisis.[17] But, so far, the plan is politically popular, and the current cuts have been accomplished with both a drop in recidivism rates and no increase in crime rates.

Georgia has a similar story of unprecedented (and ultimately unsustainable) correctional growth.[18] In the twenty or so years between 1990 and 2010, Georgia's prison population more than doubled in size and

Georgia's incarceration rate became one of the highest in the nation. The state spent a staggering billion dollars a year on corrections, much of which was spent paying for the incarceration of nonviolent offenders (who account for close to 60 percent of the state prison population). To make matters worse, prison population projections based on the criminal justice policies in place predicted growth in the next five years that would require several hundred million dollars more in taxpayer dollars. A Special Council on Criminal Justice Reform for Georgians convened to study the factors driving prison growth concluded that very little of the growth could be explained by crime—almost all of the growth was explained by the series of policies that dictated who would go to prison (increasingly, nonviolent offenders) and how long they would stay (longer than they had previously).[19] Moreover, recidivism rates among released offenders had not changed, and, while the substantial growth in incarceration might have enhanced public safety, alternatives to the most expensive form of correctional control for nonviolent offenders could potentially offer equal or greater public-safety returns at a substantial cost savings. In May of 2012, on the basis of the recommendations made by the council, Georgia's governor, Nathan Deal, signed a public safety reform bill (H.B. 1176) into law. Georgia's comprehensive criminal justice reform bill is expected "to avert all the anticipated growth in prison population and costs over the next five years."[20]

Nearly every state corrections system has some version of the Georgia or Mississippi story. The states are looking for ways to reduce spending, and that means—operationally—a reduction in the most expensive forms of correctional control: confinement (see table 1.1). We would be remiss if we did not acknowledge that some states (including Illinois, Arkansas, and Iowa) have seen continued (and sometimes substantial) increases in their prison populations in recent years.[21] Indeed, some will no doubt argue that our prediction is premature. But a visit to the Council of State Government's Justice Center website shows that each new day, a new state story unfolds.[22]

The number of states actively working to either close prisons or introduce legislation to ultimately reduce prison populations is

Table 1.1: State Efforts to Reduce Prison Populations

States that have recently closed or proposed to close prisons:[1]

Colorado	Connecticut	Florida
Georgia	Michigan	Nevada
New York	North Carolina	Oregon
Rhode Island	Texas	
Washington	Wisconsin	

States that have recently enacted criminal justice reforms designed to reduce prison populations:[2]

Alabama	Alaska	Arizona
Arkansas	California	Connecticut
Delaware	Florida	Georgia
Hawaii	Kentucky	Louisiana
Maryland	Minnesota	Missouri
Nevada	New Hampshire	New Jersey
New York	North Carolina	Ohio
Pennsylvania	Rhode Island	South Carolina
South Dakota	Texas	Vermont
Virginia	Washington	

1. Nicole D. Porter, "On the Chopping Block: State Prison Closings" (Washington, DC: Sentencing Project, 2011).
2. NGA Center for Best Practices, "Issue Brief: State Efforts in Sentencing and Corrections Reform" (Washington, DC: National Governors Association, 2011).

unprecedented—and most of this activity has taken place very recently, since 2010. It is too simplistic to say that the recession has been the sole cause of this shift and that when good times return, so will the nation's previously insatiable appetite for prisons. In the high days of the grand penal experiment, there were also recessions, with the usual clarion call for fiscally responsible correctional practices. But they never affected the prison growth trajectory much. In the midst of some of the country's toughest times in the 1970s and again in the 1980s, correctional systems seemed impervious to budgetary woes.

Moreover, the seismic shifts in the way punishment is now thought of are not simply housed in fiscal realities. For example, the Right on Crime movement, championed by some of the same Republican leaders who had been so captivated by the Punishment Imperative in prior years, is an express abandonment of the "punishment first" model of penal reform that dominated the scene for the last generation.[23] But it is not simply a fiscal reform position. Arguing that the correctional system has grown way too big and way too onerous, it uses an appeal to fiscal realities to support its recommendations but also appeals to evidence, to common sense, and to ethical thinking. The Right on Crime Statement of Principles, written as it was by some of the most conservative political thinkers in the country, is evidence that the center of energy in the prison reform has moved away from the Punishment Imperative. The third paragraph of Right on Crime's Statement of Principles explicitly addresses overreliance on incarceration:

> Conservatives are known for being tough on crime, but we must also be tough on criminal justice spending. That means demanding more cost-effective approaches that enhance public safety. A clear example is our reliance on prisons, which serve a critical role by incapacitating dangerous offenders and career criminals but are not the solution for every type of offender. And in some instances, they have the unintended consequence of hardening nonviolent, low-risk offenders—making them a greater risk to the public than when they entered.[24]

Given their exorbitant costs, prisons and prison spending have been identified as priority issues, with Right on Crime offering a number of conservative solutions to the problem of mass incarceration, several of which are expressly aimed at reducing prison populations. Likewise, Mark Kleiman's study of Hawaii's Opportunity Probation with Enforcement (HOPE), which argues for a strict model of probation enforcement, might seem at first blush to be more of the same Punishment Imperative thinking. Indeed, had it been written a decade ago, the book's title might have been "Time to Get Tough with Probationers."

Instead, Kleiman seeks to distinguish this work from the failed ideas of the past by using a provocative title: *When Brute Force Fails: How to Have Less Crime and Less Punishment.*[25] The fact that a new intervention strategy that is based on the deterrence model is sold as "less" punishment is symbolic of where we are today. The Punishment Imperative has lost energy.

So while the current fiscal crisis is *a motivating factor* for the downsizing of the correctional system, it is not by itself *the cause*.[26] The de-escalation of punishment is possible mainly because the sentiment of punitiveness has undergone an important shift. Here are some of the forces that have contributed to that change in fundamental values.

Falling Crime Rates

If the 2008 recession provides the motivation for reducing the overall costs of the penal system, the decade-long drop in crime rates has enabled that conversation to take place. Broadly speaking, crime rates across the country have declined by 35 to 40 percent in the 1990s, led by a quite remarkable decline in New York City of more than 70 percent.[27] Crime rates continued their relatively remarkable declines into and through the 2000s. In 2010, violent crime hit its lowest rate in forty years—in other words, violent crime rates across the United States are now generally lower than they were when the Punishment Imperative was launched.[28] As we entered 2012, cities across the country were still reporting record declines in crime. In Los Angeles, for example, the crime rate hit its lowest level since 1952.[29] Other large cities, including Boston, Chicago, and Dallas, also continue to report declining, and in some cases record low, levels of crime—particularly violent crime.[30] To be sure, the drop in crime has not been uniform across all places. Some cities and states have been much slower to experience these changes or have experienced more moderate declines. But these fluctuating local experiences cannot deflect the major point: partly as a result of falling crime rates, crime has fallen off the main list of concerns Americans express in public opinion polls.[31] And with crime out of the public mind, a window of opportunity for real policy reform has now presented itself. The most remarkable illustration of this new state of affairs comes from the so-called red states (Georgia, Mississippi, Kansas, South Carolina, Texas, etc.), where tough crime policy has been a mainstay of political life for decades. These states have capitalized on the lack of angst about crime in the public mind to enact relatively sweeping sentencing and prison-reform initiatives.[32]

What this means is that the politics of crime is, to an extent not seen for a generation, on the back burner. Exceptions occur when significant criminal events hit the front pages of newspapers,[33] and in cities where violence remains high, crime talk among political aspirants is significant. But there is no longer the overwhelming sense that a label of "soft on crime" is a mortal political liability.

The waning of crime from the political scene should not surprise us. There has been a gradual shift in this direction in national politics for a while. Bill Clinton de-toothed the issue with a range of policies that positioned him and his party as undeniably "tough on crime": COPS funding, truth-in-sentencing legislation, and boot camps are representative examples. Indeed, many of the policies that have since served to make a prisoner's return to the community all the more difficult (including housing and welfare restrictions that will be described more fully in chapter 4) were Clinton-era policies. Through these and other initiatives, Clinton was able to demonstrate that Democrats could be just as tough on crime as their Republican counterparts. While some of these Clinton initiatives have produced policy debacles from which states are still trying to recover, they were undeniably political winners. In the several presidential elections since *Clinton v. Bush* (1992), crime and public safety have received barely a mention in the campaign discourse. In the most recent 2012 election season, crime made an appearance only once during the presidential debates and that came during the "town hall" style debate when an undecided voter from the audience asked both Obama and Romney to address whether they supported an assault weapons ban.[34] Crime and crime control are currently not priority issues for the American public and have not been for some time.[35]

All of this may change, of course, if crime rates start to rise again. And undoubtedly there is no political vaccination against the problems of crime and public safety. But what has seemed to be a political truism, what Jonathon Simon labels "governing through crime," no longer seems as unflinchingly true.[36] And even in the face of difficult criminal statistics and those random events that always seem to come along, the political reality is far more nuanced today than it has been for a generation. A main reason is the long, steady, and national drop in crime.[37]

Reentry as a Concept

The symbolic power of the felon has also changed. Willie Horton remains one of the organizing stories in contemporary crime politics, and George H. W. Bush used visual images of the furloughed felon, a black-skinned repeat violent offender, to successfully chain his election opponent (Massachusetts governor Michael Dukakis) with racially provocative dead weight. One consequence of this political event is that we came to connect the fear of personal safety with the image of the violent felon whose black skin marked him as dangerous.[38]

It is ironic, then, that Bush's son, George W. Bush, put policies in place to soften this collective mindset. His landmark legislative effort to build a new foundation for people returning to the community from prison—the Second Chance Act—provided a new fiscal and programmatic infrastructure of services and support for people returning to the communities from prison. But it did more than that. It helped give standing to a new way to refer to the process of coming back from prison: *reentry*.

The production of the idea of "reentry" was a masterstroke of conceptual change. It reflects a nearly complete turn-around in the visualization of the problem. No longer do we refer to those people as "felons" or "parolees." They are not seen as fixed entities defined by their past, lawbreaking acts. They are instead to be seen as people in motion, people undergoing change—going through a process.[39] They are "in reentry." The term suggests that what these people face is a tough transition, a process that requires them to change the way they relate to the world and to circumstances that will be different later on than they are today. The connotations of "reentry" are ever so preferable to what reformers had to work with when the dominant public idea was Willie Horton and the many dozens of similar images on the public mind. Reentry is more subtle, more dynamic, and opens the door to the idea of transition and, ultimately, redemption.[40]

While the Second Chance Act and the rhetoric surrounding it were a central source of the emerging power of "reentry," this was not solely the work of George W. Bush. Several distinguished scholars, most notably Jeremy Travis (then director of the National Institute of Justice and now president of John Jay College of Criminal Justice) and Joan Petersilia (of Stanford Law School) made reentry the core concern of their research, writing noteworthy books on the topic.[41] Research organizations, like the Urban Institute, made prisoner reentry one of their focal issues. The public organizations associated with this work, the American Probation and Parole Association (APPA) and the America Correctional Association (ACA), eagerly adopted the terminology of reentry in day-to-day practice, and mayors and governors opened up "Offices of Reentry."

As often happens, in the end this simple change in terminology came to stand for a profound shift in thinking. Where we once saw "ex-felons and parolees" as problem people who need to be "controlled" in order for us to be protected, we came to see "people in reentry" as those who deserve a "second chance" and require support and services in order to "succeed." The public mind shifted in subtle ways from the pessimistic problem of "dangerous classes" to a more hopeful idea of "potentially productive fellow citizens." The power of this shift can be overstated, of course, but neither should it be underestimated. And the fact that it could happen is more evidence that the Punishment Imperative has run its course.

Evidence

Finally, it is becoming more widely accepted that the grand penal experiment has produced, at best, disappointing results. As our reviews in chapters 5 and 6 will demonstrate, there has been a substantial body of research on the main programs and strategies of the get-tough movement, and they have, with only isolated exceptions, been found wanting. Just as significantly, the unintended consequences of these approaches have become considerably clearer as evidence mounts about the problems created by large penal populations concentrated among minority populations.

The availability of this growing body of evidence—and the dearth of contradictory studies—has probably not been a definitive force in the waning of the Punishment Imperative, but it has had an important role. If the drop in crime made the experiment's end possible, and the fiscal crisis made it necessary, then the burgeoning evidence for its failure has made it reasonable. As we will show in chapter 3, grand social experiments develop their own "knowledge," in the sense that a shared public reality undergirds the energy for the social movement. With regard to the Punishment Imperative, this body of critical studies, now more widely disseminated among the intellectual, opinion-leading public, means that a fledgling foundation is growing for a wholesale rethinking of the idea.

In the 1970s and 1980s, when the Punishment Imperative was in its heyday, what we "knew" about penal policy could fairly be summarized as follows: (1) rehabilitation programs do not work, (2) a small number of highly active law violators are responsible for most crime, (3) the odds of these active offenders being caught and punished are too small, and (4) prisons prevent crime through incapacitation. These were the empirical foundations for the Punishment Imperative, and by the 1980s, they were widely accepted as demonstrably true statements about our penal system, shaping the reforms of the era.

The new evidence—facts and studies that have helped bring about the end of the Punishment Imperative—do not so much contradict these "truths" as they replace them with a different set of more nuanced "truths." The motivating data for new penological thinking stress a different set of points: (1) carefully designed and implemented correctional strategies can result in significant reductions in rates of recidivism;

(2) the growth in the penal system, especially prisons, has resulted in a series of collateral problems that produce inequality and reproduce injustice in ways that are inconsistent with sound democratic policy; (3) prison populations can be reduced without harming public safety; and (4) the general public supports a penal system that provides opportunities for people who are convicted of crimes to reform and return to society as productive citizens.

Along with this new factual foundation for action has come, predictably, a new set of policies to reflect them. Where once policy reform had to meet a criterion of "toughness," today the new guiding phrase is "evidence-based." Policymakers are asked to articulate the empirical foundation for the solutions they offer, which shifts the burden of proof from the heated threshold of harshness to a much cooler, more nuanced foundation of an evidence base. This shift has assigned a premium to programmatic thinking, and in place of legislative action we now see practical program strategies occupying the center of the debate. Ideas that reduce costs, increase rates of success, and support the reform of people who break the law now have an advantage over other ideas, and the shift in the evidentiary foundation of corrections is a key reason this is true.

The Argument of This Book

This book then is about an American idea that took root in the 1970s, rose to dominate discourse and practice through the 1980s and 1990s, and has, as we enter the second decade of the new century, shown distinct signs of having run its course. In the chapters that follow, we explore the dynamics of that major American idea, which we call a grand social experiment in punishment. We describe the sources of this experiment, its main elements, and its most important consequences. If we are right in our argument, then we truly find ourselves at one of those rare, momentous times in history, for after more than a generation of unremittingly punitive penal policy, we have now arrived at a new threshold of what will be normal for the U.S. penal system.

2

The Contours of Mass Incarceration

The United States has a punishment system that no one would know-
ingly have built from the ground up. It is often unjust, it is unduly severe
and it does enormous damage to the lives of black Americans.
—Michael Tonry, 1995

As the United States' prison and jail population approached, and then, in
midyear 2002, exceeded the two million mark for the first time,[1] commentators—both expert and otherwise—no longer found it sufficient to refer
to incarceration in the United States as simply incarceration: incarceration
became mass incarceration. How else could one convey the enormity of
the size of the America's incarcerated population? More than one in one
hundred Americans were behind bars,[2] and, at the beginning of the new
millennium, 5.6 million Americans had served time in prison.[3] At these
rates, almost 7 percent of the U.S. population could have expected to be
imprisoned in their lifetime.[4] We did not simply have a lot of people in
prisons and jails; we literally had *millions* of people in prisons and jails.
We had earned the distinction of having the highest incarceration rate in
the world, a rate that far exceeded the incarceration rates of our closest
allies. With just under ten million people incarcerated in prisons and jails
worldwide, America incarcerated more than one-fifth of the world's total
prison population.[5] By any measure, these numbers were staggering.

Most scholars came to agree that, on the basis of its incarceration rate alone, America could fairly be described as the most punitive nation in the world.[6] The United States' incarceration rate of 756 inmates per 100,000 residents far exceeds the incarceration rates of other Western democracies, which generally have rates of less than 200 inmates per 100,000 residents.[7] Our incarceration rate has been the highest among Western industrialized countries since at least the mid-1990s.[8] In the fifteen years since we achieved that status, the number of people incarcerated across the United States has grown by more than a million, and we now incarcerate more people than any other nation in the world, in terms of both the absolute number of people in prison and the incarceration rate per one hundred thousand people.[9] As depicted in figure 2.1, the United States leads the world in incarceration (followed by Russia, Rwanda, St. Kitts & Nevis, and Cuba) and has an incarceration rate that is more than four times that of several comparable European nations.[10]

Since 1980, we have seen the U.S. prison population increase by over 373 percent, from 319,598 prisoners in 1980 to 1,543,206 at year-end 2010, and the jail population increase by 324 percent, from 183,988 inmates in 1980 to 748,728 in 2010.[11] At year-end 2010, the overall incarceration rate had reached 731 inmates per 100,000 residents.[12] It might be tempting to think that we had turned to incarceration in lieu of community approaches to punishment—in other words, that we no longer trusted probation and parole to supervise offenders in the community—but we had seen exponential growth across those domains as well.[13] While there were just over one million probationers in 1980, by 2010 that number had grown by 284 percent, to more than four million. Parole had likewise seen unprecedented growth from a parole population of 220,000 in 1980 to one of close to 841,000 in 2010.[14] Figure 2.2 visually documents the growth experienced across all four branches of corrections.

So it was not just prisons and jails that had been affected by relentless growth. The Punishment Imperative had significantly impacted the size of the population under all types of correctional supervision. As astounding as it might sound, the 2.3 million people incarcerated in prisons and jails account for less than one-third of the total correctional

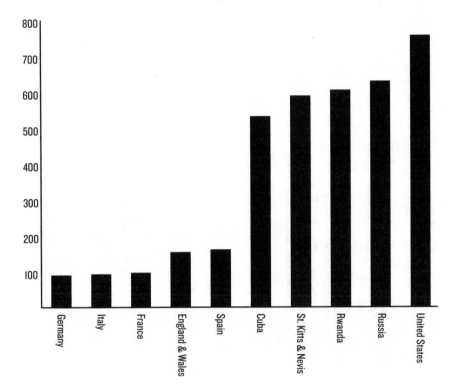

Figure 2.1: International Rates of Incarceration (per 100,000 population). R. Walmsley, *World Prison Population List*, eighth edition (London: International Centre for Prison Studies, 2009)

population. When the population under any form of correctional supervision (probation, parole, or jail/prison) is counted, the numbers are even more staggering, with one in every thirty-one adults across the United States in prison or jail or on probation or parole.[15] In other words, as 2010 drew to a close, more than 7.25 million Americans were currently living under some form of correctional supervision.[16] By way of comparison, in 1980, prisons and jails across the country housed just over five hundred thousand people, and under two million (1,840,000) people were under correctional supervision.[17] To put the growth in perspective, in 2010, we had *half a million more people* in prison or jail alone than we had under any form of correctional supervision just thirty years before.

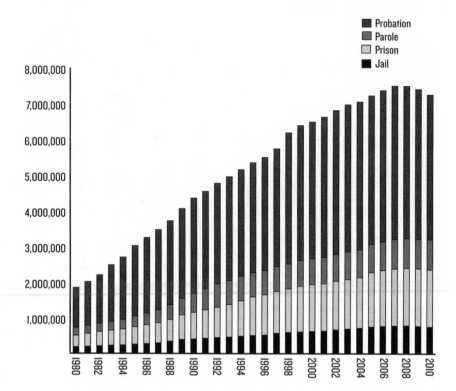

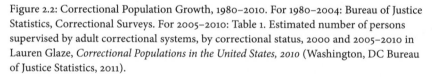

Figure 2.2: Correctional Population Growth, 1980–2010. For 1980–2004: Bureau of Justice Statistics, Correctional Surveys. For 2005–2010: Table 1. Estimated number of persons supervised by adult correctional systems, by correctional status, 2000 and 2005–2010 in Lauren Glaze, *Correctional Populations in the United States, 2010* (Washington, DC Bureau of Justice Statistics, 2011).

Of course this unprecedented growth in corrections came with quite a hefty price tag. In 2006, jurisdictions across the United States spent more than $68 billion on corrections.[18] Although the $68 billion spent on corrections was less than the more than $98 billion spent on policing, between 1982 and 2006, corrections expenditures grew more substantially than expenditures for any other criminal justice function. Direct expenditures on corrections grew from just over $9 billion in 1982 to over $68 billion in 2006 (an increase of 660 percent). By way of comparison, over the same period, direct judicial expenditures increased by

503 percent and direct policing expenditures increased by 420 percent.[19] The vast majority of correctional dollars spent—close to 90 percent— went toward sustaining mass incarceration. With a national average annual price tag of almost $29,000 per person per year of incarceration, it cost taxpayers at least ten times more to incarcerate a person than it would have cost to maintain him or her under supervision in the community.[20] The additional costs might have constituted a worthy invest- ment if demonstrable benefits in terms of public safety could have been claimed, but research had repeatedly demonstrated that prison was no more effective than community supervision (at least in terms of crime prevention). As emphasized in a report issued by the Pew Center on the States, "serious, chronic and violent offenders belong behind bars, for a long time, and the expense of locking them up is justified many times over. But, for hundreds of thousands of lower-level inmates, incarcera- tion costs taxpayers more than it saves in prevented crime."[21]

So who goes to prison? Prison population trend data, which suggest that over half of the current prison population is made up of violent offenders, exaggerate the extent to which we lock up serious violent offenders (see figure 2.3). First, the offense-type classifications (violent, property, drug, and public order) used to calculate these population trend figures can include both very serious and far less serious offenses. Within each of these offense classifications, crime seriousness could be scored on a continuum, with offenses falling at both ends of the spec- trum. "Violent offenses," for example, include very serious crimes like murder, rape, and armed robbery, but also presumably far less serious offenses like criminal endangerment, intimidation, and a whole host of "other" violent offenses. In other words, the types of offenses classified as violent offenses are perhaps more appropriately labeled something else. A similarly wide range of offenses is captured by the category "pub- lic order offenses," with crimes ranging from presumably quite serious weapons offenses at the high end of the spectrum to morals and decency charges and liquor law violations at the low end. The same can be said of each of the other two broad categories of offenses (property and drug offenses). These broad classifications capture a very wide range of behaviors. Penal code reform rarely stems from the "average" case, however; when legislators write new laws, they are almost always reacting to extreme and highly publicized cases, and newspapers cover the most newsworthy cases.

These prison population trend figures also mask the fact that hundreds of thousands of inmates have been sent to prison each year for relatively low-level offenses and cycle through the system from year to year. Those serving time for violent offenses tend to stay in prison a lot longer than those serving time for public order offenses, and thus the population of violent offenders counted in these trends builds over time while the population of property, drug, and public order offenders tends to turn over more rapidly.[22] For those released in 2003, the average (median) time served for inmates released following admission for a violent offense was thirty-one months, while the average time served for inmates released following admission for a property (fourteen months), drug (fifteen months), or public order (thirteen months) offense was substantially lower.[23] Prison admissions data tell a quite different story. Using the same broad classifications of offenses, the most recently available data on prison admissions suggest that in 2003, just under 27 percent of all admissions were for violent offenses, about 30 percent were for property offenses, 32 percent were for drug offenses, and just over 11 percent were for public order offenses.[24] In other words, in terms of who is going to prison, more than two-thirds (over 70 percent) of those entering prisons each year were convicted of a nonviolent crime.

The absolute size of the prison population versus the number going into and coming out of prisons is often referred to as the distinction between stock and flow. The stock prison population is a count of the total number of prisoners incarcerated at any given point in time, while the flow refers to the movement of persons into and out of prisons (e.g., the absolute number of admissions and releases in a set time period). The distinction between stock and flow is helpful to the development of a more complete understanding of the dynamics of incarceration. At year-end 2008, the stock prison population stood at 1,610,446. In that same year, there were 739,132 prison admissions and 735,454 prison

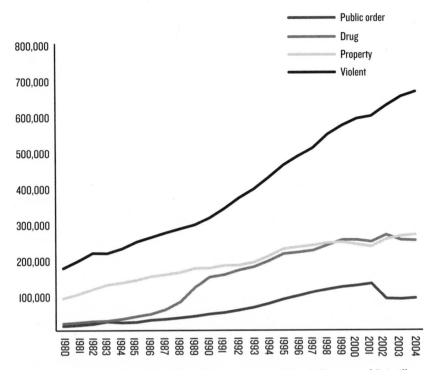

Figure 2.3: Prison Population by Offense Type, 1980-2005. Tina L. Dorsey and Priscilla Middleton, "Number of Persons under Jurisdiction of State Correctional Authorities by Most Serious Offense, 1980–2005" (Washington, DC: Bureau of Justice Statistics, 2007).

releases—together these admission and release figures represent the flow into and out of prison, respectively.[25] Until recently, in each year since the early 1970s, more prisoners were admitted to prison than had been released, and therefore the stock prison population continually increased. Moreover, the number of prisoners released in 2008 is just slightly lower than the number of prisoners admitted—although some of those released in 2008 might have served less than one year in prison, most of those released were probably not admitted in that same year. In other words, all prisoners contribute to the stock prison population— but do so for varying amounts of time. Inmates sentenced to serve long sentences (for example, serious violent offenders) contribute to the stock population for much longer than those serving relatively short sentences (like low-level drug offenders convicted of possession-only offenses). Stock prison population figures will always reflect larger numbers of violent long-term inmates than measures of the flow into and out of prison because low-level, nonviolent offenders cycle in and out of prison much more quickly.

Although for the remainder of the book we will focus primarily on incarceration generally, and prisons more specifically, it is crucial to acknowledge that America's grand penal experiment extended well beyond mass incarceration. As prison, jail, probation, and parole populations expanded, so did a whole host of alternative methods of coercive social control. The alternatives—often described as intermediate sanctions—were designed to be more restrictive than probation but less confining than prison. Intermediate sanctions were intended to reduce or limit the use of incarceration, reserving the loss of liberty for use as a punishment of last resort.[26] Virtually all of these new and innovative alternatives to incarceration, though, became add-ons to incarceration and, as Stanley Cohen noted many years ago, the net of punitive social control only widened.[27] The widening of the net of social control led others to argue that there had been both an overt punitive strategy, focusing on "control through confinement," and a more covert strategy, focused on "control through surveillance."[28] Indeed it may very well be the case that growth in control through surveillance did as much as, if not more than, growth in confinement to increase the punitive reach of the justice system.[29] It can certainly be argued that growth in surveillance and other ostensibly community-based sanctions served to fuel growth in incarceration.[30] With enhanced surveillance came an enhanced ability to detect failure and an increased chance of incarceration as a result of those failures (and with debatable implications for public safety).[31]

The Distribution of Incarceration across Places

Although the national story—and indeed the headline—should be of unrelenting growth in prison populations for close to four decades, that growth did not distribute evenly across places. Controlling for the state population, some states had incarceration rates that were as much as five times higher than other states. At year-end 2010, for example, imprisonment rates (measured as the number of prisoners per one hundred thousand residents) ranged from a low of 148 in Maine to a high of 867 in Louisiana.[32] Given the wide range in incarceration rates across states, those states that managed to maintain fairly low rates of incarceration tended to look more like some of our Western European allies than they did their fellow (and sometimes geographically neighboring) states. Although all states experienced fairly substantial prison population growth through much of the period of prison expansion, in recent years, growth has continued unabated in a few states, slowed in others, and reversed course *in at least half of the states.*[33]

There have also been some fairly prominent regional patterns to prison population growth—although these patterns become less clear when the focus is shifted to something other than the sheer numbers of people in prison.[34] Southern states certainly lead the way in imprisonment rates: at year-end 2010, five southern states (Louisiana, Mississippi, Texas, Oklahoma, and Alabama) each had imprisonment rates higher than six hundred prisoners per one hundred thousand residents. At the other end of the continuum, the low-imprisonment-rate states (those maintaining imprisonment rates of less than 250 per 100,000) were primarily northern states—with Nebraska, a decidedly midwestern state, the only non-northern state in that category.[35] A number of explanations have been offered for these relatively stable regional patterns, mostly having to do with race dynamics, but regardless of the cause, growth did not distributed evenly across places.[36]

Nor did growth distribute evenly over time. The most rapid growth occurred through the 1980s and continued well into the 1990s. Although growth has slowed since 2000, slowing growth was still growth. During the nearly forty years of sustained expansion in the use of prisons, several generations of Americans had known nothing but prison population growth. People born after 1973 had never known a time when the number of people incarcerated in this country was not rising. At no time in their lives had there been declines—let alone meaningful declines—in rates of imprisonment. High rates of imprisonment had assumed the status of social fact for these young Americans. And if high rates of incarceration were now social fact for an entire generation or two, nowhere was this more pronounced than in the places—and among the people—most impacted by these seemingly permanently high rates of incarceration.

The Concentration of Incarceration

Without question, growth in incarceration over the period concentrated among young black males from impoverished inner-city neighborhoods. Although an increasing number of Americans could claim prison experience, demographically, some—most notably young black males—were far more likely to have felt the consequences of mass incarceration. More than half of the adult prisoners are under thirty-five years old and almost nine in ten are under forty-five. Over 90 percent are men, and nearly half are African American.[37] Co-occurrence of these demographic characteristics concentrates incarceration even further: incarceration rates for black males are at least five times higher than for white males across every age group. Of black men in their late twenties, one in eight is currently behind bars.[38] Well more than half of all black high school dropouts born between 1965 and 1999 have been in (or will go to) prison, and overall, one in five black males can expect to be imprisoned sometime during adulthood.[39] These numbers are so staggering that it has become impossible to talk about incarceration without talking about its disparate impact on minority communities.

Why has incarceration concentrated so heavily in poor, inner-city communities that tend to be disproportionately comprised of minority populations? As is often the case, the answer to that seemingly simple question is complicated and multifaceted. Overly simplistic answers with a singular focus—like blacks commit more crime, or the criminal justice system is overtly or covertly racist—are woefully inadequate. A coalignment of factors, including disproportionate offending rates, the concentration of policing in inner-city communities, and (sometimes blatant) disparities in criminal justice outcomes across races all have contributed to black rates of incarceration that are more than five times higher than rates for whites.[40] Differential selection of blacks for criminal justice processing operates by moving blacks through the system at slightly higher rates at each and every stage of the system. The effect at each decision point might be small, but the overall effect, when all these small effects are added up, has been substantial.[41]

Understanding Growth in Prison Populations

Prior to the 1970s, prison populations across the United States had been remarkably stable, hovering at around one hundred prisoners per one hundred thousand population for most of the previous century (see figure 2.4). Indeed, consistency in incarceration rates over time had been so remarkable, and so seemingly impervious to fluctuations in crime, that some of the most prominent criminologists of our time suggested that imprisonment might be a self-regulating process.[42] In the mid-1970s, Alfred Blumstein and his colleagues argued that stable incarceration rates since the early 1900s suggested that society required a stable amount of punishment in order to function as a society. Drawing from the work of sociologist Emile Durkheim, they postulated that societies use punishment to affirm behavioral norms, and that a more or less standard amount of incarceration was needed in order to do so. Their point was that while actual crimes leading to incarceration might shift fairly substantially from one era to another, the rate of incarceration would stay relatively constant within a fairly narrow range of about one hundred prisoners per one hundred thousand citizens. At the time Blumstein and his colleagues wrote, their thesis—which has come to be known as the "stability of punishment thesis"—was borne out by data on the U.S. incarceration rate through most of the first three-quarters of the twentieth century. Until the early 1970s, the incarceration rate had indeed remained remarkably consistent over time despite some quite remarkable shifts in the nature and scope of the crime problem.

Unfortunately for Blumstein and his colleagues, despite notable stability of punishment until 1970, the decade prior to the 1970s had been

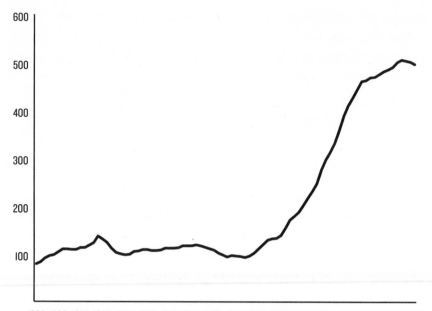

Figure 2.4: U.S. Imprisonment Rate* (per 100,000 population), 1925-2010. Sourcebook of Criminal Justice Statistics Online, Table 6.28.2009, http://www.albany.edu/sourcebook/csv/t6282009.csv.
*The imprisonment rate includes only those sentenced to more than one year in prison.

one of notable social turmoil and increasing distrust of government. Through the turbulent 1960s, the efficacy of punishment was frequently called into question, and there was a real push to develop alternatives to incarceration in the form of community-based sanctions. Prominent scholars of punishment publishing in the years preceding the era of relentless prison population growth not only failed to see it coming but, in some instances, they actually predicted that the end of imprisonment might be near. In the 1940s, Hermann Mannheim proclaimed, "The days of imprisonment as a method of mass treatment of lawbreakers are over."[43] A quarter-century later, in a tribute to Mannheim, the late Norval Morris, one of the most preeminent penologists of our time, "confidently predicted that, before the end of this century, prison in [its current] form will become extinct, though the word may live on."[44] Morris was not alone in his sense that the prison was an institution with a foreshortened life expectancy. Historian David J. Rothman, who wrote several of the more influential accounts of the history of penal institutions, offered the following observation at the end of the now-classic *Discovery of the Asylum,* originally published in 1971:

> We still live with many of these institutions, accepting their presence as inevitable. Despite a personal revulsion, we think of them as always having been with us, and therefore as always to be with us. We tend to forget that they were the invention of one generation to serve very special needs, not the only possible reaction to social problems. In fact, since the Progressive era, we have been gradually escaping from institutional responses, and one can foresee the period when incarceration will be used still more rarely than it is today.[45]

All indications seemed to suggest that the prison was an institution that was fast outgrowing its utility. The predictions of these prominent scholars, which also preceded the era of unrelenting prison population growth, made some sense in the context of the time in which they were made. In the 1960s, amid social turmoil and increasing distrust of government, there had indeed been a movement toward decarceration (albeit, in hindsight, the decarceration movement was short-lived).

In 1972 prison populations across the United States began their steep and rapid climb and continued that ascent for more than a generation (see figure 2.4). To be sure, toward the end of that period, some states began to experience small declines in the size of their prison populations, and in others growth slowed. But even as growth slowed, until 2010, overall prison populations continued to climb and our incarceration rates continued to grow. This is true even though, for at least the last fifteen years of that period, crime rates were not only falling but were doing so perhaps more dramatically than at any other time in our modern history.[46]

Partitioning Prison Population Growth

Although we witnessed almost unrelenting growth in prison populations since the 1970s, there is some evidence suggesting that the growth
was driven by different factors at different times over the period. Franklin Zimring, for example, proposed that we think about prison population expansion in terms of three distinct phases of growth.[47] According
to Zimring, most of the early growth in prison populations was best
explained by an increasing risk of imprisonment. Beginning in the mid-
1970s and continuing through the mid-1980s, imprisonment risk increased
quite dramatically—meaning that those convicted of crimes were more
likely to be sentenced to prison than they ever had been previously. This
dramatic increase in imprisonment risk was inspired in part by the growing sense that the system had been too soft and its rehabilitative orientation misguided. Proponents of this perspective argued that in a rational
cost-benefit analysis, crime actually paid, and therefore the payoff of crime
needed to be addressed. The basic premise of deterrence—that people
will avoid crime if the consequences are noxious enough—emphasized
the importance of making punishment more certain and more severe to
make offending less appealing, and this type of thinking resonated with the
American public. As renowned political scientist James Q. Wilson noted
in a widely read article published in *Atlantic Monthly* in the early 1980s,

> The average citizen hardly needs to be persuaded that crimes will be
> committed more frequently if, other things being equal, crime becomes
> more profitable than other ways of spending one's time. Accordingly, the
> average citizen thinks it obvious that one major reason why crime has
> increased is that people have discovered they can get away with it. By the
> same token, a good way to reduce crime is to make its consequences to
> the would-be offender more costly (by making penalties swifter, more
> certain, or more severe).[48]

During this early phase of the Punishment Imperative, the likelihood of
imprisonment generally increased for everyone but especially for those

low-level offenders who previously would never have received a prison sentence in the first place.

Toward the middle of the 1980s, we entered the second phase, during which prison population growth was driven largely by policies and practices associated with the increasingly ubiquitous War on Drugs. Here the focus shifted from increasing the likelihood of imprisonment for all offenders, including relatively low-level offenders, to vastly increasing the likelihood of imprisonment for drug offenders more specifically. A series of federal legislative initiatives targeting drug offenders passed in the mid- to late 1980s all but ensured that the majority of offenders entering federal prisons would be drug offenders. Not only did the likelihood of receiving a sentence to imprisonment increase dramatically for drug offenders over this period, but so too did the length of sentence they could expect to serve. So while early prison population growth was driven by our inclination to send more and more people to prison, by the mid-1980s we were increasingly becoming concerned with extending the length of time that they would stay there. Although many were affected by this shift, the focus of these initiatives was on drug offenders who, by this time, had been increasingly vilified. From the mid-1980s through at least the early 1990s, drug offenders were far more likely to be sent to prison and once there could expect to stay much longer than they ever had previously.

The third and final phase—which started in the early to mid-1990s and presumably persisted until very recently—shifted focus back to the more general offender population and emphasized increasing lengths of stay over increasing the likelihood of imprisonment. Zimring characterized the transition to the third phase as a "shift in emphasis from 'lock 'em up' to 'throw away the key'" and hypothesized that much of the more recent growth in incarceration could be attributed to increasingly long sentences.[49] As will be described in chapter 4, truth-in-sentencing legislation that required that violent offenders serve at least 85 percent of their sentence was the centerpiece legislation of this most recent era, but a wide array of mandatory sentencing laws targeting all types of offenders meant that virtually everyone sent to prison would be serving sentences that were at least slightly longer than they had been previously. When upwards of half a million people are admitted to prison each year, even very small changes in the average time a prisoner can expect to serve results in quite dramatic increases in the prison population.

Although Zimring did not empirically test his thesis regarding the three distinct phases of imprisonment growth, in a series of studies, Alfred Blumstein and Allen Beck isolated growth across each of the various stages of the criminal justice process.[50] Along the crime-punishment continuum, there are really four processing stages that might contribute to increasing prison populations: (1) crime, (2) arrests, (3) sentencing, and (4) time served. First, and most obviously, increasing crime might lead to increasing use of imprisonment. Indeed, the perception that crime had been spiraling out of control has often been cited as one of the driving forces behind increasing punitiveness.[51] And, while there certainly were some quite substantial increases in crime in the period immediately preceding the Punishment Imperative, there has been some debate about the magnitude of those actual increases given changes in the way in which crime was recorded over the same period.[52] A change in the number of *arrests* might also affect prison population size with or without a concomitant increase in crime. In fact, one might expect changes in arrest patterns to have a bigger effect than changes in crime. Only those offenders who are arrested can ultimately be sanctioned by the criminal justice system, so changes in offending will have little effect if the police do not meet that challenge of increasing crime with more arrests. Holding crime constant, increases in arrests would indicate that the police have become more effective in apprehending offenders, increasing the supply of offenders for the criminal justice system to sanction.

There are also two distinct processes associated with the sanctioning phase that could have contributed to prison population growth: commitments to prison and length of stay. The size of the prison population ultimately depends upon how many people go to prison and how long they stay (a truism recently referred to as the "Iron Law of Prison Populations").[53] A sudden increase in the number of persons sent to prison (e.g., commitments to prison) will have a pretty immediate effect on the size of the prison population while a sudden change in the length of time that they stay (e.g., time served) will have a delayed, but equally profound, effect over time.

Scholars have demonstrated that virtually all growth in prison populations over several decades could be attributed to the two sanctioning phases of the system: commitments to prison once convicted and length of stay once admitted. Eighty-eight percent of the growth in prison populations between 1980 and 1996 has been attributed to increasing commitments to prison and increasing lengths of stay.[54] The remaining 12 percent predominantly resulted from increases in crime, and particularly drug crime. Only one-half of 1 percent of the growth over that period could be explained by increasing police effectiveness at the arrest stage. Blumstein and Beck, the scholars who generated these estimates, provided empirical support for Zimring's thesis about the importance of the War on Drugs to prison population growth when they reported that virtually all of the early-stage growth in crime could be explained by drug offenses. When drug offenses were removed from the equation, changes during the two sanctioning phases accounted for more than 99 percent of the prison population growth.

In later work,[55] Blumstein and Beck extended their earlier analysis to 2001 and partitioned the period into two separate eras of growth (with 1992 as the break point). Again they found that increases in the early offense and apprehension phases explained very little prison population growth over either period, although those increases did explain some in the earlier period, and the sanctioning phases explained most of the growth in prison population. Crucially, increases in commitments contributed more to growth in the early period (1980–1992) and increases in length of stay contributed more to growth in the later period (1992–2001). Blumstein and Beck's empirical partitioning of prison population growth ultimately aligned quite nicely with Zimring's thesis that prison population growth might best be understood if parsed into three distinct eras.

Economists Steven Raphael and Michael Stoll similarly demonstrated that increasing lengths of stay account for a substantial portion of prison population growth, reporting that growth in average time served could explain roughly one-third of prison population growth.[56] Like Blumstein and Beck, Raphael and Stoll reported that changes in rates of criminal offending explained relatively little (at most 17 percent) of the growth in imprisonment between 1980 and 2005. Crucially, in their analysis of average time served, they controlled for the fact that the massive influx of relatively low-level offenders in the 1980s and 1990s will have disproportionately impacted the overall average time served (driving it downward). Those low-level offenders—who were now disproportionately represented in the prison population—served relatively short prison sentences, making it appear as though the average time served had actually changed little over time. Raphael and Stoll, however, estimated the average time served for "like" offenders and found that "prisoners today are serving longer sentences than comparable prisoners in years past, a fact that is missed in simple comparisons of the overall average release rate or the aggregate time-served distribution."[57] According to Raphael and Stoll, "collectively, changes in who goes to prison . . . and for how long . . . explain 80–85% of prison expansion over the last twenty-five years."[58] The increasingly sophisticated work of criminologists and economists has helped us to better understand the complicated dynamics of prison population growth. When changes in offending patterns could explain so little of the prison population growth, it became more and more clear that prison population growth had been driven primarily by policy choices.

The Relationship between Crime and Punishment

Work partitioning prison population growth has suggested that crime—or, more precisely, change in crime—has had a negligible impact on prison population growth, and few scholars today argue that changes in crime rates, or trends in crime over time, can adequately explain changes in the level of imprisonment. Even a quick glance at trends over the past forty years illustrates the complex and often contradictory nature of the relationship between crime and incarceration (see figure 2.5).

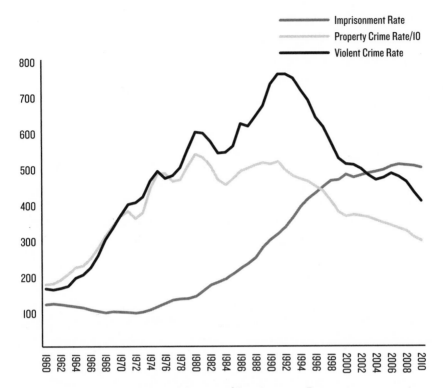

Figure 2.5: Violent Crime, Property Crime, and Imprisonment Rates per 100,000, 1960-2010*. Crime Rates: Sourcebook of Criminal Justice Statistics Online, Table 3.106. 2010, http://www.albany.edu/sourcebook/csv/t31062010.csv; Incarceration Rate: Sourcebook of Criminal Justice Statistics Online, Table 6.28.2009, http://www.albany.edu/sourcebook/csv/t6282009.csv.
*Property crime rate has been divided by ten to scale it on the same axis as the violent crime rate. Imprisonment rate includes only those sentenced to more than one year of imprisonment.

In the fifteen-year period before the incarceration rate began to rise, the crime rate doubled. Over the next decade or so, the crime rate had two accelerations and three declines, ending at about 50 percent higher than it started. The incarceration rate increased about 50 percent as well. In the decade that followed (the early eighties to the early nineties), crime rates fell and then rose again, ending up where they started that period, while incarceration rates almost tripled. Since the last crime peak in 1994, crime rates have steadily fallen for well over a decade.

Incarceration rates over the same period grew by two-thirds. Thus, there has been no straightforward relationship between incarceration and crime—during a generation-long growth of imprisonment, crime rates first increased, then fluctuated quite erratically, and have since dropped rather substantially.[59]

It seems crucial to note that in studies of the relationship between crime and imprisonment, crime might be conceived of as both an *input* of imprisonment and an *output* of imprisonment—making the nature of the relationship between crime and imprisonment difficult to model statistically (a point we will return to later in this book). Crime is quite obviously an input for prisons (ostensibly only those accused and convicted of crimes are sentenced to prison),[60] and indeed it is in some ways a truism that the size of the prison population depends upon crime—after all, without crime there would be no imprisonment (or at least very little). Most obviously, as an explanatory variable, crime clearly might explain some of the variation in imprisonment rates over time. In times of increasing crime, for example, one might expect increasing imprisonment.

Although few studies examine the relationship between crime and imprisonment singularly, most empirical work specifies crime as one among many factors potentially explaining variation in imprisonment rates. Empirical research has demonstrated that, broadly speaking, crime rates—particularly violent crime rates—tend to explain some of the variation in imprisonment rates across states and over time. In a study attempting to explain variation in imprisonment rates across states, Greenberg and West broke the crime rate down into its two component parts (violent and property crime) and additionally included a measure of drug arrests.[61] They found that violent crime and drug arrest rates each significantly predicted imprisonment rates, but property crime rates did not, and noted that "although growth in crime was not a major cause of higher prison populations, imprisonment rates have been higher, and have grown faster, in states with higher levels of victimizing crime, especially violent crime."[62] They concluded that their findings support the conclusion that imprisonment rates are neither "entirely determined" by nor "entirely unrelated" to crime rates. In other words, crime rates—particularly violent crime rates—explain some, but certainly nothing like all, of the variation in state imprisonment rates.

But variation in crime might also be an output of prisons. When crime is specified as a potential outcome, one might predict that imprisonment would either reduce crime or increase crime. To the extent that imprisonment deters, rehabilitates, or effectively incapacitates criminal offenders, imprisonment might be expected to reduce crime. To the extent that imprisonment weakens informal social control or disrupts important networks, imprisonment might be expected to increase crime.[63] Scholars of penology have long argued that prisons do little to improve the lot of those offenders sent to them for punishment and might actually be criminogenic—increasing the likelihood of future offending upon release rather than decreasing it. As will be discussed in greater detail in chapter 5, we currently release large numbers of prisoners (more than seven hundred thousand each year) into communities with very little support, almost no material resources (financial or otherwise), and few if any educational credentials or marketable skills. Given the stigma of a criminal conviction and of having served a term of incarceration, these former offenders are quite likely to find themselves in a far worse position following a stint in prison than they had been prior to entering prison. To be sure, when prison populations grow, rates of prison releases also grow, with the attendant consequence of increased crime that results from increases in prisoner reentry.

A sizeable body of research has tried to estimate the impact of the *size* of the prison population on state and national levels of crime.[64] The theory is that prison incapacitates those who are locked up, and the more people who are incapacitated, the less the crime. This research has produced a range of estimates of incapacitation effects. Very high estimates, on the order of 187 crimes prevented per year of incarceration, have been based on self-reports of criminal activity by people who were incarcerated.[65] Much more moderate effects, on the order of a 1 percent drop in crime for every 10 percent increase in the size of the prison population, have been derived from observations of the national relationship between the rate of incarceration and the rate of crime over time.[66] In general, smaller estimates of incapacitation effects are provided by more recent models, more sophisticated models, and models using smaller geo-spatial units of analysis.[67] Indeed, a recent state-level panel study of incarceration between the years 1978 and 2004 found that, after accounting for reverse causality and the lagged effects of reentry rates, incarceration had actually increased rates of violent crime.[68]

In studies of the net effect of the size of the stock population of prisoners at any given time on crime rates (through incapacitation), incarceration is usually thought of as something that happens to individuals, changing the way in which offenders are free to act in the community. But recently, the idea has arisen among scholars that incarceration is not just a process operating on individuals who go to prison but is also a social process with impact at the community level.[69] By and large, convicted criminal offenders are not simply removed from communities never to return again. Rather, these offenders typically cycle through prison (often more than once in their lifetimes). The removal of people from communities to prison and their eventual return back to the community from prison has been referred to as reentry cycling—or, more recently, prison cycling.[70] The effects of that social process known as prison cycling are typically presented as unforeseen collateral consequences of a crime-control policy that tends to exacerbate the very social problems that are thought to undermine a community's public safety.[71] It may therefore be that the effect of the stock population of prisoners on suppressing crime rates is counteracted by the community-level impact of prison cycling: that the flow in and out of prison has a different impact on crime than the stay in prison. In other words, it might be the case that in the communities that are most differentially impacted by sustained high rates of prison cycling, incarceration actually backfires and ultimately ends up increasing crime in those communities (a point to which we will return in chapter 6).[72]

Penologist David Garland has made the point that crime and imprisonment are assuredly related to one another, but not in any simple or straightforward manner.[73] A cursory understanding of this relationship is that it is almost certainly reciprocal, changes in each producing changes in the other. The precise nature of these changes has not been empirically identified. Indeed, empirical work assessing the effect of either crime on imprisonment or imprisonment on crime has often produced conflicting results. When crime has been specified as an explanatory variable, some find that crime—particularly violent crime—predicts imprisonment and others find no significant relationship. Similarly, when crime is specified as an outcome variable, some find that imprisonment reduces crime, some find that it increases crime, and others find no significant relationship between imprisonment and crime.[74]

If Not Crime, Then What?

In recent years, scholars have increasingly tried to understand incarceration as more than just a response to crime and as more than simply the end result of a collection of related policies that have been adopted largely in isolation. Although explanations for unabated prison population growth are many and varied, there are some dominant themes that occur across many of the more influential attempts to explain that growth. Central among these themes is the idea that the American sociopolitical culture is unique, producing a strong trend of control-oriented policies that emphasize the prison and "tough" responses to crime as salient political platforms and acceptable cultural starting points for crime policy.[75] We return to these themes in the chapters that follow. For now, we turn briefly to a historical development in crime policy whose influence on prison population growth cannot be overstated and should not be ignored. The framing of the crime problem as requiring an all-out "war" in response has had lasting consequences. The various war metaphors that have been used to characterize the necessary response to crime problems for at least the past four decades are important in that they served to legitimize the anything-goes approach that drove penal policy over that period. These wars also notably contributed to the increasing racial divide in punishment.

The Wars on Crime and on Drugs

There is no way to write about the Punishment Imperative without explicitly addressing the centrality of race and of the ongoing wars on crime and on drugs. The seeds for the wars on crime and then on drugs were certainly planted in the decade immediately preceding the buildup, and as has been noted by several before us, the framing of the crime problem was implicitly (and at times explicitly) racialized.[76]

The United States has a fairly long and storied history of crime wars. In fact, our crime wars have long outlasted any of our military wars, which, relatively speaking, have tended to be short-lived. Even the protracted Vietnam War, spanning more than fifteen years, seems fleeting by comparison to our ongoing crime wars. Before we launched the most recent War on Terror in the aftermath of the 9/11 attacks in 2001, we fought a protracted War on Drugs, and before that a prolonged War on Crime. All told, we have been fighting crime-related wars for close to half a century now—none of which have we won and all of which we continue to fight to varying degrees today. In other words, with the debut of each new crime-related war, we have supplemented rather than replaced the previous, yet-to-be-won (and, some would argue, unwinnable) crime-related war.

The earliest of these wars, the War on Crime, which was first initiated in the mid-1960s following what appeared to be a fairly dramatic increase in crime, has continued unabated for well over forty years now. Although labeled somewhat generically, at its inception, the War on Crime was quite specifically a war on violent crime and was the first in the series of wars that would virtually guarantee the supply of prisoners who would drive up prison populations over the next four decades. The War on Crime was initially launched following the release of the landmark 1967 report, *The Challenge of Crime in a Free Society*, authored by the President's Commission on Law Enforcement and the Administration of Justice (hereafter 1967 Crime Commission).[77] The 1967 Crime Commission report detailed the crime-related challenges facing the United States and laid the foundations of a crime-control strategy for beginning to address them. According to the report, the challenges were daunting and the task monumental. An ambitious agenda for the future, a road map for a War on Crime, was laid out in seven propositions:

> First, society must seek to prevent crime before it happens by assuring all Americans a stake in the benefits and responsibilities of American life, by strengthening law enforcement, and by reducing criminal opportunities. Second, society's aim of reducing crime would be better served if the system of criminal justice developed a far broader range of techniques with which to deal with individual offenders. Third, the system of criminal justice must eliminate existing injustices if it is to achieve its ideals and win the respect and cooperation of all citizens. Fourth, the system of criminal justice must attract more people and better people—police, prosecutors, judges, defense attorneys, probation and parole officers, and corrections officials with more knowledge, expertise, initiative, and integrity. Fifth, there must be much more operational and basic research into the problems of crime and criminal administration, by those both within and without the system of criminal justice. Sixth, the police, courts, and correctional agencies must be given substantially greater amounts of money if they are to improve their ability to control crime. Seventh, individual citizens, civic and business organizations, religious institutions, and all levels of government must take responsibility for planning and implementing the changes that must be made in the criminal justice system if crime is to be reduced.[78]

According to the President's Crime Commission, when it came to crime very little had been going well—virtually every facet of current crime prevention and control strategies had to be reassessed and the approach going forward would have to be multifaceted and comprehensive. In the three hundred pages that followed, the commission offered a litany of recommendations for waging a crime war covering everything from strengthening families to addressing underlying social problems to improving detection and eliminating disparities. Commemorating the fortieth anniversary of the publication of *The Challenge of Crime in a*

Free Society, Thomas Feucht and Edwin Zedlewski describe its impact in the following way:

> The President's Crime Commission thrust "ordinary street crime" irreversibly into policy discussions and provided the framework for the Federal Government to take new responsibility for fighting crime and enhancing public safety in neighborhoods and communities across the country. No one was under the illusion that crime could easily be banished. In fact, when Johnson accepted the Challenge of Crime report in 1967, he cautioned that the war on crime would take generations to wage.[79]

President Johnson couldn't have been more accurate. More than forty years later, the War on Crime that was launched with the publication of that report in many ways wages on.

Not long after the launch of the War on Crime, the emphasis shifted from violent crime to drug crime—a type of crime that had been largely ignored by the 1967 Crime Commission.[80] Although President Nixon can be credited with turning the focus to drugs beginning in his 1968 campaign for office, the War on Drugs was really launched in earnest under the Reagan administration in the early 1980s. The subsequent administrations, at least through Republican George H. W. Bush and Democrat William Jefferson Clinton, ensured that the War on Drugs would continue unabated long after the core problems identified as substantiating the War on Drugs—primarily the emergence of crack cocaine and the violence associated with the drug trade—had waned. Although the precise reasons for the shift have proven difficult to isolate with any precision, several have argued that drugs offered a convenient avenue through which to shift the conversation about the nature of the crime problem (and those responsible for it)—and simultaneously offered a convenient diversion from the reality that the War on Crime had seen limited success in the fifteen years since it was launched with the publication of the 1967 Crime Commission report.

The vast majority of legislation associated with the War on Drugs has targeted the supply side of the equation—targeting those who manufacture, distribute, and possess illegal drugs. Very little of the drug war legislation has focused on addressing the underlying problem of drug addiction that fuels the drug markets. Indeed, from its inception, the focus of the War on Drugs has been predominantly on enforcement of drug laws, with far less funding going to prevention or treatment. In recent testimony before a subcommittee in Congress, criminologist Peter Reuter, a noted expert on drugs and crime, explained that "total expenditures for drug control, at all levels of government, totaled close to $40 billion in 2007" with approximately three-quarters (70–75 percent) of those funds going toward enforcement.[81] The impact of the enforcement-heavy War on Drugs has been profound, and its impact on inner-city minority communities, devastating. In 1980, the number of people incarcerated for drug offenses was small in both absolute and proportional terms—the growth has been exponential. The population incarcerated for drug offenses grew from less than fifty thousand drug offenders in 1980 to more than five hundred thousand in 2007.[82] In the 1970s, before the start of the War on Drugs, people in prison for drug crimes constituted about 5 percent of the total number of the prison population. By 2010, they represented close to 20 percent of the total population. At the federal level—where the drug war has been fought most prominently, *more than half* of all incarcerated offenders are serving time for drug offenses.[83] Given the dynamics of incarceration explained above, as longer sentences for violent crime kick in, the proportion of people behind bars for drug crimes decreases, even though the number actually going to prison for drug offenses remains high.[84]

While we will return to drug policy more explicitly in the chapters that follow, suffice it to say, for now, that perhaps no series of crime control initiatives have contributed to the racialization of the crime problem and ensured the disparate impact of incarceration than those policies most closely associated with the War on Drugs. That said, although drugs (and particularly the policies associated with the War on Drugs) were central to the most precipitous period of prison population buildup, they were certainly not solely responsible for it. As we will argue here and throughout the book, the experiment was grand and the approach was multifaceted. Even without the War on Drugs, we would have seen unprecedented growth in the use of imprisonment. Sweeping changes in sentencing policy and correctional practice all but ensured that we would see prison populations reach astounding proportions.

Summary

This chapter describes the basic contours of a grand penal experiment, in which the U.S. prison population increased for thirty-seven years, growing every year since 1972. When prison growth started, the incarceration rate (per one hundred thousand residents) was about one hundred, a level that had been steady for a half-century. Systematic annual increases since then produced an incarceration rate over five times that level. By 2010, the U.S. incarceration rate was the highest in the world and three to ten times the imprisonment rate of other Western democracies.[85] The use of imprisonment in the United States has been a social policy without a parallel elsewhere in the world; it has been a long-term and seemingly inexorable policy of expanded prison use that has persisted during good economic times and bad, during periods of war and those of peace, and while crime rose and when it dropped.[86]

Beginning in the early 1970s and continuing until very recently, reliance on incarceration as a sanction increased so consistently and so steadily that we reached the point where the term "incarceration" was almost invariably preceded by the word "mass." We had become a nation addicted to incarceration.[87] Long gone were the days when incarceration was reserved for only the most serious, violent, or recalcitrant offenders. Gone also were the days when incarceration was used reluctantly as a punishment of last resort. We now incarcerated first-time offenders and career criminals; we incarcerated violent criminals, but also no shortage of drug and property offenders; we incarcerated the very young and the very old. Women and girls were being incarcerated at rates unprecedented in U.S. history.[88] In our quest to incarcerate our way out of crime, it seems few were spared. Evidence shows that we were not only quicker to send someone to prison but also more willing than ever before to send him or her there for protracted periods of time. We were also more inclined to use the prison than any other Western democracy.

During this 37-year period, the United States ceased to rely on incarceration as a punishment response of limited or last resort; our commitment to a policy of incarceration became so entrenched and our addiction to incarceration so relentless that we created the problem of mass incarceration. The penal system had always been an institution of social and political significance, but it became embedded as a cultural power.[89] In our life of symbols, the penal system came to be ever-present on television, in movies, and on the written page. Shows like HBO's *Oz* and Fox's *Prison Break*, films like *The Shawshank Redemption* and *Dead Man Walking*, and books like *In the Belly of the Beast* all contributed to the integration of the prison into mainstream popular culture. Mass incarceration, though, is not just a culturally powerful symbol; it has become a tangible fact in real lives more than was even imaginable a few decades ago. Today the United States incarcerates more than 2.3 million people— or one in one hundred of its adult population.[90] At least one in every thirty-six Americans now has "prison experience."[91] Prison is no longer an elusive, ominous, distant place that many fear but few ever experience. What was at one time a back-up institution, infrequently used and a bit curious to the everyday person, is now a core fact of present-day life. By 2010, prison and jail had become routine features in the lives of an increasing number of Americans living in the areas most affected by our incarceration policies.[92]

In the next chapter, we show how America's recent experience with incarceration might be best understood as a grand social experiment. We describe the ever-growing American use of the prison—a pattern that lasted longer than a generation—as a social experiment in the grand tradition of utilitarian political ideas in American history. We argue that for close to forty years, American penal policy was dominated by an ideology in which punishment became an imperative, and the prison became a penalty of choice. We call this social experiment the Punishment Imperative. By using the term "imperative," we imply a kind of structured intellectual economy in which the idea of punishment—as opposed to other ideas such as reform or reintegration—becomes so powerful that it drowns out any other voices in the discussion about penal policy. We hold that the Punishment Imperative arose when all options disappeared (or at least lost legitimacy) in the face of broad acceptance of the need for a punitive response to crime (or, perhaps more accurately, public alarm about crime rather than crime itself). Punitive ideas became an irresistible force in postconviction policy, and no idea could find a hearing unless it first accepted the logic of the need for more—ever more—punishment.

3

The Punishment Imperative as a Grand Social Experiment

It's a government program whose impact rivals the New Deal. It pushes
whole communities out of society's mainstream. It costs tens of billions
of dollars a year. . . . What if America launched a new New Deal and
no one noticed. And what if, instead of lifting the unemployed out of
poverty, this multi-billion-dollar project steadily drove poor communities further and further out of the American mainstream? That's how
America should think about its growing prison system.
—Christopher Shea, 2007[1]

In the previous chapter we reviewed some of the major trends in prison
population growth over the past several decades and introduced some
of the most influential explanations for that growth. We showed that the
growth of punishment—especially imprisonment—over the last forty years
has been unprecedented in U.S. history and outstrips other nations' experiences. We have made the case that this shift in U.S. policy for the most part
came about not as a consequence of changes in rates of crime but rather as
a consequence of changes in our orientation to crime and in the policies
that were used to deal with crime as a social problem. In a very real sense, it
may be said that when it came to the problem of crime, America engaged in
something of a grand social policy experiment of dramatic proportions. In
this chapter, we consider this metaphor of grand social experiments. There
has, in U.S. history, been a tradition of grand experiments to confront vexing social issues. We argue that it is useful to think of punishment in the late
twentieth century as one of those grand social experiments, and we call the
grand penal experiment of our time "The Punishment Imperative."

Grand Social Experiments

America, some suggest, was founded as a grand social experiment.[2] The new country in the new world offered a new vision for what a society could aspire to and offered the first full-scale attempt to fully incorporate democratic principles into the governing structure. Alexis de Tocqueville was impressed with many aspects of the American experiment in democracy—the energy and optimism of the people, their entrepreneurial capacity, and their faith in democratic ideals. He did not declare the American Democratic Experiment a success (or a failure). He was wise enough to know that history would have to answer that question. Rather, he judged the American idea as worthy of note, interesting and exciting. For our purposes, Tocqueville's unique evaluation of the early days of the nation remind us that, founded as a social experiment, America has had a long tradition of ongoing and grand social experimentation.

By "grand social experimentation" we mean pursuing expansive social programs—in wholesale fashion—to address a social problem of some import.[3] We refer to the idea of "grand social experiments" as comprised of a higher order of policy shifts, historical moments when a rare combination of public will and political energy coalesce to change, fundamentally, the way a dominant social concern is addressed.[4] What happens, then, is less the creation of a few new programs than it is an overhaul of thinking about and strategy for a pressing problem of concern. Social experiments of this type are often controversial when implemented and frequently take some time to fully realize their potential. After all, grand social experiments offer seismic-like shifts in the sociopolitical ground.

In this conception, grand social experiments have three defining characteristics. First, they take place around a pressing social problem, one that so galvanizes public attention that it calls for a transformative kind of action, something that turns the status quo on its head. The immensity of the problem is defined, in part, by how substantially extraordinary a solution is called for. By definition, a small problem does not present itself as in need of a grand solution; only grand problems qualify.

Second, there is a coalescence of political will and public enthusiasm for a "new approach." What makes a grand experiment possible is not the mere fact of an overarching problem, but the companion fact that public frustration with the problem opens the door to new possibilities for tackling the problem—a "window of opportunity" in the policy arena.[5] The status quo—the old way of doing business—comes to be widely seen as a failure. This, in turn, suggests that new strategies are called for. Those with political agendas offer new definitions of the underlying nature of the problem, and these new definitions promote changes in action, often calling for radical change.

Third, there is an idea that gains momentum as a widely accepted new way of addressing the pressing problem. Coming out of the shift in the way the problem is perceived by the broad public—the way the problem is socially "defined"—is a logical strategy for attacking the problem. The "grand social experiment" is thus the adoption of a new, largely unproven strategy for a high-priority social problem based on a reformulated understanding of that problem. By these criteria, it is an "experiment."

Grand social experiments gain momentum from three facts. First, the immensity of the problem, at least as it is present in the public consciousness, creates a sense that "something must be done." Second, constituencies that often oppose one another in other political contexts become aligned in this one, enabling a wide acceptance of the need not just for a new strategy but for a particular type of strategy. The ordinary kinds of compromises required for political change are diminished, as the potential opposition to the "grand idea" is suppressed in the face of the coalesced forces. Third, the action itself is the solution to the problem. That is, merely passing laws that enact the new strategy abates the pressure for action. This implies that "grand" social experiments are evaluated less by their accomplishments in the long-term alleviation of the problem than they are by their ability, in the short run, to address the public demand for action.

Grand social experiments do not just calm public anxieties—they also have "results," or, perhaps more precisely, consequences. Because the experiments are grand, the results and consequences are often far-reaching and multifaceted. Some of the results are so detached in time and effort from the original social change that the link to the experiment is not obvious and is historically debatable. For these reasons, grand social experiments are "studied" rather than "evaluated" in the usual sense of that term. We can illustrate this by a brief discussion of two grand social experiments that fit our description.

Because it has frequently been argued that punishment and welfare are social policies that target the same socially marginal populations,[6] we review two grand social experiments that had widespread welfare reform at the center of their programs of social change. We focus on Franklin D. Roosevelt's New Deal federalization of welfare and Lyndon B. Johnson's Great Society War on Poverty programs. These grand social experiments each sought to address what seemed like the most pressing social problems of their time (unemployment and poverty, respectively) and included a series of sweeping reforms that came about following substantial social pressure. The New Deal federalization of welfare was launched in response to the devastating 1929 stock market crash and the Great Depression that followed,[7] and the Great Society programs of the 1960s were integral to the newly declared "War on Poverty."[8]

The New Deal

In the 1930s, President Franklin D. Roosevelt launched a series of federal initiatives aimed at recovering a U.S. economy reeling in the aftermath of the devastating1929 stock market crash. Together these initiatives are collectively referred to as the New Deal. When the stock market crashed in 1929, the Great Depression—lasting more than six years—led to increasing cries for the federal government to do something proactive to speed the recovery of the American economy. Americans everywhere were feeling the crippling effects of an economy in crisis and, in the words of historian Mimi Abramovitz, "the dispossessed—both middle and working class—took to the streets."[9] The highest unemployment rates and most deplorable living conditions this country had ever seen generated such substantial public outcry and protest that the impetus for the New Deal can only be described as a broad-based social move-ment. Through social protest, the poor, the unemployed, the working and middle classes were able to exert considerable political pressure on the government to get something done.[10] The New Deal was not simply a response to an economy in crisis; it was a response to an economy in crisis and a growing and increasingly vocal class of unemployed citizens demanding an immediate and far-reaching response. Tackling a prob-lem as enormous as the one that Americans faced at the beginning of the 1930s required a radical rethinking of the structure of the U.S. economy.

By most historical accounts, the New Deal, a series of economic recov-ery programs launched between 1933 and 1940, actually involved two New Deals.[11] The First New Deal was marked by an array of economic reform initiatives designed to stimulate the U.S. economy. These policy reforms included the creation of fair competition regulations, a series of banking reforms, and the passage of the National Housing Act and the Security and Exchange Act. Virtually all of the first New Deal initiatives were ush-ered in through legislation swiftly enacted in 1933 following the election of Franklin Delano Roosevelt.[12] The Second New Deal, which began follow-ing further democratic electoral successes in 1934, included another series of federal initiatives related to banking, fair labor practices, and further regulation of industry and utilities. The second New Deal was marked most notably by the 1935 passage of the Social Security Act that essentially created the federal welfare system. The Social Security Act of 1935 pro-vided for unemployment insurance, income assistance and insurance for the aged, and public assistance for the poor through the Aid to Dependent Children (ADC) program, which ultimately became the Aid to Families with Dependent Children (AFDC) program.[13]

Although they can be chronicled, and indeed the above is an incom-plete list, the New Deal initiatives were not a series of singular economic policies enacted in isolation, each intended to address its own specific problem; rather, the New Deal was a collection of policies that together represented an attempt to create a seismic shift in the structure of the U.S. economy. There were some rapid "results" of this seismic shift. As Frances Fox Piven has described, the cash assistance that came as part of the First

New Deal quite literally "poured out" to more than twenty-three million people so that, by 1935, 5 percent of the U.S. gross national product was going toward cash assistance and work relief programs.[14] This initial surge in assistance that followed the First New Deal was scaled back by the Second New Deal's Social Security Act. By all accounts, the American welfare state, which was launched with the New Deal initiatives of the 1930s, was slower to develop and less comprehensive in scope than the welfare states of other comparable nations.[15] Nonetheless, the New Deal led to shifts in economic policy that remain with us today, and although welfare has gone through a series of reforms in the seven decades since it was established, the Social Security system remains largely intact.

The Great Society

In the 1930s, the United States used the New Deal initiatives to stimulate the recovery of the national economy; in the 1960s, we launched an all-out War on Poverty. While Roosevelt's New Deal economic-growth initiatives established the federal welfare system in the United States, Lyndon B. Johnson's Great Society programs sought to greatly expand a more broadly conceived social welfare safety net. During the 1960s, the problems of social and racial inequality—made increasingly salient by the civil and women's rights movements—made their way to the top of Johnson's national agenda. America was embroiled in an unpopular war, structural inequality was widespread, and racial tensions were at an all-time high. As in the New Deal, social movements played a crucial role in the impetus for widespread social change.

The Great Society, though, was more than a set of federal initiatives aimed at a particular social problem or set of social problems; it was a vision for what America could become. In a speech given in May of 1964 to an audience at the University of Michigan, President Johnson described his vision for the Great Society:

[W]e have the opportunity to move not only toward the rich society and the powerful society, but upward to the Great Society. The Great Society rests on abundance and liberty for all. It demands an end to poverty and racial injustice, to which we are totally committed in our time. But that is just the beginning. The Great Society is a place where every child can find knowledge to enrich his mind and to enlarge his talents. It is a place where leisure is a welcome chance to build and reflect, not a feared cause of boredom and restlessness. It is a place where the city of man serves not only the needs of the body and the demands of commerce but the desire for beauty and the hunger for community. It is a place where man can renew contact with nature. It is a place which honors creation for its own sake and for what it adds to the understanding of the race. It is a place where men are more concerned with the quality of their goals than the quantity of their goods. But most of all, the Great Society is not a safe harbor, a resting place, a final objective, a finished work. It is a challenge constantly renewed, beckoning us toward a destiny where the meaning of our lives matches the marvelous products of our labor.[16]

The scope and breadth of the vision for the Great Society called for expansion of social programs across multiple domains, including education, health, housing, income redistribution, public assistance, and urban renewal.[17] Programs and initiatives developed during the Great Society era included federal support in the areas of primary and secondary education, the establishment of not only Medicare (the use of Social Security funds to provide for health insurance for the aged) but also Medicaid (federal-state health insurance for the poor), and the passage of the landmark Economic Opportunity Act of 1964 that "made poverty itself, and not only age or physical disability, an object of government policy."[18] Many of these initiatives were designed to "break the cycle of poverty" and confront the problems of social and racial inequality.

The New Deal and Great Society as Grand Social Experiments

Recall that we have argued that grand social experiments have three characteristics: they develop when (1) a sizeable and pressing social problem emerges that requires a transformative kind of action; (2) a coalescence of political will and public enthusiasm for a new approach develops; and (3) an idea gains momentum as a widely accepted new way of addressing the social problem. The New Deal and Great Society each qualify as grand social experiments under these criteria. With regard to the New Deal, an economic crisis served as the pressing social problem requiring transformative action. The crisis was so acute that it became apparent that nothing less than a radical restructuring of the U.S. economy was required. The package of New Deal programs emerged as a viable solution to the economic crisis and the grand social experiment was underway. Similarly, during the Great Society era, social and racial inequalities emerged as pressing social problems. Obviously, they were hardly new problems; indeed, some of the legislation associated with the Second New Deal has been described by Harvard Sitkoff as instrumental to the later civil rights movement:

> [The New Deal] played its part by substantively and symbolically assist-
> ing blacks to an unprecedented extent, by making explicit as never before
> the federal government's recognition of and responsibility for the plight
> of African Americans, and by creating a reform atmosphere that made
> possible a major campaign for civil rights.[19]

Although the seeds for civil rights reform were likely planted long before the 1960s, it was in the decade leading up to this time that these problems took on a new significance. We were, after all, in the midst of multiple highly visible social movements that brought stark attention to the problem of inequality. This experimental mindset began, perhaps, with ending the desegregation of public functions in the 1940s and 1950s, beginning with President Truman's executive order that desegregated the U.S. Army in 1948, followed by the Supreme Court's ruling in *Brown v. Board of Education* ordering the desegregation of public schools six years later.[20] These desegregation efforts dominated social and political life in the middle of the twentieth century, bringing a public focus on the dual problems of racial and social inequality.[21] By the mid-1960s, the problem of inequality could no longer be ignored. The Great Society was offered as a vision for what America could become, and the collection of opportunity programs that accompanied that vision were widely accepted as practicable ways to address poverty and widespread inequality.

From the New Deal to the Great Society to the Punishment Imperative

Despite some resistance, public assistance programs and economic opportunity initiatives grew through the period spanning from 1935 through the mid-1970s.[22] Although conservatives fought vocally against the expansion of social programs through the 1960s, it was during the 1970s that the backlash against government spending on social welfare programs was launched in earnest. In this sense, the Great Society programs are particularly relevant to the notion of incarceration as a grand social experiment. Indeed, it has been argued that the punitive turn in criminal justice policy was largely a response to the excessive permissiveness of the welfarist approach to social problems.[23]

It is frequently argued that social policy and penal policy are so tightly intertwined that together they constitute a relatively coherent "policy regime."[24] According to this line of argument, both social and penal policies target the same group—those who are socially marginal. When social causes of marginality (poverty, unemployment, inequality, and the like) are emphasized, as they were during the Great Society War on Poverty era, we can expect to see more concerted efforts to integrate those in society who are deemed socially marginal (the poor, the unemployed, the homeless, the criminal). In these times, we tend to see expansion in integrative policies such as welfare assistance, educational and occupational opportunity initiatives, and rehabilitative programs. By contrast, when the causes of social marginality are attributed to the individual and constructed as the result of (poor) rational choices, idleness, innate badness, and the like we tend to depict the socially marginal as undeserving of our sympathy or our aid and develop more punitive and exclusionary policies for the control of these populations.[25] Under this conception, imprisonment, an exclusionary penal policy for dealing with those who are socially marginal, can be contrasted with welfare, an inclusionary social policy for dealing with that very same population.

The Punishment Imperative as a Grand Social Experiment

As noted in the previous chapter, criminologists writing in the years prior to the beginning of the grand penal experiment that would result in mass incarceration certainly did not see the experiment coming. The preeminent punishment scholar, Norval Morris, argued in 1965 that the end of imprisonment was near.[26] In his acclaimed history of penal institutions, David Rothman suggested that we had been "gradually escaping from institutional responses," and foresaw a "period when incarceration will be used still more rarely than it is today."[27] Relying on trends in imprisonment over the previous century, in the early 1970s criminologist Alfred Blumstein and his colleagues argued famously that punishment was probably a self-regulating system.[28] And Marc Mauer, who has served as executive director of the Sentencing Project since 2005, has speculated that had the social experiment in mass incarceration been announced as a concerted policy strategy for reducing crime, public outrage would have ensued.[29] As rates of imprisonment began their steep uphill climb, scholars of punishment and social control (who tend to be critical of institutional responses and exclusionary approaches) remained optimistic and would never have predicted that growth in imprisonment would continue unabated for close to four decades.[30]

To be fair, few criminologists could have known at the time that the wars on crime and drugs would be fought with such fervor and with a marked determination to enact policies that all but ensured the massive buildup in incarceration. As Kevin Reitz recently argued, "the U.S. has embarked upon one of the greatest experiments in the use of governmental coercion known to history" and has done so "without advance planning and without an articulable rationale that can be reconstructed with confidence after the fact"—let alone as it was happening.[31] This is what makes the Punishment Imperative a particularly insidious social

experiment—the goal was never articulated, the full array of consequences was never considered, and the momentum built even as the
forces driving the policy shifts diminished.

The Seeds of the Punishment Imperative: Public Alarm about Crime

Just as the New Deal and the Great Society initiatives were envisioned
as potential solutions to the most pressing social problems of their time,
so too was incarceration. In claiming that mass incarceration can be
understood as the end result of a grand social experiment in punishment, we are arguing that increasingly harsh punishment was offered as
an answer—indeed, perhaps the only politically viable answer—to one
of the most pressing social problems facing Americans at the time. In
the late 1960s, crime emerged as a social problem of increasing urgency
in the American consciousness. As crime increased markedly through
the 1960s and into the early 1970s, public fear of crime and the sense
that informal social control was breaking down increased alongside it.[32]

Between 1960 and 1970, the crime rate doubled. In retrospect, commentators have looked critically at this figure and found much reason
to question its accuracy, but at the time there was no denying that crime
was the core concern of the day.[33] The very first recommendation of the
1967 Crime Commission report conveys the growing sense of urgency
around the problem of crime: "The Commission finds, first, that America must translate its well-founded alarm about crime into social action
that will prevent crime."[34] Capitalizing on public alarm, the nightly news
increasingly began to feature crime stories and Gallup poll after Gallup poll found that crime had risen to the top of public concerns. The
rapid and multiyear rise in crime was the 500-pound gorilla of public
policy. It is important to stress that while increasing crime rates actually may have been a "real" problem for people, especially poor people
at risk of victimization, this is not what served as a foundation for the
grand penal experiment. Rather, it was the way crime posed a political
problem—and thereby offered a political opportunity—that became the
basis for the grand social experiment in punishment. Concern about

crime became an orienting idea that defined political camps and political agendas, and building a platform about crime that incorporated the punitive ideal became a kind of truism in U.S. politics.

Public Alarm Meets Political Convenience and a New Conceptualization of the Problem of Crime Arises

The Punishment Imperative was made possible by a pair of fundamental shifts in orientation—a shift in our understanding of the nature and causes of crime and a related shift in our understanding of the purpose of punishment.

Our understanding of punishment has historically been related to our understanding of the nature and causes of crime. Until the early 1970s, many believed that crime was just one of a cluster of social problems related to poverty, inequality, and lack of opportunity. The dominant criminological theories of the era that immediately preceded the buildup in incarceration tended to emphasize the social and ecological causes of crime (poverty, inequality, lack of opportunity, high rates of unemployment, social disorganization, and the like). Many would have argued that crime was an inevitable byproduct of the social problems associated with vast inequality and that the Great Society's War on Poverty, with its economic and educational opportunity programs, would also go a long way toward reducing crime.

The post-Nixon era of national policy saw a profound pessimism emerge as the dominant idea regarding crime. A number of scholars have commented upon this era.[35] The broad contours of these commentaries are the same: after the Great Society, a national doubt emerged that social programs, either directed at poverty generally or at criminals specifically, could do much to alleviate rising crime. Instead, a new dedication to swift and certain punishments was necessary in order to give the criminal law the teeth it needed to guide us out of the abyss of an ever more unsafe society. Nobody described this new idea better than political scientist James Q. Wilson, in his 1975 book, *Thinking about Crime*.[36] Wilson's view was that the deterrent power of the law had been increasingly dissipated by a misplaced desire to reform criminals and create social equity. The result of this mistaken desire to "help" people avoid crime was that the basic reason not to be criminal—the undesirability of being punished—had all but disappeared. Instead, he said, we needed laws that punished firmly and were imposed uniformly. Wilson's work foreshadowed a four-decade-long policy shift following that formula. We discuss the influence of this and other works in the paragraphs that follow.

CRIME AND THE PUNISHMENT IMPERATIVE

It is tempting to think—and broadly believed to be true—that the rise in punitiveness was a straightforward response to the politics surrounding rising crime rates. This is at once essentially true but also too simplistic a casting of the problem. There are two significant facts that are inconsistent with the idea that punitiveness arose in the United States as a consequence of crime.

First, the rise in crime rates predate the punitive response by a full decade. Crime rates, historically stable for much of the twentieth century, began to rise during the second half of the 1950s. Incarceration rates did not rise until the first half of the 1970s. In fact, there was a fairly short-lived but important move toward decarceration in the 1960s. It is fair to expect a lag between the rise of a social problem and a movement to address it, but the dynamic here reflects more than a decade's delay between rising crime and the coalescence of a response. A fully satisfactory explanation of the rise in punitiveness must take into account this delay, and incorporate it into the overall theory.

Second, the punitive agenda continued long after the crime rate stabilized, and well into a period of dropping crime rates. From the late 1970s to the late 1980s, crime rates fluctuated, but around an essentially stable level. Yet this was a period of almost frenzied harshness in punishments. It was amid this frenzy that many of the determinate sentencing and mandatory minimum sentencing schemes were enacted, that we witnessed a substantial drop in the use of probation and other community sanctions, and that we saw the beginning of a series of targeted sentencing reforms meant to deal with drug offenders, recidivists, and people convicted of sex crimes. Indeed, after more than a decade of declining crime from the early 1990s, punitive rhetoric remained strong. It has been tempered by hard fiscal realities in the states during the end of the first decade of the new millennium, but abating interest in the punitive ideal seems more a consequence of money than of ideology.

So the punitive era in U.S. penal policy, while it corresponds with a signal rise in crime in the previous decade, does not map very closely onto that shift in crime. While it would be naive to say that the punitive turn had little to do with the rise in crime, the mere fact of rising crime rates is an insufficient explanation for U.S. punitiveness. In fact, as others have pointed out, penal harshness was consonant with several other social dynamics that characterize the onset of the closing decades of the twentieth century.[37] Concern about crime was only one of these.

Indeed, concern about crime became shorthand for a broader concern about what many perceived as the general breakdown of order. The term, "law 'n' order" came to stand for the bedrock idea that social control had broken down, and strong measures were needed to reestablish it. To adherents of the "law 'n' order" ideal, there was plenty of evidence that things had gone awry. Mass demonstrations were common, with protests against the Vietnam War in the late 1960s following on the heels of regular civil rights protests in the first half of the decade. To a somewhat lesser extent, the social challenges represented by the women's liberation movement also contributed to the idea that the long-standing order of things was breaking down—or at least seemed threatening to those wed to more traditional gender roles. To people who might have been entirely comfortable with the extant social order, it may have seemed that the there was an onslaught of new values that undercut virtually everything they cared about.

We have already pointed out that conservative political leaders developed a rhetoric and a perspective that spoke directly to these concerns. But the way this occurred offers important insights into the dynamics of "law 'n' order" politics. In particular, it shows how the politicization of crime was closely linked to white backlash in the politics of race.

In the southern states, there was in the 1960s a strong political tradition of opposition to the changes arising as a consequence of street demonstrations. This is best exemplified by Alabama twice electing George Wallace its governor, in 1962 and 1970, and Georgia electing Lester Maddox its governor in 1967. Wallace gained his voters' support when he personally stood in front of two black students, seeking to block their enrollment as the first black students in the University of Alabama. Maddox refused to serve blacks in his Atlanta restaurant, and, brandishing a handgun, threatened Georgia Tech students when they came to be served there while handing out axe handles to his customers so that they could confront the "racial agitators." These and other southern figures, such as Strom Thurmond of South Carolina, were polarizing figures who represented a mostly white viewpoint that people were using threats and disruption to fundamentally alter the social order. These feelings became set in stone following the passage of the Civil Rights Acts in 1964, and Barry Goldwater made his opposition to civil rights legislation a core aspect of his campaign for the presidency in 1964. He was trounced, but he was the first Republican presidential candidate to win electoral votes in the South after Reconstruction. The South was no longer reliably Democratic in national electoral politics, and white reaction to changes in race relations was key to this transition.

It was left to Richard Nixon to reap the benefits of Goldwater's breakthrough. He linked street disruption to street crime and proposed a new War against Crime as a way to mobilize support in the South, but in a way that was consonant with growing media attention and public concern about crime. Linking crime to social order cleansed the backlash against disorder from the contaminating backdrop of racial injustice, and enabled the rhetoric in favor of restoring order to be more palatable to a general public increasingly troubled by fear of crime. In national public opinion surveys, fear of crime had shot to the top of the list, and "law 'n' order" spoke directly to that fear in a way that almost no other idea could.

Ronald Reagan continued this strategy of running a campaign as though his opponent's support for constitutional rights and social justice

were the same as being soft on crime. Crime politics hit its apex when
Reagan's successor, George H. W. Bush, famously used the images of
black murderer-rapist Willie Horton to paint his opponent, Massachusetts Governor Michael Dukakis, as "soft on crime" because he presided
over the state when Horton received his furlough.[38]

RACE AS A FOUNDATION FOR PUNISHMENT

Three points can be made about the crime politics era from Goldwater
to Bush Senior. First, the modern punitive movement owes much of its
energy to the abiding discomforts Americans have about race. "Getting
tough" got its first burst of energy in the South, arising as part of a gen-
eralized reaction against civil rights and the street demonstrations that
facilitated the end of Jim Crow. It became a full-fledged agenda when
Richard Nixon was able to coalesce the hidden fears of a white majority as not a problematic resistance to civil rights but rather an entirely
understandable desire to be free of fear of crime—he even called his
agenda "toward freedom from fear." By the 1980s, this linkage was complete. No politician could afford to be successfully painted with the label
"soft on crime."[39] The result was that the national conversation about
crime became a one-sided debate about how tough we needed to be, and
issues of racial justice were completely decoupled from the conversation about safety, with the remarkable outcome that the nation faced its
concerns about crime as though they could be confronted without even
thinking about race.

Second, the growth of the penal system maps much more successfully
onto the dynamics of crime rhetoric than onto crime itself.[40] As we said,
the most substantial jump in penality occurred in the 1980s, even after
crime rates had reached their apex. And the waning of punitiveness has
been associated not with a drop in crime but rather with the growth of
international threat and economic insecurity as public concerns while
fear of crime drops down the list.

Third, and not surprisingly, given this history, the punishment
experiment has had dramatic racial effects. No social group has borne
the brunt of the get-tough movement more than African Americans.

Overall, blacks are locked up at six times the rate of whites.[41] When the full apparatus of the formal systems of social control are taken into account—prison, probation, parole, and other correctional methods— one in thirty-one adult Americans is entangled within it. By contrast, one in eleven African American adults is currently under correctional control.[42] With at least one in nine young black men between the ages of twenty and thirty-four currently in prison,[43] young black males are the group most demonstrably affected by the policies of the Punishment Imperative.

So we might say that the grand penal experiment was about crime. But it was also very much about race, and its foray into the dynamics of race relations and race politics in America has had significant staying power.

CHANGE IN CORRECTIONAL ETHICS

At the same time, the correctional project was also undergoing change. Until the 1970s, corrections had been guided by a long-standing belief in the potential for rehabilitation. Although the rehabilitative strategy had varied over the past century, a belief that rehabilitation could work—through enabling individual change, through treating pathology, through providing educational and employment skills and opportunities—remained the backbone of the correctional orientation. All of that changed when the rising crime rates of the 1960s were met with a series of critiques of our understanding of the nature of criminal offending and calls to modify our strategies for addressing crime.

Decline in faith in the rehabilitative ideal coalesced around the publication of Robert Martinson's now-infamous 1974 article, "What Works? Questions and Answers about Prison Reform."[44] In that article, Martinson reviewed an abundance of empirical work on rehabilitative programming and ultimately argued that with regard to rehabilitation, it seemed that nothing had worked very well. Prior to the publication of this article, rehabilitation and the indeterminate sentencing schemes that typically accompany the correctional goal of rehabilitation had been attacked from both the Left and the Right. Those on the right, who had begun to depict criminal offenders as intractable, irredeemable, and undeserving of our sympathies, argued that indeterminate sentences often led to lenience in punishment and lobbied for the pursuit of more retributively oriented, deterrence-inducing punishment. In a word, this equated to calling for more certain, swift, and severe sentences that more appropriately communicated social disapproval and increased the costs associated with committing crime. Those on the left, dismayed with the amount of discretion afforded to judges and correctional authorities, argued that when the sentence was indeterminate and release was dependent upon the whim of a parole board, abuses had almost certainly followed.

Central to all of this was a shift away from the uneasy ideology of the Great Society notion that an individual's problem behavior comes about as a consequence of embedded social problems—namely, economic, social, and racial inequality—that act as the foundation for behavior. At question here were the core claims of a social-service platform that maintained that people in difficult circumstances find it hard to overcome the barriers of an unfair society and that the remedy is to increase fairness. In place of this general idea, a new paradigm gained momentum in which individuals were seen as responsible for their own actions, agents of their own making, whose choices were based on calculations about costs and benefits. Those rational calculations were shaped, in part, by the weaknesses on the cost side. The irony was that both models saw people who commit crime as creations, in part, of their contexts, but the ideology of punishment held that the main context of concern was not "opportunity" but "costs." Society simply did not impose enough hardship on those who engaged in criminal activity, and the result was that they did so with near impunity. No work better laid bare this idea than Wilson's *Thinking about Crime*, with its admonition to stop worrying about root causes and start fighting crime by managing the risks.[45] Wilson's work popularized the notion that it was time to stop "coddling criminals" and start punishing. Criminologist Malcolm Feeley has described this transformation in the following way:

Martinson's and Wilson's pieces had enormous influence in shaping subsequent crime policy. Martinson's article crystallized opposition not only to rehabilitation programs but to social programs designed to prevent crime more generally. Wilson's writings set forth an alternative set of concerns. Rather suddenly, social workers and traditional (i.e. structural) criminologists were out of fashion and out of favor.[46]

This shift in orientation away from the Great Society and toward the Punishment Imperative was offered in a historic moment when mounting concern about crime offered a window of opportunity for a new approach to crime control.

Strategies Arise That Meld Political Interests and Lead to a Reformulated Understanding of the Problem

We saw, then, in the 1970s, a seismic shift in orientation—a shift toward the Punishment Imperative. Given that criminal offenders were calculating rational thinkers choosing crime because crime paid, our approach to addressing crime had to include increasing the costs associated with committing crime. In a return to the classical school foundations of criminal justice, increasing the cost of crime involved increasing the probability that crime would result in punishment. Arguments in favor of retribution and deterrence held the day, and opposition, where it existed,[47] was relegated to the stoic halls of academia.

It is almost impossible to overstate the get-tough character of the ensuing paradigm shift in criminal justice. Where crime was the question, it seemed incarceration was inevitably the answer. Twenty years on, this equation was still viable. As recently as 1996, John DiIulio asked, "If incarceration is not the answer, what, precisely, is the question?"—and then answered his own rhetorical question: "if the question is how to restrain known convicted criminals from murdering, raping, robbing, assaulting and stealing, then incarceration is a solution, and a highly cost-effective one."[48] DiIulio went on to espouse the benefits of a policy of mass incarceration:

On average, it costs about $25,000 a year to keep a convicted criminal in prison. For that money, society gets four benefits: Imprisonment punishes offenders and expresses society's moral disapproval. It teaches felons and would-be felons a lesson: Do crime, do time. Prisoners get drug treatment and education. And, as the columnist Ben Wattenberg has noted, "A thug in prison can't shoot your sister."[49]

The power of this incapacitation rhetoric was evident in how popularized such sentiments became. "You do the crime, you do the time" or "lock 'em up and throw away the key" rapidly became slogans that most grade school children could recite. Moreover, although violence and violent offenders may have been a symbolic target, we did not just go after the thugs with guns. Throughout the 1980s and 1990s, politicians and policymakers made conscious choices that virtually ensured the mass incarceration that we have today. These will be described in more detail in the chapter that follows, but by way of example, the War on Drugs generally, and the Anti–Drug Abuse Acts of 1986 and 1988 specifically, included sentencing provisions that ensured that the supply of drug offenders eligible for imprisonment would increase exponentially. Mandatory minimum sentences for drug offenses, violent offenses, weapons offenses, and habitual offending ensured that a wide array of sentenced offenders would spend more time in prison than they ever had previously. As though mandatory sentences were not enough, almost half of the states passed three-strikes laws to provide for extraordinarily lengthy terms of incarceration for third-time violent offenders. Truth-in-sentencing, the most significant contribution of the late 1990s, added insurance to our investment in keeping offenders in prison for more protracted periods of time.

With so many policy initiatives across so many fronts over such an extended period of time, it should come as no surprise that the Punishment Imperative ultimately had such a profound effect on the size and scope of prison populations. Perhaps what has made our grand penal experiment most remarkable is that until very recently incarceration rates remained strong regardless of the usual social forces that we have, for many years, thought were the source of those rates. Prison popula-tions grew during periods when crime grew (1960–1980; 1985–1991), but also while crime fell (1981–1984, 1992–present); they grew in times of war/conflict (1983, 1989, 1990–1991, 1995–1996, and 2001–present) and during times of relative peace (mid-1970s through most of the 1980s, 1992–1995, 1996–2001); and they grew during good economic times (1982–1988, 1999–2001) and bad (1973, 1979, 1980–1982, 1988–1992, 2001–2003, 2007–2009). The Punishment Imperative has been a con-stant for an entire generation, remaining a staple of American policy even while other aspects of the nation changed remarkably.

Limits of the Grand Social Experiment Metaphor

Although we propose the experiment metaphor as a useful one for understanding the extraordinary pattern of sustained growth in the penal complex between 1970 and 2010, we recognize that there are some hazards in using the metaphor because it connotes a level of intentional-ity that does not easily apply to the changes in the penal system. There is a certain clarity to the grand social experiments of the New Deal and the Great Society. The legislation putting these experiments into place was clearly defined as such and most of the legislative initiatives associ-ated with these grand social experiments were enacted over a relatively brief period of time. The policy initiatives most closely associated with the first New Deal were mainly contained in the 1933 Emergency Bank-ing Act creating the Federal Deposit Insurance Corporation (FDIC), the 1934 Securities and Exchange Act creating the Securities and Exchange Commission (SEC), the 1933 Agricultural Adjustment and National Industrial Recovery Acts, each of which was intended to rescue key industries (and both of which were ultimately struck down by the U.S. Supreme Court). The vast majority of legislation associated with the first New Deal was passed within the first one hundred or so days of the Roosevelt administration in 1933. Similarly, the legislation associated with the Second New Deal was passed in a relatively confined period of time (1934 to 1936). Johnson's Great Society legislation took the form of a series of federal legislative achievements, including prohibitions against housing discrimination, civil rights laws, and the establishment of Medicare and Medicaid.[50] Both of these grand social experiments consisted almost exclusively of packages of federal laws; neither of them required much local initiative or legislation.

By contrast, education reform involved a combination of local and federal action. Mandatory education became U.S. policy as a series of state-by-state laws were enacted, beginning with Massachusetts in 1852 and continuing until the last state passed such a law in 1918. In 1954, in one fell swoop, legislatively segregated schools became a thing of the past with the unanimous U.S. Supreme Court decision in *Brown v. Board of Education* (1954).[51] Although the women's suffrage movement experienced a series of small but important local victories between the 1850s and the 1920s, women's suffrage formally became the nation's standard in 1920 when the Nineteenth Amendment was ratified.

In each of these cases, a grand social experiment to deal with a pressing social issue can be linked to a fairly finite point in time. If a scientist were inclined to do so, he or she could meaningfully propose an evaluation of the experiment based on an examination of social circumstances before and after the changes were put into place. Inevitably, some version of a time series would apply in the effort to measure the impact of the change on some outcome of interest.

As we have described it, the Punishment Imperative shares many of the characteristics we have described for other grand social experiments. Like education reform, the changes in the penal system occurred as states passed a host of legislative changes designed to grow the penal system. And yet, as we have seen, the federal government also played a role with its heavy sentencing guidelines (especially for drug distribution offenses) and the Violent Offender Incarceration and Truth in Sentencing Incentive Grant Program (VOI/TIS), passed during the Clinton administration. The "intervention" of the penal experiment was, thus, a complex series of varied laws passed primarily by the many states one by one, extending over more than a decade's period of time. In fact, rather than a single policy experiment, it is in some ways more reasonable to think of the Punishment Imperative as a series of fifty-one different experiments occurring across the fifty states and the federal jurisdiction. Elsewhere the point has been made that there is not really a single American penal story, but rather fifty-one of them, each somewhat different in its themes.[52]

As with the Great Society, there was also a social vision that served as impetus for the penal reform movement. Advocates for change envisioned a tough "war" on crime in which any meaningful point of leverage would be used to increase the punitive response to crime. And like all of these social changes, the political context was crucial, as potentially diverse political viewpoints coalesced to set the groundwork for legal and policy shifts of substantial importance.

With all of its limitations, we think the "grand social experiment" metaphor remains a useful one for several reasons. Most particularly, we think each of the elements of the "grand social experiment" idea is well represented in the case of the Punishment Imperative. There is a galvanizing problem (crime) and an orienting take on it (eradicating leniency). Diverse interests—emerging from the Left and the Right—coalesce to see the need for action in a similar light. Solutions are proposed that relate directly to the problem as perceived; laws are passed and new institutions born. The fact that in the case of the Punishment Imperative these debates extend over a protracted period of time and lead to heterogeneity of local legal responses does not mean that we cannot call it a grand social experiment. It merely means that certain evaluation tools, such as before-after time series impact models, cannot meaningfully be constructed. Fair enough. But for other grand social experiments, we might point out that these evaluation models are rarely employed anyway. And besides, our interest in the experiment metaphor is not actually to conduct a formal evaluation but to provide an intellectually useful structure for understanding what happened in the latter half of the twentieth century in the U.S. penal system. We use the metaphor not as a scientific device, but as a rhetorical one.

Conclusion

Unlike many grand social experiments, enacted by political leaders taking advantage of the co-alignment of forces taking place at a particular point in time, the Punishment Imperative was an experiment that maintained strength for decades and was embraced across the political spectrum. It represented a major change in social policy enacted in order to gain certain utilitarian ends, and may thus be seen as a classic kind of grand social experiment in the pragmatic American tradition. The metaphor of an experiment also helps us understand that after decades of ascendance as an idea, the strength of the Punishment Imperative is waning, as evidence accumulates about the consequences of the changes and policy attention on public safety turns elsewhere.

4

The Policies of the Punishment Imperative

Virtually all contemporary commentaries on correctional policy begin, almost ritualistically, by chronicling—and most often decrying—the seemingly endless roster of policies designed in recent years to inflict increasing amounts of pain on offenders.
—Francis T. Cullen, Bonnie S. Fisher, and Brandon K. Applegate, 2000[1]

When the President's Commission on Law Enforcement and Administration of Justice (hereafter 1967 Crime Commission) convened by President Lyndon B. Johnson released its report, *The Challenge of Crime in a Free Society*, in 1967, the influence of the Great Society ideas and ideals was still very evident. In the summary that preceded the lengthy report, the 1967 Crime Commission offered three overarching recommendations. The very first recommendation emphasized attention to the root causes of crime:

> The Commission finds, first, that America must translate its well-founded alarm about crime into social action that will prevent crime. It has no doubt whatever that the most significant action that can be taken against crime is action designed to eliminate slums and ghettos, to improve education, to provide jobs, to make sure that every American is given the opportunities and the freedoms that will enable him to assume his responsibilities. We will not have dealt effectively with crime until we

have alleviated the conditions that stimulate it. To speak of controlling crime only in terms of the work of the police, the courts and the correctional apparatus, is to refuse to face the fact that widespread crime implies a widespread failure by society as a whole.[2]

The second and third recommendations addressed the need for investment in the justice system and for innovation across criminal justice system agencies, respectively. The Crime Commission, it seemed, recognized that confronting crime would prove challenging, but appeared confident that its recommendations would go a long way toward meeting those challenges.

It is one of the great ironies in U.S. penal policy that during the forty-year period following this 1967 Crime Commission recommendation, it was so completely ignored. It is as though, with great fanfare, a major pronouncement was made about the path toward justice, and nobody heard it. Despite this clarion call for a social agenda to combat crime, precious little happened. Following the police riots of the 1968 Chicago presidential election, law 'n' order quickly became a main topic in the political conversation. Rather than an agenda to confront the causes of crime, we elected a Nixon administration that promised a War on Crime. That this kind of 180-degree shift could occur is stunning, but that it happened so quickly and so completely is astonishing.

Cognizant of the ways in which we are surely oversimplifying, we argue that it is useful to think of crime policy change as having occurred across three eras that roughly coincide with the passing of decades (and with three administrations). In the first (the 1970s) both violent and nonviolent offending became the target of a Nixon administration hell bent on doing something about crime. Here we would see upheavals of sentencing structures that had been at least a century in the making. In the second (the 1980s), the Reagan administration launched an all-out War on Drugs with drug offenders and offenses fueling much of the growth in penal populations. In the third (the 1990s), with violent crime reaching new heights, the Clinton administration pushed a crime control agenda that would target the most violent or intractable offenders.

Targeting Crime (1970s)

While the seeds of the Punishment Imperative were planted in the 1960s, the grand social experiment really began to take shape in the 1970s. Barry Goldwater's posturing around crime during his failed 1964 presidential bid and Johnson's subsequent establishment of the 1967 Crime Commission brought crime into a spotlight whose intensity has not since dimmed. Crime rates, which were believed to be at an all-time high when the Crime Commission published its report, only grew in the interim years.[3] Just five years after the publication of the 1967 report, James Vorenberg, who had served as executive director of the 1967 Crime Commission, wrote,

> No one can say for sure what accounts for the enormous increase in the danger which Americans face from each other. We do know that those agencies on which we are accustomed to rely for crime control—police, courts, and corrections—seem less capable of that task today than they did five years ago, and many police chiefs, judges, and prison officials openly acknowledge that there is nothing they can do to help.[4]

For all its fanfare and prescriptions for confronting the challenge of crime, it seems the report with its many recommendations had done little to assuage crime or fear of crime.

Shortly thereafter, political scientist James Q. Wilson, sociologist Ernest van den Haag, and other conservative commentators began to argue for a new, more punitive approach to crime control.[5] Gone were the references to society's failure in terms of its ability to eliminate poverty, address inequality, and provide opportunity. In their place, the neoconservative commentators ushered in a new rhetoric aimed at placing responsibility for crime squarely on the offenders themselves. Emphasizing rational choice and individual responsibility, these neocons endorsed expansion in the use of imprisonment as the principle mechanism by which to effectively fight the new war on crime. While this argument took a long time to become a commonly held view among academic criminologists, it was quickly a dominant view among political elites, and it comported nicely with a general public that had been placing public safety at or near the top of social concerns for a decade.

Targeting Drug Offenses and Offenders (1980s)

In the 1980s, partly because of concern about a "crack epidemic," the focus shifted toward drug offenders. The Sentencing Guidelines created by the U.S. Congress, in the Sentencing Reform Act of 1984, established strong penalty thresholds for drug-related offenses. The already stiff penalties were made even more severe by the Anti–Drug Abuse Act of 1986. Mandatory prison sentences of five years were required for anyone convicted of selling five grams or more of crack cocaine, and ten-year terms were required for fifty grams or more. (A major dispute arose regarding the racially disparate consequences of the enormous difference between penalties for crack as compared to powder cocaine, but by any measure all the penalties were far more severe than under prior law.)

The federal experience was not isolated. Almost every state passed some version of a drug-related sentencing reform measure in this same time period. Many of these statutes were based on the federal guidelines, requiring prison terms for small amounts of prohibited drugs. An example is Delaware's 1989 law that set a threshold of five grams of illicit drugs to require a mandatory five-year term in prison.[6]

The effect of this spate of state-level legislation, in combination with the federal law, was to vastly increase the population of prisoners serving time for drug offenses. The number of new court commitments for drug-related crimes increased from about 12,000 in 1980 to about 102,000 in 1991. Many of these new commitments served short sentences, but their collective impact on the overall populations was profound. The number of people incarcerated for drug crimes increased tenfold between 1980 and 2001.[7]

The poster child for these changes was the state of New York, whose drug law changes in 1973 (called the "Rockefeller Drug Laws" because of the enthusiastic support from then-governor Nelson A. Rockefeller) were the bellwether for the rest of the country. The penalty for selling two ounces of controlled substances (including marijuana) was set at a minimum of fifteen years to life (larger amounts were twenty-five to life). The New York prison population started to balloon. By 2010, there were more than ten thousand people serving time under these laws, close to one-fifth of the state's total prison population.[8]

The changes in sentencing for people convicted of drug crimes makes the most obvious case that the unprecedented growth in imprisonment in the 1980s and 1990s was a consequence of deliberate policy decisions, and not some natural product of changes in crime. Changes in drug penalties were not an external force over which policymakers had little control; they were instead a series of decisions policymakers made to change things. They were a legal reform idea: a rather deliberate social experiment.

Targeting Violent Crime and Repeat Offenders (1990s)

Although we continued fighting the War on Drugs well into the 1990s, in the early 1990s the focus of the Punishment Imperative returned once more to violent offenders. Between the mid-1980s and the early 1990s, violent crime spiked, increasing by more than one-third. Political rhetoric about violent crime also grew. Among the more strident voices was that of President William Jefferson Clinton (1993–2001), who was determined to prove himself to be as tough on crime as anyone else on the political scene. The dominant rhetoric singled out repeat offenders, especially violent offenders, as particularly important sources of the rapid increase in crime. The general public was exposed to repeated news stories about previously convicted felons who engaged in dramatic violent incidents. A kind of public outrage developed that people who are punished once do not desist from crime, but rather account for such a disproportionate share of mayhem.

No analysis illustrated this line of thinking better than then–Princeton University professor John DiIulio's essay warning us of the coming onslaught of violent juveniles, who came to be referred to as super-predators.[9] His language seemed intentionally designed to alarm, calling forth an image of teeming gangs of "stone-cold killers," as he put it, "an estimated 270,000 more young predators on the streets." They would be "the youngest, biggest and baddest generation any society has ever known."[10] He was not alone. Northeastern University professor James Alan Fox called these juvenile super-predators "the young and the ruthless."[11]

These intellectuals did not produce the public froth about repeat violent criminals, but their work and their rhetoric certainly reflected it. They also provided a scientific legitimacy to politicians who proposed initiatives focused on repeat criminality. After all, if the usually circumspect halls of academe were in an uproar over the scourge of young predatory criminals in our midst, what is a politician to do but to take on this exploding social problem?

And they did take it on. The 1990s saw a spate of legislative reform, the general thrust of which was to make sentences longer for those people who it seemed had shown, by their repeat behavior, that the usual punishments did not work. Under the Punishment Imperative, the solution when punishments fail is, of course, more punishment.

The Policy Shifts behind the Punishment Imperative

The collective experience was indeed an imperative: the penal system *must* be made harsher, more unforgiving, more punitive. In order for the Punishment Imperative to have such a profound and far-reaching effect, many policies had to be changed. In the rest of this chapter, we describe some of the policies that produced the enormous changes over an extended period of time. As we will argue in chapter 7, these are the very policies that will need to be undone if we are to successfully reverse course and substantially reduce our reliance on incarceration. The most expansive sentencing shifts were those that altered the structure of sentencing across the United States: most notably the shift to determinate sentencing and the introduction of sentencing guidelines.

From Indeterminate to Determinate Sentencing

An early sweeping change in sentencing policy came with the introduction of determinate sentencing structures and the often simultaneous
abolition of discretionary parole release.[12] For much of the past century,
the structure of sentencing systems had been fairly uniform across the
states. Rehabilitation had been the core goal of the correctional system,
and sentencing schemes had been designed to allow for a fair amount
of individual variation in the amount of time it might take to treat different offenders. All states had a form of indeterminate sentencing
wherein the criminal statute specified a fairly broad range of sentences
that would allow for release (at the discretion of the paroling authority)
upon sufficient evidence of rehabilitation. Beginning in the mid-1970s,
states began to switch from these indeterminate sentencing schemes to
determinate ones. In determinate sentencing, a precise sentence (or a
far more narrow sentence range) is prescribed, and release is generally
determined by the statutorily imposed sentence minus any good time.[13]

The advent of the determinate sentence coincided with the decline of
faith in rehabilitation that coalesced around the publication of Robert
Martinson's now-infamous 1974 article, "What Works? Questions and
Answers about Prison Reform." In that article, Martinson asked what
worked, reviewed an abundance of empirical studies, and ultimately
argued that, with regard to rehabilitation, it appeared that the evidence
suggested that nothing seemed to have worked very well.[14] Prior to the
publication of this article, rehabilitation, and particularly the indeterminate sentencing scheme that generally accompanies the goal of rehabilitation, had been attacked by those on the left and on the right of
the political spectrum. Those on the right, who had begun to depict
criminal offenders as intractable, irredeemable, and undeserving of our
sympathies, felt that indeterminate sentences all too often led to lenience
in punishment and lobbied hard for the pursuit of more retributively
oriented punishment.[15] Those on the left, dismayed with the amount of
discretion afforded to correctional authorities in the granting of discretionary parole release, argued that when the sentence was indeterminate

and release was dependent upon the whim of a parole board, abuses had followed and would persist. Nobody, it seemed, was particularly content with the sentencing structures that had been in place since at least the turn of the previous century.[16]

Moreover, the impact that the transition from indeterminate to determinate sentences had on prison populations remained contested. Some argued that a switch to determinate sentencing would increase prison populations because the switch was often accompanied by the abolition of discretionary parole release.[17] Discretionary parole release—wherein a parole board would review the inmate's case and institutional conduct to make an early release decision—had always served as a back-end safety valve for the correctional system. Having a discretionary parole system allowed the justice system to bark louder than it would bite in terms of punishment.[18] At sentencing, lengthy sentences could be handed down signifying strong condemnation of the act and the person could be escorted out to begin serving this outwardly harsh prison term. Discretionary parole release, however, almost invariably meant that the inmate would serve far less time than had been pronounced at sentencing.

A switch from indeterminate to determinate sentencing could potentially increase prison populations through increasing the contribution of either of the two functional determinants of prison population size. In other words, a transition to determinate sentencing could potentially increase prison admissions or length of stay or both.[19] Under the indeterminate sentencing schemes in place across all states until the 1970s, judges had relatively unfettered discretion in the assigning of a sentence. Determinate sentencing with its prescribed sentences often reduces the ability of a judge to impose a community sentence, particularly for felony offenses, and prison admissions might therefore increase. Moreover, because determinate sentences specify either a specific term or a very narrow range of term, the sentences imposed under these structures might be lengthier in the first instance and, coupled with the absence of a discretionary parole release mechanism at the back end, might lead to longer lengths of stay.

Others though have pointed out that the anticipated effects of sentencing laws generally, and sentencing structures specifically, depends to some extent on the objectives and intentions of those choosing to make the transition.[20] In places where the objective of adopting determinate sentencing was to get tough on crime and increase the deterrent value of penalties through increasing prison terms, then clearly these laws could potentially increase prison populations. If however, the intent was to restrict or control prison population growth or to endorse a just-deserts sentencing philosophy—where every offender would get what he or she is deemed to deserve but no more and no less—then these laws might be expected to ultimately result in a decrease in the size of the prison population.[21] In other words, the underlying objectives behind the adoption of determinate sentencing schemes matter. As Kevin Reitz has argued, "there is, in short, no obvious correlation between the overarching structure that a jurisdiction chooses to erect for sentencing decisions and such things as the harshness, lenity, or distribution of punishments."[22]

Crucially, although during this period many states effectively abandoned rehabilitation as their correctional goal, a majority of states have retained the indeterminate sentencing scheme that can be described as the backbone of a rehabilitative correctional orientation, and most states continue to allow for discretionary parole release.

The Introduction of Sentencing Guidelines

Shortly after the transition to determinate sentencing, states began to consider and adopt sentencing guidelines. Sentencing guidelines, which in their simplest form specify a fairly narrow range of sentence for a convicted offender based on his or her current offense and prior criminal history, were heralded as an effective way to reduce disparity in sentencing. Concern about disparity had been evident in the publication of the 1967 Crime Commission report and had only grown in the years that had followed. Sentencing guidelines were popular in states with both determinate and indeterminate sentencing structures.[23] They can be either presumptive or voluntary, and most were developed by independent sentencing commissions.[24] Presumptive sentencing guidelines provide the expected or presumed range of sentence based on an offender/

offense score and require that the judge impose a sentence within that narrow range. While permitted, departures from the guidelines (e.g., imposing a sentence outside of the presumptive range) are discouraged and often require written justification. Voluntary guidelines, on the other hand, are purely advisory, are meant to be informative, and offer appropriate ranges of sentence that the judge may choose to consider in coming to a sentencing decision. In places in which guidelines are voluntary, judges can sentence outside of the recommended range at their own discretion. In all, nineteen states had adopted guidelines between 1980 and 2002.[25]

Sentencing guidelines were initially envisioned as a way to provide a mechanism for greater judicial control over the size of prison populations and were therefore expected to potentially slow prison population growth.[26] A handful of states that had adopted sentencing guidelines had explicitly required that the sentencing commission consider institutional capacity in their formulation of guidelines, and had in some cases been quite successful in slowing the growth of their prison populations relative to other states.[27] Conversely, states wishing to expand their prison population could instruct their sentencing commission to develop pro-growth sentences, and some apparently did so quite successfully.[28] Overall, sentencing scholars largely agree that sentencing commissions had a positive effect on justice systems in that they "managed to make sentencing more accountable, more consistent, and less disparate in its impact on minority group members" and had "proven themselves the most effective prescription thus far offered for the ills of lawlessness, arbitrariness, disparity, and discrimination that were widely believed to characterize indeterminate sentencing."[29]

It is important to note that although sentencing guidelines received a more positive reception than any of the other sentencing policy changes, the experience of the states that have adopted guidelines stands in marked contrast to the experience of the federal government. There was a decidedly more critical response to the federal sentencing guidelines that took effect in 1987 and remained in effect for almost twenty years.[30] Until they were ruled advisory by the U.S. Supreme Court in the landmark case *United States v. Booker* (2005), the federal sentencing guidelines were routinely criticized for their rigidity and for their virtual elimination of judicial discretion.[31]

In contrast to the federal experience, Minnesota, which was the first state to enact sentencing guidelines, managed to maintain an imprisonment rate far below the national average, and its guidelines, which mandate consideration of prison population size, were frequently credited for playing a central role in that control. State guidelines differ in some key respects from the federal guidelines. State guidelines are both more flexible and less complicated than their federal counterpart. Indeed, some state guidelines "are so flexible that they are hardly 'guidelines' at all."[32] Despite the dismal federal experience with sentencing guidelines, state sentencing guidelines have proven more resilient, with at least one expert arguing that state sentencing guidelines "have proven to be much better than any other sentencing system which has been tried or proposed."[33]

The introduction of determinate sentencing and the development of sentencing guidelines were two fundamental shifts in the foundation of criminal sentencing because each signaled a sea change in correctional orientation. In and of themselves, neither the transition away from indeterminate sentencing nor the introduction of guidelines would have inevitably led to huge increases in the size of prison populations. Indeed, as mentioned previously, if the intent of the legislature had been to limit or restrict prison population growth, then both of these structural changes to sentencing could have been designed to accomplish those goals. These underlying structural shifts, however, took place in the context of multiple wars on crime and concomitant with a series of other policy shifts that were almost certainly designed to increase either the number of people going to prison or the length of time that they would stay there. Mandatory sentencing, three-strikes (and related habitual-offender sentencing policies), and truth-in-sentencing are among the most frequently cited punitive "tough on crime" initiatives, and all three have resulted in significant prison population growth. We refer to these specific shifts in policy orientation as the substantive changes that made up the grand penal experiment that we have called the Punishment Imperative.

The Substantive Changes That Made Up the Experiment

With a better understanding of the functional determinants of prison population growth and sweeping changes to the structure of sentencing, we now turn to the task of identifying the categories of policy changes that helped to produce the remarkable trends in prison population growth described in chapter 2.

Increasing the Likelihood of Prison and Lengthening Penalties for Certain Offenses and Offenders

As explained previously, early prison population growth was driven in part by a rapidly increasing likelihood that a person convicted of a felony offense would be sentenced to a term of imprisonment. One of the principal ways in which the likelihood of prison was increased was through restricting the availability of probation for those convicted of felony offenses. Indeed, although imprisonment certainly did not replace community sanctions such as probation, it did go from serving as a penalty of last resort for the hardened, intractable, or violent offender to serving as the penalty of first resort for offenses that would never have previously resulted in a term of incarceration. There is also evidence that judges became less willing to impose probation, regardless of legislative restrictions on its use. In the early 1980s, about three-quarters of those convicted of a felony received a probation term; by 2005, the number had dwindled to less than one-quarter.[34]

Legislative initiatives to increase penalties for serious and repeat criminality took three main forms. A first thrust was to create mandatory prison terms for people who committed offenses of particular concern to the public. Many states had already done this, of course, for drug crimes, and so the logical foundation for mandatory penalties existed in most states. Because the penalties for drug crimes were already in place in many states, they established a kind of floor for the new legislative initiatives. Almost all the crimes targeted by the new initiatives—sexual assault, homicide, and armed robbery, for instance—were *prima facie* more serious crimes than drug offenses. The logical conclusion was that whatever new penalties were imposed, they should exceed the existing mandatory terms for drug crimes.

The second thrust involved time served. Repeated news stories showing all manner of mayhem committed by people recently released from prison provoked the logical question, then why were they released? There were many critiques of sentencing systems in which lengthy terms were imposed for violent crimes, and yet people were released from prison having served only a fraction of the sentence. A "truth-in-sentencing" movement arose advocating that a judicial sentence should closely reflect the actual penalty to be imposed. Of course, that could be accomplished by reducing the often overly long judicial sentencing maximums available under the law, but that strategy was rarely taken.[35] Instead, legislative initiatives sought to make the maximum sentence the "truth," by establishing required proportions of that sentence that must be served.

Third, repeat criminality, especially violent crime, became a target as well. The logic of the Punishment Imperative is that if the quota of punishment is set too low, it cannot work. What better evidence is there that a penalty was too lenient than a recidivist felon? And so the solution is obvious: up the penal ante. This idea came to be known as the "three-strikes" movement because its most extreme version reflected the baseball metaphor: "three-strikes, you're out!" For the most vociferous advocate of harsh time, people who are convicted of a third serious felony should be sentenced to prison for life.

The collective effect of these three penal reforms movements—mandatory sentences, truth-in-sentencing, and three-strikes—was a decade of lengthened time served for the vast majority of people entering the prison system.

Mandatory Sentencing for Serious Felonies

Mandatory sentencing statutes stipulate that offenders sentenced for an offense for which there is a mandatory punishment be subject to that punishment without exception. Some have argued that the mandatory-sentence approach is perhaps best understood as the adoption of determinate sentences offense by offense.[36] Between the mid-1970s and the mid-1980s, this offense-by-offense determinate sentencing approach was pursued by all states for some types of offenses regardless of whether the state retained indeterminate sentencing or had formally switched to a determinate sentencing structure.[37] A number of states, for example, have enacted mandatory terms of life in prison without the possibility of parole for aggravated murder even if they have maintained indeterminate sentences for the majority of other offenses. This alone was a change of no small consequence. In 2010, there were 140,000 people serving life sentences in the United States, many without eligibility for parole, and this represented a fourfold increase from 1984.[38]

Mandatory sentences might require either that a term of incarceration be imposed (affecting the in/out decision) or that specific terms of incarceration apply (affecting the length of stay). In the case of the latter, these sentences are referred to as mandatory minimums. Mandatory *minimum* sentencing provisions stipulate the minimum time to be served for a conviction for a particular offense. When there is a mandatory minimum in effect, the sentencing judge, while not required to impose the maximum sentence for the offense, is not permitted to sentence to less than the statutorily mandated minimum. In addition to specifying minimum terms, some state mandatory minimum provisions specifically restrict eligibility for parole to ensure that parole boards do not release offenders serving mandatory minimum terms until the minimum term of incarceration has been served. Like determinate sentencing structures, mandatory sentencing provisions were enacted to reduce judicial discretion and decrease disparities across sentences: "The motivating rationale [behind mandatory sentences] is that every scenario of that type should result in an identical sentence, with perfect uniformity across offenders and zero discretion exercised by government officials (such as judges and parole boards) at the case level."[39]

Although mandatory sentences date as far back as 1790 at the federal level, the mandatory sentencing approach really gained traction beginning in the 1970s.[40] Since 1970, all fifty states and the federal government have adopted mandatory minimum sentencing provisions. Although a jurisdiction might have adopted mandatory minimum sentences for any offense or class of offenses, these sentencing provisions have typically applied to one of five classes of offenses or offenders: (1) repeat or habitual offending, (2) drunk driving offenses, (3) drug offenses, (4) weapons offenses, or (5) sex offenses.[41] Although these five classes of offenses dominated mandatory minimum provisions, states increasingly passed mandatory minimums for other types of offenses as well.[42]

For some time now, critics from across the political and ideological spectrum have been denouncing mandatory minimum penalties as too often unjust and unfair. Moreover, these penalties are often depicted as unnecessary, with scholars like Franklin Zimring and his colleagues arguing that "the mandatory term is a huge expansion of punishment, rendering excessive outcomes in many cases to ensure sufficiency of punishment in a very few that might otherwise escape their just deserts."[43] It seems that even some traditionally more conservative members of the nation's highest court agree. In an address to the American Bar Association, moderately conservative Supreme Court Justice Anthony Kennedy spoke out against mandatory minimum penalties, proclaiming that he "[accepts] neither the wisdom, the justice, nor the necessity of mandatory minimums," adding that "in all too many cases they are unjust" and that "our resources are misspent, our punishments too severe, our sentences too long."[44]

Mandatory sentences were expected to contribute to growing prison populations by both increasing the number of offenders sentenced to terms of imprisonment and increasing the average severity of sentences imposed on the classes of offenders or offenses sentenced under these provisions. Some have argued that mandatory minimum sentencing provisions have failed even on their own terms—neither achieving the expected increases in sentence severity nor reducing sentencing disparities. Although mandatory minimums have contributed to an increase in the severity of sentences for some of the targeted offenses, there is some evidence that mandatory minimums might have failed to drastically increase sentence severity overall.[45] Moreover, although judicial discretion has been severely restricted by mandatory sentencing, in some instances judges have managed to successfully circumvent the mandatory minimum. Perhaps most importantly, the mandatory sentence failed to eliminate discretion from the system, but instead simply displaced that discretion, transferring discretionary power from one system actor (the judge) to another (the prosecutor). The discretion to determine the sentence for mandatory-minimum-eligible offenses now rests almost entirely in the hands of the prosecutor who for all intents and purposes gets to determine the sentence when he or she files the charges.

Truth-in-Sentencing for Violent Crimes

Of all the sentencing policy changes associated with the Punishment Imperative, truth-in-sentencing legislation, unless repealed, will ultimately have the largest impact on prison populations into the future. Truth-in-sentencing laws, passed across the country in the late 1990s, required that violent offenders serve a substantial portion of their court-imposed sentence (usually 85 percent) before even becoming eligible for parole.[46] Prior to the enactment of truth-in-sentencing laws (hereafter TIS laws), most offenders served only a relatively small portion—on average about one-third—of their court-imposed sentences prior to release.[47] This was true for the majority of offenders, regardless of offense type. The system was designed to work in this way for a variety of relatively straightforward reasons. First and foremost, our entire correctional complex was built on the principles of rehabilitation that had served as the foundation for corrections for well over a hundred years. Even as enthusiasm for rehabilitation waned, the system still needed a way to make back-end adjustments to sentences. The criminal justice system has always been organized to "bark louder than it bites," presumably in the interest of furthering the deterrent value of sentences.[48] Parole, as an early-release mechanism, allowed for the pronouncement of lengthy sentences in court at sentencing to be followed by often quite substantial back-end adjustments to those sentences once the inmate was incarcerated. Truth-in-sentencing laws curtailed the ability of the system to make those back-end adjustments.

Although the first TIS law had been enacted in Washington in 1984, prior to 1994, less than ten states had TIS laws in effect.[49] As part of the omnibus 1994 Violent Crime Control and Law Enforcement Act, Congress authorized up to $10 billion in "incentive grants," referred to as Violent Offender Incarceration and Truth-in-Sentencing, or VOI/TIS, grants, to encourage the adoption of stringent truth-in-sentencing legislation across the states.[50] To receive the grants, which would provide financial assistance in the form of additional federal funding for prison construction and expansion, the states had to either already have in place or enact legislation that met the federal standard that violent offenders serve a minimum of 85 percent of their sentence prior to release.[51]

Although TIS laws were expected to quite dramatically increase time served for violent offenses, there has been debate over how much any increase in severity could be attributed *exclusively* to TIS laws. Having analyzed the effect of TIS laws in seven states, William Sabol and his colleagues argued that while "truth-in-sentencing reforms are associated with large changes in prison population outcomes . . . the changes are more appropriately associated with broader sentencing reforms than with truth-in-sentencing in particular."[52]

A Bureau of Justice Statistics analysis of time served by violent offenders who were released in 1993, 1995, and 1997 revealed that although the percentage of the sentence served for these offenders had indeed been going up (from 47 percent in 1993 to 51 percent in 1995 to 54 percent in 1997), the average maximum sentence had simultaneously been going down (from ninety-eight months to ninety-five months to ninety-three months, respectively).[53] Nonetheless, the declining maximum sentence length was not enough to counteract the effects of more stringent percent-of-sentence requirements, and the average time that inmates served prior to first release had increased over time. The Bureau of Justice Statistics researchers additionally projected that while violent offenders actually *released* in 1996 had served an average of forty-five months (or just over half of their average sentence), violent offenders *sentenced* in 1996 (and required to serve 85 percent) would probably serve an average of eighty-eight months before release.[54] Funding for VOI/TIS was discontinued in 2002, but most of the TIS laws on the books remain intact. To the extent that they continue to be implemented, TIS laws can be expected to continue to increase the average length of stay and to contribute to continued growth in prison populations.

Three-Strikes Legislation for Recidivist Felons

In addition to the mandatory minimum laws targeting specific classes of offenses and the truth-in-sentencing laws aimed at extending the length of stay for those convicted of violent offenses, the mid-1990s also saw the passage of ever more punitive habitual offender statutes. Habitual offenders, or those who continue to offend despite multiple criminal justice system interventions, have always been singled out by the system for more harsh treatment. The number of prior convictions and prior incarcerations has always been a consideration at sentencing, with more lengthy criminal histories triggering lengthier sentences, but in the mid-1990s a series of highly publicized, sensational crimes committed by offenders with rather extensive criminal backgrounds led to the passage of a peculiar type of habitual offender law: the three-strikes law.

Three-strikes laws, which are a type of mandatory sentencing law, required lengthy sentences upon the third conviction for a serious, usually violent, felony offense. The "three-strikes and you're out" laws are unusual in that they were enacted across twenty-four states over a period of just three years (1993–1995)—in other words, they were remarkably popular in the mid-1990s when crime reached peak levels across the country, and their popularity has waned since.[55] State laws varied as to how many strikes are needed for an offender to be considered "out," what offenses count as strikes, and what it means to be "out."[56] First, not all states actually required three strikes for the often dramatically enhanced penalties to ensue. While twenty states have a third-strike provision, some states impose enhanced penalties on the second strike for certain serious or violent felonies, and three states count someone "out" upon commission of the fourth felony.[57] Definitions as to what constituted a strike also varied across states, with most states including an array of statutorily specified violent felonies. A few states, however, counted non-violent offenses, such as drug offenses, as strikes or simply specified that penalties could and perhaps should be significantly enhanced following the commission of any three felonies.[58] Just as the number of strikes required and the strike offenses varied, so too did the meaning of "you're out." In some states, the sentencing judge could double or triple the sentence specified by statute for that offense. In other states, the sentences on the second, third, or fourth strike ranged from twenty-five years to life in prison with or without the possibility of parole. Some states mandated that the sentence be imposed, while others simply allowed for the enhancement. In sum, there was no such thing as a three-strikes-and-you're-out law—there were twenty-four states that enacted some sort of more stringent habitual offender sentencing over a fairly confined period of time, conveniently borrowing the "so many strikes and you're out" metaphor from baseball.

These three-strike-type sentencing enhancements were, at least in theory, particularly punitive sentencing enhancements for repeat offenders (of which there are many) and therefore were expected to quite significantly increase prison populations through lengthening the average time served for certain offenders with certain offense histories. Many contended, however, that for the most part these laws were written to "bark louder than they bite,"[59] thereby appeasing the public's ongoing thirst for retribution while having a negligible effect on the size of prison populations.[60]

With the exception of California's atypical three-strikes law, which was recently scaled back as the result of a 2012 ballot initiative (Proposition 36), these laws were expected to have minimal impact on prison populations for several reasons. First and foremost, most states already permitted quite substantial sentence enhancements for repeat offenders. All but one of the states passing three-strikes-type legislation in the mid-1990s already had significantly enhanced penalties for the commission of second, third, and fourth offenses—some even already had the manda-tory life-without-parole requirement in place.[61] In some of the states, the new law expanded the types of offenses that counted as strikes, and in others it lengthened the sentence that was to be imposed, but in practice these changes had a minimal impact because offenders sentenced under the provisions were already serving long sentences prior to the passage of the legislation. Moreover, in many states, the three-strikes laws were quite narrowly tailored, requiring that each strike be one of just a few statutorily prescribed violent felonies. In other words, an offender could commit any number of felonies, and while the sentence imposed would probably have increased with each consecutive offense under preexisting habitual offender laws, he or she would only be eligible for the lengthy third-strike sentence after having committed the prescribed number of *strike-eligible felonies.*

In sum, while three-strike laws indeed imposed harsh sentences for repeat violent offenders, the new provisions were, according to many, not much harsher than the laws that already existed in almost every state; after all, by the time these were passed, we were already twenty years into the Punishment Imperative. Additionally, the vast majority of offenders serving three-strike sentences were serving them in Cali-fornia.[62] By the late 1990s, more offenders were serving strike sentences in California than in all other three-strikes states combined, and most of the three-strike inmates in California are serving second-strike enhancements rather than the third-strike 25-to-life sentences.[63]

Three-strikes legislation was in many ways emblematic of the heyday of the Punishment Imperative. The pattern was a cycle: media cover-age of a serious crime would generate substantial public alarm about the failure of the penal system to prevent that crime from occurring. That failure was attributed to some manner in which the system was not tough enough. In response, a public figure—governor or legisla-tor—would draft legislation to toughen the system back up. With much fanfare and little resistance, the new legislation would pass. In the 1990s, such cycles brought the Punishment Imperative to its precipice.

Enhanced Surveillance of People in the Community

Over this same period, policies were enacted that were aimed at strengthening the surveillance of people in the community. The punitive capacity of both probation and parole supervision was intensified through the advent of increasingly intrusive surveillance technologies and through the enhanced monitoring of sex offenders.

INTENSIVE SUPERVISION IN THE COMMUNITY

The intensive supervision (ISP) movement in community-based penalties coincided with the early days of the get-tough movement. Probation had been under severe criticism, perhaps best illustrated by criminologist Robert Martinson, who referred to it as "a kind of standing joke."[64] Yet, in the mid-1980s, when the country was in an economic recession, increasing rates of incarceration began to press state budgets. Public officials wondered if a community-based penalty could be devised that would cut into expensive prison population growth.

In the face of fiscal pressures, the state of Georgia responded by designing the first important example of what was often called "the new ISP movement." Georgia designed its ISP to provide for extremely close supervision by a probation team—more than weekly contact in some cases—for probationers who had prior felony records, many of whom might otherwise have been sentenced to incarceration. Early results showed promising recidivism outcomes for Georgia's ISP probationers, and its developers cautiously claimed success.

The Georgia model's claims received a great deal of publicity, and many states sought to replicate that work. But scholars publicly worried that the results of ISPs were misleading because lower recidivism rates could be attributed to the relatively low risk of those who were selected for it. The U.S. Department of Justice funded a series of field studies of ISP, the most important of which occurred in California and were carried out by criminologist Joan Petersilia and her colleagues at Rand Institute.[65]

ISP was sold as a new idea, but probation-based intensive supervision programs had been tried before, with unimpressive results.[66] What marked the new ISP movement as being apart from its predecessors was the degree to which it embraced surveillance and control as a central organizing principle. Urine testing was a routine aspect of this work. Electronic monitoring devices often restricted movement. Stringent reporting requirements were strictly enforced. The rhetoric was strong, and probation administrators bragged that their ISP programs were "tougher than prison." They were not wrong; at least one study found that some people in prison would rather stay there than come out onto ISP with an early release.[67]

The strong emphasis on surveillance and control had predictable results: people under ISP failed at high rates. Petersilia and Turner found that under ISP, California probationers were no more likely to be arrested than regular probationers, but they were far more likely to be found in violation of the rules of intensive supervision—and end up in prison as a result.[68] Overall, the ISP studies of the "new" movement mirrored their predecessors. They found that ISP did not contribute to public safety by reducing crime; rather, ISP increased the costs of corrections by putting more people behind bars for violating its own hyped-up rules.[69]

The problem of technical revocation is not a minor one, and supervision policies have exacerbated it. In 1980, 17 percent of people entering prison were doing so as a result of a technical revocation. By 2005, after years of intensifying probation and parole supervision, the proportion had doubled to 35 percent.[70] In other words, getting tough on probationers and parolees was a central cause of the expanding prison population. In California, the leader in tough supervision nationally, in recent years almost 60 percent of prison admissions have been of people who suffered probation/parole technical revocation.[71]

One would think such disappointing results would have doomed the ISP movement, at least insofar as it emphasized the tough supervision approach. But that is not how the Punishment Imperative worked—when punishment is an imperative, positive results or demonstrable benefits are simply not required. Intensive supervision thrived, and almost every probation or parole system had its version of the strategy. And every one of those systems played its part in maintaining a steady flow of offenders into the prison system.

INCREASED MONITORING OF THOSE CONVICTED OF SEX CRIMES

Although increasing surveillance was evident in prisons and among probation and parole populations, perhaps nowhere was increasing surveillance of ex-offenders in the community more apparent than in the case of those convicted of sex crimes. Widely acknowledged as the most reviled of all offenders—even drawing the ire of other offenders—sex offenders in many ways served as the poster children for the punitive laws that have made it more difficult for people to survive community supervision without a return to prison. These laws played an important role in making it ever harder for people who have been convicted of serious crimes to stay out of the penal system's clutches. They also illustrate well the one-dimensional logic of the Punishment Imperative.

Most of the early laws targeting sex offenders specifically provided for some form of sex-offender notification and registration. These represent distinct, though related, initiatives. Sex-offender registration involves the postrelease registering of sex offenders with local, state, and federal law enforcement agencies. Few dispute the utility for law enforcement of maintaining a *confidential* database for monitoring the whereabouts of known sex offenders. Access to the registry, however, has become increasingly open, with many states posting information regarding some or all of their registered sex offenders online. Sex-offender notification laws, on the other hand, require the release of limited information regarding sex offenders to the communities in which they plan to reside after release. In most states, the registration and notification provisions apply to any sex offenders who were either incarcerated or on probation or parole at the time the law took effect.

Advocates of sex-offender notification typically advanced at least two claims as to the purpose and utility of notification laws. First, they contended that notification laws involved the community in crime prevention by providing the community with information necessary for it to protect itself from a class of dangerous criminal offenders. These advocates, borrowing their rhetoric from the community-policing and community-justice movements, often described notification as a partnership between law enforcement and citizens. They contend that these laws exist so that community members can take a more active role in ensuring their own personal safety and community safety.[72] Second, advocates argued that the notification requirements would serve as an effective deterrent and would reduce the likelihood of offender recidivism. Advocates suggested that notification "helps deter sex offenders from repeating their crimes by keeping a spotlight on them and by giving nearby residents the ability to warn and protect their families."[73] Thus advocates contend that notification laws serve both crime-prevention and crime-control ends.

Like many of the 1990s crime-control initiatives, sex-offender notification statutes were passed hastily, often with little in the way of legislative discussion, and usually in the aftermath of sensational cases. In the Kanka case to be discussed below, House Assembly Speaker Chuck Haytaian "declared a legislative emergency" and prohibited committee hearings on the sex-offender legislation. The Senate similarly rushed the legislation through the process. Within three months of Megan Kanka's death, New Jersey enacted ten bills targeting sex offenders, one of which was the notification law that has come to be known as Megan's Law. While perhaps the most famous, New Jersey's Megan's Law, which was signed into law by Governor Christine Todd Whitman on October 31, 1994, was not the nation's first notification law.[74]

In 1990, in response to a particularly brutal sexual crime against a child, Washington State enacted the nation's first sex-offender notification law of its kind as part of an omnibus crime control bill known as the Community Protection Act (CPA).[75] Washington's CPA perfectly demonstrates that get-tough atmosphere in which these notification laws were typically passed. The CPA was a comprehensive crime-control bill that not only enacted a notification statute but also included provisions that increased prison sentences and allowed for the postrelease civil commitment of sexual offenders. The notification provision of the Washington statute authorized state agencies "to release relevant and necessary information regarding sex offenders to the public when the release of information is necessary for public protection." Although Washington passed the first community notification law of its type, community notification did not attract widespread national attention until the 1994 murder of Megan Kanka in New Jersey.

On July 29, 1994, seven-year-old Megan Kanka was sexually assaulted and then strangled to death by Jesse Timmendequas.[76] Timmendequas, a twice-convicted sex offender, lived with two other convicted sex offenders in a house across the street from the Kanka family.[77] Only after Megan Kanka's death was the community notified of Timmendequas's two previous convictions for sexual abuse. The community was outraged that a child sex offender could live in such close proximity to children under a cloak of virtual anonymity. Megan's mother, Maureen Kanka, vocally protested, arguing that had she known about the presence of a dangerous sex offender, she could have protected her child, and she successfully lobbied for both state and federal laws requiring the release of information regarding sexual predators to members of the community. The laws enacted at both the state and federal level both carry her daughter's name, and the case drew such widespread attention that community-notification laws are now frequently referred to simply as Megan's Laws.[78]

While all states have, under the threat of a loss of substantial federal funding, enacted a version of Megan's Law, the laws across states vary quite substantially.[79] Notification laws vary as to which sexual offenses are actually covered by the notification provision, who is to be notified, and the nature and extent of the notification. While a few states have limited the notification requirement to those convicted of sexual offenses against children, most include all sex offenses, and some states define sexual offenses in an unusually broad way. Washington characterizes any offense committed "for the purpose of sexual gratification" as a sex offense for purposes of registration and notification. In California, a conviction for "lewd and lascivious conduct" or a misdemeanor indecent exposure can trigger

registration and notification.[80] New York's notification provision is triggered by thirty-six offenses, seven of which are misdemeanors and several
of which require no sexual conduct at all. Restraining anyone under the
age of seventeen with or without sexual contact, for example, qualifies as
a sexual offense and triggers notification.[81]

Throughout the country, sex-offender registration and notification
laws enjoyed widespread popular appeal.[82] Despite such popular appeal,
the statutes remain controversial. Much of the contention surrounding
sex offender notification laws revolves around the ways in which such
requirements may infringe upon an offender's constitutional rights.
While legal issues abound, and indeed are important, some of the more
policy-oriented debates are more directly relevant here.

Among the most frequently voiced of all criticisms of notification
laws as policy is that they are overwhelmingly ineffective at achieving the ends they were enacted to serve. As noted above, proponents
advanced two central claims as to the purpose and utility of notification laws. First, they described notification as an effective way to build
partnerships between law enforcement and the community, alleging that
notification provides citizens with the information necessary to protect
themselves and their families from this type of offender. Proponents also
contended that notification would provide for more eyes and ears watching over offenders and that the increased supervision (or surveillance)
would deter future sex offending and ultimately reduce recidivism. As
an added benefit, advocates argued that, due to increased (community)
supervision, if and when sex offenders did reoffend, they would be more
quickly apprehended. Critics contend that community notification laws
have been ineffective at achieving any of these ends because they (1)
have relied too heavily on offender cooperation; (2) have failed to provide a forum either for educating the community or for constructive
community involvement and, as a result, have provoked vigilantism; (3)
have resulted in the displacement of offending and of offenders; and (4)
have branded and stigmatized offenders without concern for the effects
such labeling might have had on their prospects for treatment and successful return to the community.[83] These laws have also provided a false

sense of security,[84] and more recent research has suggested that although people typically know about the registries, most have never bothered to access them, and few have taken any sort of preventive action upon learning of sex offenders in their communities.[85]

The most basic reason for the ineffectiveness of sex-offender notification is that the registration necessary to trigger the notification has primarily been a voluntary affair. In many states sex-offender registration relies heavily on the offender literally coming forward to place his or her name on the registry. Most states have further required that the offender reconfirm his or her registered address periodically and reregister every time he or she changes residence. While penalties can be imposed for failure to register, in the rush to pass notification statutes, states typically allocated little in the way of time or resources for the enforcement of registration provisions (let alone for the implementation of active notification).[86] Moreover, there is a distinct possibility that the penalty for failing to register (if and when apprehended) may seem more attractive than the repercussions often associated with registration. When offenders do register, they often provide false or misleading information. In some places more than one-quarter of all registered sex offenders were not living at the address that they had registered.[87]

As some critics have noted, notification laws have done little to educate the public and indeed may have served to promulgate some of the popular myths surrounding sex offenders and their risk for reoffense.[88] These laws, it has been argued, project the image of sex offenders as ticking time bombs just waiting to go off.[89] Indeed, notification seems to send a clear message to the public that the criminal justice system cannot help but fail with this class of offender. As Seattle University law professor John LaFond once argued, "Registration provides a database that might be useful to discourage sex offenders from reoffending, but the community notification part in effect tells people, 'This man is going to reoffend and we can't do anything about it.' The burden is shifted to the neighbors, 'Defend yourself, we can't help you.'"[90]

Despite well-established concerns about the efficacy of these laws and policies, sex offenders remained the target of growing legal restrictions.

At least forty-four states placed restrictions on employment and/or housing.[91] Housing restrictions have meant that in some urban areas, only small geographic areas are available for legal housing for released sex offenders. In some cities, like Miami, there is quite literally nowhere to legally place sex offenders, so officials have resorted to literally housing them under bridges.[92] The imposition of these restrictions means that in at least one of the areas so crucial to reentry success—housing—people convicted of a sex-related crime are at a distinct disadvantage.

The scrutiny of people convicted of sex offenses is an apt illustration of the way the Punishment Imperative has built a powerful prison cycling machine. It is also ironic, because as a group, people convicted of sex crimes do not represent nearly the level of public safety risk that the policies and restrictions against them would imply. A recent follow-up study of people released from prison found that two-thirds of all releases were rearrested for a felony or serious misdemeanor within three years, but less than one in forty of those convicted of rape were rearrested for another rape.[93] Research has repeatedly demonstrated that sex offenders are among the least likely of all offenders to be rearrested for any offense.

The Problem of Prison Cycling

Prisoner reentry and reintegration have always been challenging because ex-offenders are among the most stigmatized and least sympathetic of all marginalized groups. By virtue of their criminal convictions, ex-offenders are deemed less trustworthy, less honest, and among the least deserving. The stigma associated with having served time in prison remains long after release and can affect an ex-offender's life chances well into the future. Moreover, the stigma can affect an ex-offender across multiple domains of life: for the ex-offender, housing is more difficult to secure, jobs are more difficult to come by, and relationships are more difficult to mend. Although one might assume that the stigma of prison is attenuated somewhat as more and more people experience prison, research suggests that this is not necessarily the case: formerly incarcerated persons are even stigmatized in neighborhoods where prison experience is relatively common.[94] Equally troubling, not only is the probability of experiencing prison elevated for African Americans, but due to the pairing of images of race with images of crime, the stigma associated with prison is amplified for African Americans as well.[95]

The Changing Nature of Postrelease Supervision

The landscape of prisoner reentry has undergone a fairly substantial shift over the past several decades. Some of these changes have made navigating reentry to the community more difficult in and of themselves, but these difficulties have been compounded by legislation that has erected more and more barriers to full reintegration. In the mid- to late 1990s, when crime was a particularly salient issue and the Punishment Imperative was in full force, the United States Congress enacted a series of legislative initiatives that would ultimately hinder rather than help ex-offenders as they negotiate the reentry process.

Legislative Barriers to Successful Reintegration

In the late 1990s, the challenges of prisoner reentry were many—there were increasing numbers of offenders returning to communities from prisons and most had received little in the way of programs and services while they were there.[96] Scholars concerned about the reentry process particularly emphasized the importance of the periods immediately preceding and following release, with many arguing for release planning that would begin on the day of admission.[97] Most agreed that the most pressing needs of prisoners returning to the community were in the areas of education, employment, housing, health care, and substance abuse treatment. Perhaps not surprisingly, the chances of success in reentry were expected to diminish precipitously if a returning prisoner's needs in any of these areas were not addressed or could not be met. For example, a returning offender who was unable to secure viable employment soon after release from prison might be expected to resort quite quickly to criminal activity in order to "make ends meet." Similarly, the inability to secure housing could result in ex-prisoner homelessness, and with homelessness would come increased risk for reoffense. Although the risk of reoffense is heightened in the period immediately following release when the challenges are greatest, it was widely recognized that it was important that reentry initiatives focus not only on the point of release but also on the period of time leading up to release (reestablishing ties to the family and community) and on the months and years that follow release. Reentry is a process, not a moment.

Before turning to a discussion of Punishment Imperative policy developments that ran counter to a renewed interest in addressing the problem of prisoner reentry, a brief discussion of the difference between reentry and reintegration seems warranted. Given that only a relatively small (though growing) portion of the prison population has been sentenced to life in prison without the possibility of parole,[98] the vast majority of prisoners sentenced to a period of incarceration will "reenter." In other words, the vast majority of prisoners will eventually be released from custody and return to communities. Although most will reenter, far fewer will be able to successfully reintegrate. Success in terms of reintegration would require that the formerly incarcerated person become a fully functioning member of the community eventually afforded most (if not all) of the rights and responsibilities of those who have never been incarcerated. A fully reintegrated ex-offender would be that person who was able to remain crime-free, to secure and maintain employment and housing, to (re)establish positive ties to the community, and to successfully reconnect with family and friends after an often extended period of separation.[99]

Policies That Inhibit Reentry

Although it is widely recognized that offender reintegration is crucial to the successful reentry experience, those trying to make this transition face multiple challenges (as do the organizations trying to assist offenders in navigating the reentry process). Laws enacted across most states in the mid- to late 1990s have restricted ex-offender access to benefits in the areas of housing, education, employment, and welfare assistance—in other words, across all of the areas that have been identified as crucial to successful prisoner reentry.[100] These restrictions, which have been referred to as "collateral consequences" and "barriers to reintegration," typically attach upon felony conviction and have impacted the ability of returning prisoners to successfully make the transition to communities. Laws such as those restricting the extension of housing benefits to convicted drug or violent offenders may make sense from a public (housing)-safety perspective, but have been counterproductive from a prisoner-reentry perspective.

Most of these counterproductive policies were enacted in the mid- to late 1990s under the Clinton administration (shortly after crime rates had reached an all-time high and just before they began what would become a steady and substantial decline). All of these policies have had a particularly disparate impact because they have had little to no effect on convicted offenders who are financially stable but have had profound effects on those in the lowest socioeconomic strata. The Wall Street broker convicted of insider trading has probably never lived in public housing or collected welfare. Only those in the lowest socioeconomic strata are in need of public housing, welfare, and food assistance, so only those offenders have been affected by these harsh provisions. Due to structural inequalities in American society, policies designed to target the most disadvantaged felony offenders will also inevitably have a disparate impact on minorities. In explaining racially disparate increases in incarceration more generally, Michael Tonry has argued that, whether intentional or not, "the rising levels of Black incarceration did not just happen . . . they were the foreseeable effects of deliberate policies."[101] It could similarly be argued that the collateral consequences that have attached to felony convictions would also have had foreseeable disparate effects. These troubling Clinton-era policies in the areas of education, housing, public assistance, and parental rights are discussed in the sections that follow.

Policies Limiting Access to Education

Although the link between employment and crime is complicated and not particularly well understood, few deny that there is an important link between the two. Securing and maintaining work has long been seen as particularly critical to successful offender reintegration. Years of research have consistently indicated that the stigma of having a criminal conviction can have a demonstrable impact on a person's ability to secure employment.[102] The criminal conviction, however, is not the only reason why ex-offenders have a hard time securing employment. Those convicted offenders sentenced to prison, and thus those ultimately released from prison, have notable deficits in the area of educational attainment that increasingly go unaddressed in the prison setting.[103] These deficits in education then impact the ability of ex-offenders to secure and maintain employment postrelease. Recognizing that deficits in educational attainment limit opportunities for gainful employment and that lack of such employment is conducive to criminal behavior, educational programs have long been among the most common and most popular forms of prison programming. Historically, these prison-based education programs had been financed, in part, through federally funded educational opportunity programs that have all but disappeared from prisons in recent years.

As one of the landmark Great Society achievements, the United States Congress passed the Higher Education Act (HEA) in 1965. When the Higher Education Act of 1965 passed, it established the education grant opportunity program that is commonly known as the Pell Grant program.[104] More than forty years old, the Pell Grant program still represents the single biggest investment in higher education that the federal government has ever made. With its Pell Grant program as one of its centerpieces, the original Higher Education Act was designed to open the door to higher education for those who otherwise could not afford it through providing federal funding to low-income individuals. Between the 1970s and mid-1980s, Pell Grants served as a major funding stream for prison-based education because prisoners tended to come from precisely the population that the Pell Grant program targeted (e.g., those with most demonstrable financial need). The Higher Education Act requires regular congressional reauthorization, however, and subsequent amendments have had a profound effect on access to education for prisoners both while they are in prison and upon their return to the community.[105]

In the years since it first passed, the original Higher Education Act of 1965 has been modified in ways that initially limited and have since completely eliminated prisoner access to Pell Grant funding for higher education. Frequently the target of punitive legislation, incarcerated drug offenders became the first class of offenders who were restricted access to Pell Grant funding. They were denied access to Pell Grants with the passage of the Anti–Drug Abuse Act of 1988, passed during the height of the Drug War. Shortly thereafter, during the 1992 HEA reauthorization, lifers and those sentenced to death were denied access to Pell Grants. And, in 1994, Clinton's much-heralded Violent Crime Control and Law Enforcement Act completely eliminated prisoner access to Pell Grants while an offender was incarcerated.[106]

Amendments to HEA have not just targeted those who are incarcerated. During its 1998 reauthorization, the HEA of 1965 was amended to include a provision that suspended eligibility for federal grants, loans, and work assistance programs for those convicted of drug-related offenses. The Free Application for Federal Student Aid (FAFSA) includes a question that specifically asks about drug convictions—both an affirmative response and no response can trigger ineligibility. Between 2000, when this question was added to the FAFSA, and 2005, at least two hundred thousand students—or one in four hundred applicants—were denied federal student aid on account of drug convictions.[107] Under the 1998 HEA Amendment (P.L. 105-244), the period of ineligibility following a drug conviction depends in part upon the type of conviction offense (possession or sale) and the offense history (with more substantial periods of ineligibility for second and subsequent offenses). A second offense for sale of controlled substances or third offense for possession of controlled substances results in indefinite suspension of eligibility. The education assistance eligibility suspension, whether time limited or indefinite, can only be lifted upon proof of rehabilitation or if the conviction is ultimately overturned or set aside. Although federal legislation often give states the option to opt out of various provisions, states are not permitted to opt out of (or modify) the ban on federal student assistance.[108] States, however, have denied state aid on the basis of federal criteria set out in the 1998 HEA Amendment.[109]

Policies Restricting Access to Public Housing

Most would agree that securing suitable housing upon release from incarceration is one of the most fundamental needs of prisoners facing reentry. Despite the centrality of securing suitable housing to success during the reintegration process, and with the full knowledge that the vast majority of offenders leaving prisons come from the lowest socio-economic strata, through the mid- to late 1990s, the federal government made access to public housing all the more difficult for ex-offenders. It did so by passing a series of increasingly restrictive housing policy initiatives explicitly designed to exclude ex-offenders from public housing.[110] As in the context of Pell Grant eligibility, the move to exclude ex-offenders from public housing began with the Anti–Drug Abuse Act of 1988. The 1988 Anti–Drug Abuse Act (ADAA) was actually the second of two Anti–Drug Abuse Acts to impose increasingly harsh penalties on drug offenders. The first Anti–Drug Abuse Act, passed in 1986,[111] had established the bulk of the mandatory minimum sentences for drug offenses that have since become so inextricably associated with the War on Drugs, including those mandatory minimums providing for a 100:1 distinction in penalties for possession of crack vs. powder cocaine.[112]

With the passage of the second Anti–Drug Abuse Act in 1988, the federal government began to tighten the proverbial noose on drug offenders, requiring that local public housing authorities include clauses in their public housing leases prohibiting tenants from engaging in drug-related criminal activity on or near public housing premises. Shortly thereafter, the law was amended to read that "any criminal activity that threatens the health, safety, or right to peaceful enjoyment of the premises by other tenants, or any drug related criminal activity" could result in eviction.[113] These public housing laws were passed amid concern about growing crime and violence associated with the drug trade in and around public housing complexes. Although the clause broadly references criminal activity, in its enforcement it has been particularly focused on evictions for drug-related criminal activity, which during the height of the crack epidemic had been characterized as the scourge of public housing. After a series of revisions, the criminal-activity provision was extended to apply not only to the tenant signing the lease but also to "any member of the tenant's household, or a guest or other person under the tenant's control," and it applies to behavior not just in and around the public housing complex but also "on or off such premises."[114] In other words, a mother living in public housing with her children can see her whole family evicted on the basis of the drug-related activity of her son even if that activity occurs several miles away from the housing projects where they reside. As an enforceable provision of the tenancy lease, engaging in criminal activity can result in the termination of the lease at the discretion of the housing authorities. As a result, entire families have seen their public housing leases terminated on the basis of the actions of one household member, a visiting relative, or even just a guest.

The move to exclude convicted offenders from public housing continued through the 1990s with Congress strengthening the force of its public housing exclusions when it passed the Housing Opportunity Program Extensions (HOPE) Act[115] and the Quality Housing and Work Responsibility Act in 1996.[116] President Clinton used part of his 1996 State of the Union Address to challenge Congress to strengthen the force of the public housing provisions. In that address, he emphasized that "criminal gang members and drug dealers [were] destroying the lives of decent tenants" and argued that "from now on, the rule for residents who commit crime and peddle drugs should be one strike and you're out."[117] Although the one-strike provision had technically been part of the original legislation, the 1996 HOPE Act tied bonus federal funding to the enforcement of the one-strike provision.[118] Crucially, with this remarkably broad provision no criminal conviction is required to trigger the eviction—evidence of engagement in criminal activity is enough.

Increasingly strict enforcement of the one-strike-and-you're-out provision led to a series of tragically sad eviction cases that garnered attention when they were ultimately heard before the U.S. Supreme Court. The cases served to highlight what some believed were overly broad criteria as to whose behaviors could trigger an eviction under the one-strike eviction policies. The details of the public housing eviction cases under consideration were provided in the appeal to the U.S. Court of Appeals for the Ninth Circuit in the case *Rucker v. Davis*.[119] The cases before the court were those of Pearlie Rucker, Barbara Hill, Willie Lee, and Herman Walker, four public housing residents from Oakland, California, who had been evicted by the Oakland Housing Authority on the basis of the criminal activity provision. Rucker, Hill, Lee, and Walker were all elderly tenants (aged sixty-three to seventy-five) who had been residing in their public housing units for many years. In the first three cases (those of Rucker, Lee, and Hill), the tenants had been evicted on the basis of the drug use of either their children or their grandchildren. Rucker's mentally disabled daughter had been convicted of cocaine possession not on the public housing premises but rather three blocks away. Hill's and Lee's grandsons were caught smoking marijuana in the parking lot of the public housing complex. Walker, a 75-year-old disabled man with a live-in caretaker, was evicted after that caretaker and some guests were found in possession of cocaine. In each of these cases, the primary tenants denied any knowledge of drug use.

The central question before the Ninth Circuit Court of Appeals was whether the U.S. Congress, when it passed the ADAA of 1988 and subsequent bills affecting public housing, intended for the Department of Housing and Urban Development (HUD) to write broad guidelines that would result in the eviction of "innocents" (e.g., those who were not aware or in control of the conduct of the criminally offending party). Circuit Judge Michael Daly Hawkins opened his opinion in *Rucker v. Davis* (237 F.3d 1113 (2001)) with a description of the plight of those living in public housing that had in many ways led to the passage of these provisions:

> Many of our nation's poor live in public housing projects that, by many accounts, are little more than illegal drug markets and war zones.

Innocent tenants live barricaded behind doors, in fear for their safety and the safety of their children. What these tenants may not realize is that, under existing policies of the Department of Housing and Urban Development ("HUD"), they should add another fear to their list: becoming homeless if a household member or guest engages in criminal drug activity on or off the tenant's property, even if the tenant did not know of or have any reason to know of such activity or took all reasonable steps to prevent the activity from occurring ("innocent tenants").[120]

The Court of Appeals for the Ninth Circuit ultimately concluded that HUD's policy was overly broad and that Congress did not intend the eviction of innocent tenants. The decision of the Ninth Circuit Court was overturned by the U.S. Supreme Court when it rendered its decision in *Department of Housing and Urban Development v. Rucker* in 2002.[121] In overturning the Ninth Circuit Court, Chief Justice Rehnquist, writing for the majority, held that the original statute "unambiguously requires lease terms that vest local public housing authorities with the discretion to evict tenants for the drug-related activity of household members and guests whether or not the tenant knew, or should have known, about the activity."[122] Given the U.S. Supreme Court's 2002 definitive ruling, public housing evictions for criminal activity are constitutionally permissible and can be initiated at the discretion of housing authorities.

With the 1996 and 1998 housing policy acts, Congress also introduced stricter mandates strengthening the ability of Public Housing Authorities (PHAs) to summarily deny admission to public housing to those with criminal histories.[123] Under the housing legislation, local PHAs can require criminal history checks for new applicants and can deny access to public housing to those who have engaged in criminal activity in the past. These developments in public housing policy have had potentially profound impacts on those attempting to reintegrate following prison release because "without access to decent, stable, and affordable housing, the likelihood of an ex-offender being able to obtain and retain employment and remain drug- and crime-free is significantly diminished."[124]

Policies Limiting Eligibility for Public Assistance

Closely related to the move to exclude ex-offenders (and particularly ex–drug offenders) from public housing is the move to permanently restrict their eligibility for public assistance. As with the policies strengthening restrictions in the areas of higher education and in public housing, the move to deny welfare benefits to drug offenders was championed during the mid-1990s. In his 1992 presidential campaign, Bill Clinton famously promised to "end welfare as we know it" if he were to be elected. After almost two decades of failed efforts to reform welfare, Bill Clinton followed through on that campaign promise with the signing of the Personal Responsibility and Work Opportunity Reconciliation Act (PRWORA) in August of 1996.[125] With the passage of PRWORA, the welfare system in the United States underwent its largest overhaul since its establishment in the 1930s as part of Roosevelt's New Deal. Under PRWORA, the traditional welfare entitlement program known as Aid to Families with Dependent Children (AFDC) was eliminated and replaced by the block-grant program known as the Temporary Assistance to Needy Families (TANF) program. The PRWORA signaled the end of entitlement (TANF requires work and is therefore often referred to as a "welfare to work" program) and limited TANF assistance to five years.

With the passage of PRWORA came the introduction of the so-called welfare ban that restricted access to public assistance for convicted drug offenders. The public assistance eligibility ban imposed on drug offenders as part of PRWORA was introduced as an amendment to the initial welfare reform bill and was debated in Congress for just two minutes.[126] The provision allows states to impose a lifetime ban on public assistance for those convicted of felony drug offenses. Under the federal legislation, states were permitted to completely opt out of the ban, but only twelve states did so.[127] Twenty-one states opted to enforce the ban with some modifications, but fully seventeen states enforce the ban in full—permanently denying public assistance to those convicted of drug offenses.[128] The welfare ban was written to apply only to those convicted of drug offenses, so a conviction for an offense other than a drug offense has no bearing on access to public assistance or food stamps. Like the ban on public housing, this collateral consequence affects only ex–drug offenders of limited means who need public assistance; however, unlike the ban on public housing, which is—at least in theory—time limited, the ban on public assistance can be permanent. Those released from prison for drug offenses in states that fully enforce the ban never recover their eligibility for this type of public assistance no matter what steps they may take to move past their criminal histories and no matter how desperately they may need the assistance.

Policies Affecting Child Custody

A final policy initiative associated with the Clinton administration that can have a damaging effect on the reentry process and the goal of eventual full reintegration relates to family reunification. The importance of maintaining (or if necessary reestablishing) family ties upon release from prison has been underscored by research that consistently shows that both maintaining those familial bonds and reestablishing parental roles after release increase the likelihood of successful reentry.[129] The Adoption and Safe Families Act (ASFA) passed in 1997 authorized the termination of parental rights for children who had been in state custody for fifteen of the most recent twenty-two months.[130] Although the ASFA did not specifically make reference to children in state custody because of parental imprisonment, the policy clearly has the potential to affect parents (and particularly women) who face periods of incarceration of greater than fifteen months. In 2007, there were at least 1.7 million children under the age of eighteen who had a parent in prison.[131] Although not all incarcerated parents had physical custody of their children in the period leading up to their current incarceration, women in prison were more likely than men (64 percent vs. 44 percent) to report having lived with their children immediately prior to their incarceration.[132] Many children of the incarcerated—particularly children of the incarcerated with financial means—live with a member of the extended family (an aunt, a grandparent, etc.) during a parent's incarceration, but it has been estimated that more than 10 percent of those children with a parent in prison live in foster homes or agencies.[133] As recently pointed out in a report addressing trends in the prevalence of parental incarceration, "following release from prison both parents and children face challenges in reuniting their families. Parents have to cope with the difficulty of finding employment and stable housing while also reestablishing a relationship with their children."[134] For the more than 170,000 children probably living in foster homes while a parent is incarcerated, with the passage of ASFA, the involuntary and permanent termination of parental rights has become a real possibility.[135]

In conclusion, the policy initiatives ushered in during the mid- to late 1990s were certainly not kind to those convicted of felony offenses (and, because of the drug war, particularly harsh on those convicted of felony drug offenses). Crucially, the consequences of these policies have not been evenly felt. Most have affected only those of limited socioeconomic means—and because of the focus on drug offenses and offenders will have potentially profound effects on the poor, minority communities that have largely been the battleground for the War on Drugs. Although the War on Drugs led to increases in admissions to prison for drug offenses across the board, the increases in admissions for African Americans have been staggering.[136] Given the racial disproportionality in prison admissions, it should not be surprising that at least 70 percent of children with a parent in prison are minority children.[137] Women too have been disproportionately affected by drug laws, with women of color bearing the brunt of the impact.[138] The stigma of a felony conviction has always meant that offenders exiting prison would come up against challenges when trying to reintegrate, but the erection of further barriers through the series of policy initiatives in the areas of education, housing, welfare, and child custody has only served to make that transition from prison to community all the more difficult.

Summary

The Punishment Imperative dominated penal reform for almost four decades, with shifting foci of concern but fairly uniform results. In the

1970s, structural sentencing changes led to increases in the likelihood of imprisonment across the board. In the 1980s, mandatory sentencing reform limited the availability of probation for people convicted of drug and other serious felonies, increasing further the numbers of people going into prisons. In the 1990s, sentencing reforms lengthened the terms people served once in prison. Throughout that same decade, tougher policies regarding community supervision increased the rate of technical revocations that would lead to return to prison. And over the last twenty years, new laws have been passed that restrict the avenues by which people in reentry can succeed by limiting housing, employment, and welfare options and through restricting support for education.

The result was that by 2010, the United States had created the largest and most imposing penal system in the world. As this chapter shows, we did not *have* to have this scope of a penal system—we chose it; we created it through policy. Working on every legislative and policy front, targeting every component of the system—from probation to prisoner reentry—we made the penal system harder, bigger, tougher, and sterner. This was the Punishment Imperative: no matter what the problem, punishment had to grow. This analysis gives rise to three questions to which we devote ourselves in the remainder of this book.

The first question is, "Why did this happen?" In the chapter that follows, we describe two perspectives on the Punishment Imperative, one that sees it as a largely irrational response to the problem of crime, and the other that sees it as the social manifestation of problems in class conflict and labor-market inadequacies.

The second question is, "What has been the result of this policy—how did the experiment fare?" In chapter 6, we survey research on the impacts of the Punishment Imperative, showing that it has failed to accomplish its own main objectives while at the same time producing a host of problematic collateral consequences.

The most pressing question, of course, is, "What should be done, now that we know what we know?" We turn to this question in chapter 7, our concluding chapter. In that analysis, we rely heavily on what we have shown here: that the Punishment Imperative is represented in a host of policies intentionally designed to quite dramatically increase the number of people who go to prison and the length of time they stay there. We have argued that many signs are signaling the end of an era—the Punishment Imperative has lost steam. As we move away from the Punishment Imperative and toward something more constructive, these two numbers (who goes and how long they stay) must be the initial targets of any remedial action.

5

Two Views on the Objectives of the Punishment Imperative

We have argued that the Punishment Imperative should be thought of as a "grand social experiment," and we are not alone in using this term. Increasingly, scholars make reference to a "policy experiment" or an "experiment in mass incarceration."[1] Without being as explicit, these scholars recognize what we have said in chapter 4, that the forty-year vast increase in the size of the penal system, especially the prison population, has many of the markings of the kind of social experiment that is characteristic of American social reform movements.

It is tempting to think of the punitive agenda as a cynical political appeal to the baser human attitudes and beliefs. This would be too simplistic. To be sure, punitive rhetoric is often harsh and sometimes deliberately invokes racial fears, a point we return to toward the end of this chapter. But there is a substantive defense of punishment that cannot be dismissed so easily. Advocates for more punitive penal policies have typically portrayed the justice system as "broken," arguing for stiffer penalties as an essential step in fixing it.

Our purpose in this chapter is to explore the social impetus for the Punishment Imperative. Typically, when people think about this great change in penal policy, they offer an analysis of a burgeoning crime rate and a justice system incapable of doing much about it. There are three principal starting points for such an analysis. The first point of departure holds that the law is responsible for producing public safety; secondly, different levels of importance are given to the ideal of deterrence and the practical result of incapacitation. In these lines of reasoning, weak criminal laws promote criminality through inconsequential penalties that fail to control the actions of people who are committed to criminal conduct.[2] A third complaint about lenient laws holds that insufficient penalties denigrate the suffering of victims of crime. This argument claims that the symbolic functions of the criminal penalty are crucially important, and that the legitimacy of the law is undermined when penalties are too lenient.

What emerges from this discussion is that the Punishment Imperative did not arise from a single issue or in reaction to a particular event but instead emerged from a general alarm about crime but eventually took the form of a broad narrative about crime and justice. In chapter 4, we argued that public alarm about crime eventually coalesced as a political and policy narrative that shaped every aspect of public and private thought about justice policy, beginning in the 1970s and continuing until very recently. That so many of the underlying claims of this analysis are not factually accurate cautions us against accepting it too easily. There is, it turns out, an alternative explanation for the Punishment Imperative, one that is housed not in the working of crime and justice but in the struggle of a society coping with shrinking labor markets, burgeoning inequality, and racial injustice.

Controlling Crime and Fear of Crime
through a Punishment Imperative

We have already described the sociopolitical dimensions of the Punishment Imperative.[3] To be sure, the rise of the punishment ideal was a public event. But the punishment experiment was also an exercise in penal management. Accompanying the noisy public conversation about increasing crime and fear of crime was a technical agenda, in which laws and policies were changed in order to achieve certain objectives. To some extent, the objectives were political, as Jonathon Simon has argued.[4] But it would be a mistake to see them as solely political. The agenda included concrete proposals for changes in law and policy, and these proposals had substantive intentions and justifications. It can be argued that the many changes in penal policy described in detail in the previous chapter can all be justified by reference to one or more aspects of a technical agenda that emphasized (1) controlling judicial discretion, (2) controlling crime by controlling active criminals, (3) making community penalties more onerous, (4) ratcheting up the collateral consequences, and, perhaps most symbolically, (5) expressing coalignment with the victim.

Controlling Judicial Discretion

The early target of legal/policy change was the judiciary. A fairly standard critique had emerged that judicial discretion at sentencing promoted a kind of logic-free policy in which different judges sentenced similar cases in wildly different ways.[5] There was also a profound attack on parole board decision making.[6] From these two critiques, legal initiatives grew to restrict the discretion available to judges in determining the sentence to be imposed and that of parole boards to determine the proportion of the sentence to be carried out. While the original critics of sentencing disparity and parole board discretion were not particularly concerned with an overabundance of lenient penalties, the general public seemed to feel this way—certainly that was the perception of their elected representatives. So the distrust of the judiciary and parole was soon coupled with the "get-tough" mood, with the result that sentencing reform had as one of its primary aims the restriction of lenient decisions.

As we suggested in the preceding chapter, three major waves of sentencing reform occurred.[7] The first, in the mid-1970s, involved a transition to determinate sentencing, either eliminating parole or vastly restricting its discretion. The second, in the 1980s, reduced the discretion of judges, largely by restricting the availability of probation and by introducing mandatory sentences for drug and violent offenders. The third, in the 1990s, lengthened sentences for serious and repeat criminality. Taken together, these waves of sentencing reform joined a host of specific legislative changes to alter the way sentencing functions in the United States.[8] There was never any explicit argument to purge judicial and correctional control of sentences, but that was the consequence of these reforms. Increasingly, the sentence judges imposed on people convicted of crimes and the amount of time they served behind bars became determined by legislative act and sentencing commission policy, not judges and parole boards. Mandatory sentencing and truth-in-sentencing laws, then, have simply shifted the control of the sentence from the judiciary and corrections to the prosecutor and the legislature.

While mandatory minimum sentences might have been successful in reducing judicial discretion, they have not been particularly successful in achieving some of the other ends that they were intended to serve. Circumventing judicial discretion, it was thought, would have the useful side effects of reducing disparity and producing greater equality in sentencing. In fact, it has been argued that mandatory sentencing laws have done more to create disparity than they have to eliminate it. While the judge is relatively restricted at sentencing, the prosecution now has the power to determine the sentence when deciding the charge. According to some, prosecutors have liberally used their discretion in the charging of offenses when mandatory minimums apply and have tended to use the threat of a mandatory minimum term as a useful card to play in their favor during the plea-bargaining process.[9] With regard to federal mandatory minimums, the U.S. Sentencing Commission reported that prosecutors infrequently charged mandatory minimum offenses, in effect circumventing the laws before the case even made it to court.[10] Others have reported that prosecution, defense counsel, and judges have at times conspired to alter the facts of cases simply to avoid the mandatory minimum sentence that would apply or have willfully disregarded the stipulated sentence.[11] Attempts to circumvent mandatory sentencing laws would be less of a concern were they consistent and universal, but sentencing scholar Michael Tonry has explained that "patterns of circumvention are generally ad hoc and idiosyncratic with the result that sentencing disparities are often extreme: among like situated offenders, some will be sentenced to the ten- or twenty-year minimum sentence and others, benefiting from circumventions, will receive much less severe sentences."[12]

While much of the disparity created by mandatory minimums comes from attempts to circumvent the laws, in some cases disparities are written right into the law. Nowhere are intentional legislative disparities more apparent—or accusations more racially charged—than in the federal sentences mandated for convictions related to the possession of powder versus crack cocaine. The mandatory sentencing laws—passed as part of the Anti–Drug Abuse Acts of 1986 and 1988 during the early phases of the War on Drugs—included a 100:1 disparity for possession of crack vs. powder cocaine. Under the original federal sentencing law, possession of five grams of crack cocaine triggered a five-year sentence, and possession of fifty grams triggered a ten-year mandatory minimum sentence. You needed to possess one hundred times that amount (e.g., five hundred grams and five kilograms) of powder cocaine to trigger those same penalties. In other words, as written, these laws penalized crack cocaine *one hundred times* more severely than powder cocaine.[13] The distinction in mandatory minimum punishment for the possession of crack cocaine versus powder cocaine was possibly the most widely criticized individual sentencing policy to have come to pass over the past few decades.[14] Recently, the U.S. Sentencing Commission implemented changes in the law that maintained the penalty disparity but reduced it to 18:1.[15]

Mandatory sentencing does no better with regard to equality. The equality principle requires not only that similar cases be treated similarly but also that different cases be treated differently. As Tonry has pointed out, mandatory sentences focus entirely on treating similar *crimes* similarly "but at the cost of ignoring differences in [offenders'] lives and circumstances that many judges (and others) believe ethically relevant to thinking about just punishments."[16] Mandatory sentencing laws, with their no-exceptions and no-excuses orientation, leave no room either for an assessment of individual culpability beyond the prior offense history or for the tailoring of a sentence to fit that individual culpability.[17] On paper, all offenses might seem alike, but in reality both the offenses and the offenders have their individual circumstances—and these differences are important.

Controlling Crime by Controlling Active Criminals

By far, the most influential ideas underlying the Punishment Imperative have been some version or another of incapacitation or deterrence. The term "incapacitation" refers to the use of physical restraint to impede the ability of a person under correctional authority to commit a crime. Usually, when people think of incapacitation, they think of imprisonment. But there are other forms of incapacitation that are practiced throughout the postarrest justice system. For example, electronic monitoring devices attempt to display the whereabouts of someone who is under correctional supervision so that he or she can be prevented from committing crimes. Some jurisdictions sentence people to home confinement as a way of restricting freedom while imposing a punishment. And drugs that control moods and restrict certain appetites are sometimes prescribed.[18]

Incapacitation has always been a justification of imprisonment, but the philosophy got a significant boost in the 1980s when research began to show that a small proportion of people who get caught for crimes are responsible for a vastly disproportional number of total crimes. People began to calculate the likely benefits for public safety if this highly active portion of the criminal population could be identified and prevented from committing crimes through incapacitation.

Most of the arguments made in this form used retrospective methods to identify the people who were most criminally active, and then posed a "what if" idea: what if they had been in prison instead of at large? The work of Edwin Zedlewski illustrates this line of argument.[19] Even though his short paper was neither the most sophisticated nor the most well-documented incapacitation estimate, it was in some ways the most important, both because it was widely disseminated by the U.S. Justice Department (and thus it was widely known) and because its estimates of incapacitation effects were so high: 187 crimes prevented for every year a person spends behind bars.

An even modestly critical reading of Zedlewski would have identified important problems with the promise of incapacitation via increased use of incarceration. His estimates of the number of crimes averted through a year's incarceration were based on a single study, carried out by RAND researchers who asked a sample of California, Michigan, and Texas prisoners how many crimes they committed in the year *prior to* their incarceration.[20] The average number was 187 per person. He estimated, then, that each year of incarceration prevents 187 crimes, and using estimates of the costs of crimes, he concluded that prisons save money. The numerous technical problems of Zedlewski's estimates have been well documented.[21] And the problematic external validity has also been given wide attention: Zimring and his colleagues have pointed out that between 1976 and 1986, the prison population tripled, but crime rates rose nationally anyway.[22]

There are many other problems with this method. For one thing, prisoners from just three states are not necessarily representative of the national prison population. What people do in the year before their incarceration may not represent their activity in the following year. And a few people in the sample who reported thousands of crimes in their preincarceration year drive up the numerical average number. If they were to be dropped from the sample, the average number would be much smaller. So at the most basic level, the math is problematic.

So is the concept of incapacitation. We have since learned that many crimes are not prevented through incapacitation, because a replacement offender comes along to commit the crimes anyway. This is particularly true for drug crimes, but is also true for many of the crimes that are committed by young men in groups. Replacement may explain why crime rates have remained remarkably unaffected by rates of incarceration.[23]

But these problems were little more than academic quibbles in the public arena, and policymakers became enamored of the possibility that they could achieve substantial public safety gains by growing the prison population. A key objective of a host of sentencing reforms became the enactment of policies and laws that would provide for very long sentences for the most active criminals—these recidivist offenders could presumably be identified through criminal histories and risk assessments and targeted through recidivism statutes that target repeat lawbreakers. Much of this legislation came under the rubric, "three strikes and you're out." The most extreme example occurred in California, where many third-time felons would be subject to mandatory sentences to life in prison.[24] The explicit aim was to isolate the most active criminals and prevent the crimes they would commit by taking them off the street.

Changing the Payoff of Crime

A second way to control active criminals is to change the payoff of crime. The economic model of crime is rooted in the idea of general deterrence, which holds that people will avoid committing crimes when they sufficiently fear the penalty for doing so. Critics of the justice system held that penalties in that system were insufficiently severe to deter people from crime. There are plenty of examples of this argument, but one of the more influential voices was the late economist Morgan O. Reynolds of Texas A&M University, who linked the drop in crime to increases in penalties:

> When expected punishment plummeted after 1950, the rate of serious crime soared. And as expected punishment increased since 1980, the rate of serious crime leveled off and then fell. (Serious crime is defined as the reported violent crimes of murder/non-negligent manslaughter, forcible rape, robbery, and aggravated assault, plus the property crime of burglary.) By 1995, expected punishment had risen to almost 22 days from an early-1980s low of fewer than 10 days. In response, serious crime per 1,000 persons has decreased by 27 percent since its high point in 1980.[25]

The calculation of "average costs" is an appealing, straightforward idea. But it is difficult to interpret the figure directly. It is a ratio of crimes to penalties, and all things being equal, it will get larger when crime drops and smaller when crime declines, even if the prison population does not change. Thus, if some different variable is causing the crime rate to change, the "expected penalty" will automatically adjust to fit the theory of deterrence.

Nonetheless, increasing the deterrent impact of penalties would make perfect sense in protracted wars on crime and drugs but for the scant evidence supporting the efficacy of deterrence generally. Scholars point out that the research on deterrence reveals numerous problems with this strategy. Daniel Nagin and his colleagues have shown that speed and certainty of punishment have a much stronger empirical foundation in shaping compliance with the law than does severity of punishment.[26] None of the policy changes associated with the Punishment Imperative seem well suited to tackle celerity or certainty. Moreover, it has been demonstrated that people who are likely to choose criminal activity have a poor understanding of the actual penalties they might face.[27]

The practical difficulties with deterrence are among the reasons national advisory panels, including the National Academy of Science's Panels on Research on Deterrent and Incapacitative Effects[28] and on Understanding and Control of Violent Behavior,[29] have each concluded that the evidence for deterrence is marginal at best. With regard to the deterrent effects of mandatory penalties more specifically, research suggests that even assuming that deterrence can be effective, the deterrent effect of mandatory sentencing provisions is likely to be compromised because, as we pointed out in the previous section, many of the central actors in the criminal justice system view these mandatory sentences as too harsh. Police, prosecutors, and judges often go out of their way to circumvent the laws, thereby avoiding the mandatory penalty.

Making Community Penalties More Onerous

The technical ideas that took hold in the Punishment Imperative did not apply only to prison. Community supervision underwent its own program of changes during this period, as well. The story of this change is illustrative of the ubiquity of the punitive agenda throughout the 1980s and 1990s.

Community supervision has, for most of its history, been a function that claims a mission of aiding in the "adjustment to the community." This self-proclaimed justification has always allowed community supervision advocates to entertain a wide and complex variety of supervision strategies, but by giving priority to the positive—that is, "adjustment"— the core mission promotes a vision of support and assistance. After all, "adjustment" seems an unlikely response to strategies that involve hounding and antagonism. By contrast, taking "adjustment" seriously connotes supervision strategies that are problem-solving in nature and not at all at odds with the self-interests of the person under supervision. It is not far-fetched to think of community supervision of the "adjustment" variety as being comprised of all manner of help: getting a job, improving educational preparation, obtaining child care, receiving counseling and even a bit of social advocacy.

That somewhat rustic view of community supervision applies little to the job as carried out by most probation and parole officers today. Contemporary probation and parole work emphasizes strategies of "control" over those of "adjustment." Urine samples are taken and analyzed, and lie detector tests are administered. Houses are searched. Probationers and parolees pay fines as the opening ceremony of "reports" to the office.

The state of community supervision is well illustrated by the hottest new program in the field, Hawaii's Opportunity Probation with Enforcement (also known as HOPE).[30] The strategy begins with a stern warning by the judge, talking from the bench, to the person on probation, saying something like, "You are being given a chance to straighten out your life. We can help. But we will also be keeping track of you. You will be drug tested on a regular basis with a few hours' notice. And you'll be required to show up at the probation office on a day's notice. If you fail to show up, or you turn in a dirty urine sample, you'll be picked up that day and you will go to jail for a couple of days. If it happens again, you'll be picked up immediately and go to jail again. If you persist, you'll go to prison and serve the remainder of your sentence. The onus is on you. You can succeed or you can fail."

The results of the HOPE program have been impressive. According to a recent evaluation, those probationers randomly assigned to HOPE were significantly less likely to skip probation appointments, use drugs, get arrested for new crimes, or have their probation revoked.[31] But that is not what is notable for our purposes here. What stands out is what the HOPE approach is *not*. It is not a traditional treatment program. It is a sanction.

The underlying idea of HOPE is that the key to probation success is enforcement. This theory of behavior change—swift and certain sanctions—has driven most of the innovation in probation for the last quarter-century. At the core of the idea is surveillance, more of it applied with greater promise of consequence. Thus the signal shift in probation and parole supervision in the era of the Punishment Imperative has been to turn away from the ethic of support and reintegration, replacing it with a wholesale embrace of the ethic of surveillance and control.[32]

To be sure, there is much about HOPE that is different from earlier iterations of this idea. Indeed, the proponents of the HOPE model promote it as "less punishment, less crime."[33] They argue, marshaling impressive data, that by imposing short, immediate jail sanctions they avoid longer prison sentences down the road. The strategy is to find the optimum calibration of sanctions needed to shape the behavior of recalcitrant probationers, even if the promise is that less is required than ordinarily believed.[34]

There is also a harsher, more unpleasant side to this argument—the sense that community penalties should be generally unlikable and distasteful. Earlier, we described the development of "shaming" methods of community-based sanctions, in which public degradation becomes a purposeful mechanism to shape behavior. Like HOPE, these methods were frequently promoted in part for what they were *not*: prison. And they are based on an idea that if the community penalty is sufficiently undesirable, people will reorient their behavior in response to the threat.

Thus, under a Punishment Imperative, the objective of community-based correctional methods becomes redirected, from "reintegration" and "adjustment" to compliance, not only with the law but also with the behavioral rules imposed by the agents of the law. The central objective requires a reshaping of the tools of community correctional work to emphasize the methods of surveillance and control, because these methods—properly employed—will produce the desired compliance. Interpersonal techniques of behavior change that emanate from the counseling tradition are far less important.

This shift comes, ironically, at a time when evidence mounts in support of the potential for certain kinds of interpersonal methods to achieve impressive results, as well. The "evidence-based movement" in corrections has used systematic evaluation research to identify a series of such methods that consistently work at reducing recidivism.[35] Those who look to the programmatic intervention evidence advocate for a "treatment" model of community supervision. We might think of them as the "treatment" camp of scholars (as opposed to the "punishment" camp that emphasizes sanctions).

The treatment camp points to myriad studies of clinically appropriate supervision strategies, such as motivational interviewing, and assessment-based supervision, and argue that a growing literature makes two points. First, when supervision strategies focus on higher-risk people and use targeted strategies designed to change particular, risk-related aspects of the person's circumstances, recidivism rates drop markedly. Second, when community supervision workers try to use sanctions to shape behavior, failure rates rise. This latter point is often emphasized by advocates of treatment, because they believe it gives the treatment regime a distinct advantage over the sanction regime.[36]

The debate continues about the best community methods, given the evidence. But our point here is more straightforward. At a time when evidence has mounted in support of supervision strategies that promote change through interpersonal and programmatic interventions, policy has taken a different tack. The aim of community supervision has been to increase the capacity of community penalties to be punitively repugnant, with the belief that their effectiveness will be enhanced in the process.

Ratcheting Up the Collateral Consequences

The same kind of hard-edged deterrent argument that changed probation and parole practice applied to a wide range of collateral consequences of felony conviction.[37] A main target was drug crime, and a hot period for drug policy was during the heady days of the drug war. As described in the previous chapter, policymakers sought to make convictions for drug-related crime as painful as possible, and so laws and policies were put into place creating disabilities for people who received drug convictions. These ranged from exclusion from public housing eligibility and welfare benefits to denial of college loans.[38] But they also included a host of employment restrictions. People convicted of sex-related crimes were also targeted for societal restrictions, which include housing and employment.[39]

For the most part, these new restrictions were individual legislative or administrative enactments, put into place as a one-off change gesture of public sentiment about crime. But their effects on the formerly convicted have been additive. Taken together, these restrictions came to constitute a sizeable wall that isolated those who have felonies from full participation in society: one study of New York, for example, counted 250 legal exclusions of services and employment for people convicted of felonies.[40]

These legal and administrative restrictions were put into place under a mix of aims. Some sought to increase public safety by protecting vulnerable populations from people who might put them at risk. For example, when people convicted of drug crimes are prohibited from pharmaceutical work or those with prior sexual crimes are barred from school employment, the objective seems to be to reduce access of prior felons to potential criminal situations. On the other hand, when a person convicted of a felony crime is prohibited from voting or from obtaining college loans, the objective seems to be more clearly punitive, to make the consequences of criminality more onerous.

The empirical foundation for these policies is at best weak and to some extent counterindicative. Recent scholarship on reentry policy suggests strongly that connections to legitimate sources of income and educational advancement are substantially associated with potential for successful postconviction adjustment. The implication is that rather than *improve* public safety, this piling up of restrictions can have the opposite effect, by making it that much harder for many people who have served their sentence to take a fully participating place in the societal arena.

Expressing Coalignment with the Victim

The Punishment Imperative was not solely a technical agenda designed to reduce crime. As is true for so many social movements that gain such traction, there was not just a practical program but a substantial normative component as well. The public sentiment was not simply that the law had become ineffective. The claim became that the law had become aligned with the wrong moral cause. The complaint "What about the victim?" was shorthand for a more substantive concern that the court system generally and the sentencing function specifically ignored the legitimate interests of the victims of crime and became instead a contest centered on the accused. Too often, it was said, the accused gets the benefit of the law while the victim gets nothing but ignored (and, by inference, insulted).

We are now used to seeing the victim occupy a prominent role in the justice process. But this was not always so, and dispute about the relevance of the victim's "point of view" was at one time a subject of some debate.[41] No longer. Victims are routinely consulted about charging decisions and are asked to speak at the sentencing hearing. They are kept apprised of the defendant's progress through the justice system and are informed about probation decisions and prison release dates. As a result of a long and vigorous "victim's rights" movement, these pro-victim sentiments are a matter of accepted practice.

One of the rallying points for the movement that produced these rights was vociferous complaint about lenient sentences and (especially) parole decisions that enabled people who had been under justice system authority to be free to commit new crimes. The pattern would be repeated time and again: a sympathetic person would become a victim of a shocking violent crime, committed by someone who had been previously under criminal justice authority. The case would receive broad publicity, and public sentiment would emerge that the system should have prevented the crime from occurring. This would lead to a new law, often referring directly to the victim, creating new policies that purportedly would have prevented the crime had they already been in place. Good examples are Polly Klaas's abduction and murder in California, which galvanized the push for three-strikes laws, and Megan Kanka's abduction and murder in New Jersey, which led to the passage of sex offender registration and notification laws (e.g., "Megan's Laws") across the country.

The import of all these laws is that the Punishment Imperative is on the side of the victim. It provides a moral voice to undergird the punishment movement, a voice that calls public attention to the plight of innocent victims of crime—a voice that adds emotional pitch to the cold, hard argument that punishment must be reset in order to prevent more crime.

There is no obvious evidentiary problem with a claim that victims ought to receive more attention in the way the system does its business. But the unstated claim that the best way for victims to be represented in the system is to increase the harshness of penalties is not only a poorly tested hypothesis; it has substantial experiential flaws. The restorative justice movement has shown that the severity of the penalty imposed has negligible impact on a victim's ability to recover from serious crimes.[42] And many victims leave the justice process feeling used by the system to "get" the defendant. To the extent that the victim's movement has become a caricature of the get-tough mantra, it may hold little promise for providing the restoration victims so deeply need.

The Manifest Objectives of the Punishment Imperative

The technical aims of the punishment experiment, then, can be easily summarized. There was something of a "perfect storm" that gave rise to the Punishment Imperative: rising crime, failing rehabilitation programs, increased attention to the plight of victims, and a powerful political movement that made "get-tough" policies salient with the public and its leaders. These were obviously not independent forces but mutually reinforcing aspects of the polity. The intersection of these forces is well characterized by the phrase "law 'n' order," which connotes a desire to bring an out-of-control society back under control. This desire arose in the late 1960s and early 1970s and went on to produce the Punishment Imperative—a generation-long era of growing punishment.

The Punishment Imperative was in no way a coordinated effort to ameliorate the underlying problem of social insecurity and perceived instability. Instead, it was a haphazard, helter-skelter social actuality, defined by a kind of legislative piling on—a relentless drive to enact serial policies and laws that would change the penal system, remaking it into a more potent instrument of social control. The architects of this new penal system may never have stated their guiding vision for it, in part because the production of this new system occurred in too piecemeal a fashion. Had they articulated their objectives, here is what they might have said:

Sentences are too lenient. So we need to place restrictions on the ability of the judiciary to impose the sentences they might want, by restricting probation and requiring long sentences in as many situations as possible. Prison time is too lax. We need to increase the disciplinary capacity of prisons by adding cells that are maximum or super-maximum security and imposing more severe losses on those who do not follow the rules. Parole is too common. We need to restrict the use of parole so that it affects only a small portion of the overall sentence—and for some people is never available. Community supervision is too soft and ineffectual, requiring too little of those who are under correctional authority while living among us. We need to increase the pressure we put on probationers and parolees. They must be regularly tested for drugs and subjected to a multiplicity of rules, strictly enforced. When they fail to follow the rules, they should go to prison.

The people who break the law have gone too long without having to suffer the consequences of their actions. Crime now pays, and that needs to stop. Moreover, a handful of those who break the law are irremediable miscreants who can never be trusted to live in free society. We need to identify them quickly and deal with them harshly, so that we are safe from their predations. If we do this with impunity, a few of those who might be

on the fence will be convinced to forego their lives of crime, and both we
and they will be saved.

But the problem is not just for people who have broken the law. Kids are
not scared enough of the consequences of breaking the law. So we need to
show that the law is serious, by promising to take away educational access
for those who break the law and, if they deal in drugs, potentially taking
away housing for their entire family. We need to impose costs upon the
families of lawbreakers, because that will not only give the lawbreakers
reason to think twice about their behavior, but it will convince those at risk
when they break the law—their loved ones—of the folly of that choice.

When we look at the places where crime is the most rampant, we plainly
see places defined by disorder: homeless people, young boys in noisy and
troubling groups, graffiti and litter. These places need to be cleaned up, and
the cleanup starts with moving the homeless off the streets and breaking up
the collections of youngsters on the corner.

Finally, because we know that lawbreaking concentrates in poor com-
munities and among the young people who live there, we need to watch
those places closely. The earlier we can see any indication of lawbreaking,
the sooner we will nip it in the bud. Getting the system involved in the lives
of those who are drawn to drugs and gangs as soon as possible—and with
as much control as possible—is the goal.

This, then, is the manifest agenda of the Punishment Imperative: to
reduce crime by imposing legal control and social order. One doubts
that there would be much in the preceding narrative that the proponents of the Punishment Imperative would dispute. In this simple,
straightforward description, what can be seen is a simple, bedrock claim.
Things have gotten out of control at every stage of the state's obligation
to provide a safe place for people to live, work, and raise their families.
Extreme measures are required to reexert control.

And most important: if this were done, crime and fear of crime would
drop.

The simple statement of aims illustrates something more. The Punishment Imperative agenda is riddled throughout with a host of untested
assumptions, unsupported claims, and simplistic formulations. Will

harsher punishments deter? Does wholesale incarceration deliver incapacitation? Is the behavior of youth well shaped through deterrence? Is disorder a proximate cause of crime? And perhaps most important, what are the collateral consequences of the Punishment Imperative?

Although the punishment agenda was the dominant voice for close to forty years, it was not the only voice. Just as the sociopolitical world embraced punishment as the central theme in society's response to crime and fear of crime, there were at the same time critical voices. As we have seen, scholars and social critics pointed to strong evidence that the main underpinnings of the Punishment Imperative were based on shaky—or even contrary—evidence. They pointed out, for example, that punishment severity has an extremely weak impact on behavior,[43] attempts to predict the most serious lawbreakers were prone to error,[44] disorder by itself did not predict crime very well,[45] and overcontrol of people under community supervision was counterproductive.[46] Most significantly, the critics pointed to a host of potential collateral consequences that would erase any potential public safety gains of ratcheted-up punishments. It seems crucial to note then that the manifest aims of the Punishment Imperative are seriously disputed among social science scholars. The more critical literature makes the point that the growth of the punishment regime was never primarily about creating a safer society; it was, rather, about other, less justifiable ends—latent goals that if explicitly stated would have exposed a putrid foundation.

Latent Aims of the Punishment Imperative

The degree to which this traditional view is at odds with established knowledge regarding crime and justice suggests that something else is afoot here. Critical social scientists, noting the poor factual foundation for the get-tough movement, have come to see it in a different light. Theirs is an alternative narrative about why we engaged a grand social experiment in punishment.

For these critical social scientists, the seeds of the Punishment Imperative were planted, not with the rise in crime but with a crisis in the labor market. Sociologist Loic Wacquant has been the most eloquent voice in describing the way the devolution of labor provided the foundation for the growth of the penal system.[47] Other writers have contributed similar analyses, providing a rather consistent literature about the causes of the penal boom.[48]

The change began when jobs for semiskilled and unskilled labor dropped precipitously, and fierce competition grew for unskilled labor positions. Whole swaths of the socioeconomic strata lost relevance to the labor market. Chief among this group were young black males living in concentrated urban ghettos. As manufacturing jobs disappeared and service sector jobs came to be dominated by women, unemployment among black men grew precipitously; and as large numbers of young black men entered the workforce, there were no jobs for them. A fundamental problem facing contemporary political leaders was what to do about this large class of young men—mostly black—for whom there was no place in the labor market and increasingly bleak employment prospects.

At the same time that the labor market was losing well-paying jobs for laborers, the political system was undergoing two important shifts. The first was what has been called a neoliberal shift away from government-funded social support systems toward work-oriented, time-limited welfare policies.[49] The second shift was a gradual federalization of justice policy.[50] These trends worked in tandem to create a policy backdrop to our justice system that was heavily symbolic, because the federal government is very limited in the ways it can directly affect local crime policy, and so the federal debates are largely about the symbols of crime. But at the same time these forces had consequences that were extremely practical, because they provided both the theory and the practice by which the problem of large numbers of unemployable black men would be managed.[51]

The symbolic and the practical come together in the rhetoric that identifies young black males as "a dangerous class," for which an ever-expanding penal system must be created in order to keep them confined.[52] In his critical appraisal of California parole, Jonathon Simon shows how public fear of recidivist parolees fueled a strategic shift in the work priorities of parole officers, in which a surveillance-oriented philosophy led to large numbers of "technical" revocations, not for new crimes, but for failures to follow parole rules.[53] Under this new policy, parole (and probation) revocations became a *majority* of prison admissions, producing a class of quasi-permanent prisoners who spend brief periods on the streets before being returned to confinement. Parole, historically thought to be a form of community-based corrections, was transformed into one more way in which the prison system expanded its capacity.

Race is a crucial factor in this. The discovery of the powerful political salience of white fear of black men is generally demonstrated by reference to Willie Horton, the black man who, after being furloughed in Massachusetts, absconded to Maryland where he committed an assault and a rape against a young white couple.[54] Horton became the subject of the most powerful political ad against former Massachusetts governor Michael Dukakis in his presidential race with George Bush. The blackness of Horton and the whiteness of his victims were boldly portrayed in the ads (and repeated in the news media), building a white backlash against Dukakis and his campaign. The war against crime became inexorably linked to "a politics of resentment toward categories deemed unworthy and unruly."[55]

The astounding success of the Willie Horton ads in mobilizing white sentiment during the election was not lost on aspiring political leaders, and there arose a kind of political formula of using crime-talk (which served as a proxy for race-talk) to claim to be "tough" on dangerous criminals. For much of the 1980s and 1990s, various types of proposed crime legislation formed the cornerstone of many local and state elections.[56] A nexus was created in the public mind linking black men to crime, with tough policies as the solution. Inflation was the rule, as each new political season saw an ever harsher round of proposals for responding to crime. No sooner had "three strikes" become a political slogan than new electoral hopefuls started to propose "two strikes."

Changes in the labor market decimated inner cities with extraordinary unemployment, and reductions in public welfare exacerbated the economic crisis in these areas.[57] Drug markets arose to fill the void created by the loss of legitimate labor markets, providing the kind of cash and employment not available through other means. The emergence of drug markets, in turn, offered to the polity a new opportunity to expand penalties, because punishments for drug crimes had historically been less severe than those for other felonies. In the 1980s, following the legislative leadership of the Bush presidency, a wave of statutes passed making prison terms mandatory for people convicted of drug crimes.

This was a perfect, if nefarious, strategy. The exogenous forces of the labor market created a crisis of unemployment in black inner cities. People who were already worried about the dangerousness of young black men had their fears stoked by the public alarm about crime. Drug markets became a public agenda, linking black inner cities, young black men, and rampant criminality in the public consciousness. Concomitantly, government was withdrawing from its fiscal support of the kinds of welfare programs that might have helped reduce the severity of the problem. But what could be done with all these young men? Political leadership had the solution: prison.

It was the perfect solution, because it attacked the very market that had grown to fill the void created by the disappearance of labor. It turned drug markets into the enemy of society, and made these markets the central mechanism for moving young black men from the streets into the prison system. This was a cynical policy action, the critics say, because few informed policymakers could have expected a "war on drugs" to have any impact on drugs, given the elasticity of the drug market and the high rate of replacement of drug market workers.[58] But the cynicism was matched by a phenomenal indifference to the racially disparate effect of the policies, for as Michael Tonry has pointed out, nobody could have credibly claimed not to know that the new policies to attack drugs would have devastating effect on black men, their families, and their neighborhoods.[59] The problem was a broken job market; the solution was to make its illicit replacement a heinous crime. When Congress set crack penalties to be one hundred times more punitive than those for powder cocaine, it did so with the certain knowledge that the effect would be borne by black men, the dangerous class.

Western and Beckett have shown how significant the incarceration rate is in suppressing official unemployment figures.[60] Throughout the 1990s, when a strong economy kept official unemployment figures low, growing prison populations masked an increasingly unproductive young black male cohort who, instead of being on unemployment lines, were behind bars. When their numbers were taken into account for 1995, the relatively satisfactory unemployment rate of 5.6 percent becomes a quite anemic rate of 7.5 percent.[61] Indeed, they argue that, far from economic vitality, we were experiencing a period characterized by a relatively weak job market, cloaked by a rapid growth in imprisonment that took many young men out of that market.

In offering this critical review, writers make another point. The Punishment Imperative helped political elites to deal with a related problem: how do they maintain control at a time when the economic benefits are increasingly concentrated in an ever smaller portion of society? Here, the symbolic politics of crime provide a wedge. Between 1979 and 1996, the height of the prison boom, 95 percent of the economic wealth went to the wealthiest 5 percent of Americans.[62] People ordinarily might resist the dismantling of the welfare foundation in favor of a net-free economic market slanted toward existing wealth and influence. But when the dismantling is overlaid by a drug war signaling the reasonableness of fear of blacks, it diverted the attention of the white working class from what was happening. The public policy agenda was about getting control over the rampant drug crime in the cities. That the economic rules were being rewritten to benefit the most wealthy was background noise.

The critical view of the rise of the Punishment Imperative offers an appealing alternative explanation of its aims. There is good evidence to think that the manifest objectives described in the opening of this chapter are not the whole story. For one thing, the onset of the growth of incarceration, in 1972, began at least ten years after crime rates were rising. The biggest burst in penal reforms, in the early 1980s, took place during a period of time when crime rates were stabilizing, and preceded the late 1980s rise in crime. Likewise, the most severe drug laws were enacted after self-report studies showed that rates of illicit drug use by youth had been *dropping*.[63] And three-strikes and truth-in-sentencing laws were enacted just after the beginning of a period of precipitously declining violent crime rates.[64]

To the extent that the biggest driver of incarceration rates today is drug enforcement policy, there is also good evidence that the impetus for those policies is not primarily crime control. The skepticism about the ability of a law enforcement approach to reduce drug use has been constant from the beginning, and study after study of drug eradication methods showed the weak or nonexistent results, but equally showed the devastating impact on people who live in the poorest neighborhoods. To return to Tonry's point, anyone who had studied the issue would have to know that the consequences of a drug war would be borne by young black men and their families. That they carried the war forward, given this knowledge, means that they did not care to avoid those consequences.

Summary

All grand social experiments involve sets of underlying operating assumptions, and the grand penal experiment is no exception. At a minimum, the operating assumptions of the Punishment Imperative were that the system was too lenient and that there was a class of people needing enhanced control. These operating assumptions led to a series of legal and policy changes that enhanced punishments in three ways. First, community penalties, long the most frequent sentence for most felony crimes, became deemphasized and of secondary importance. Second, drug crime became the focus of the penal system, and large numbers of people who might have received nonprison sentences went, instead, to prison, under mandatory penalties. Third, the length of stay in prison increased, in many cases doubled, as release programs that might have ameliorated long sentences were restricted.

The manifest object of this Punishment Imperative was quite straightforward. Its enactors want to reduce crime and disorder. From this point of view, if crime drops then the approach must have worked. If there is collateral damage inflicted in the process of making society safer, then that is regrettable but probably not avoidable.

There is an alternative explanation. This view holds that the Punishment Imperative was a method to manage the economic problems that have arisen as labor market shifts decreased jobs for the low- and unskilled. Finding no place in the legitimate market, they live in decrepit inner cities and, by their very existence, threaten the existing order.[65] There are real problems of crime, of course, but the methods undertaken in the Punishment Imperative are designed to *control people*, not prevent crime. Oscillation in crime will be irrelevant, this view holds. What is essential is to have a penal system capable of managing large numbers of people, especially men, through their most economically viable years, keeping them out of the job market and isolated from the economic world.

We should not view this debate as a contest between two views, one of which will be "proven right." Instead, we should think of these two perspectives on the Punishment Imperative as complementary. One view explains the debate that was going on and the public agenda that was at stake. It describes the functional policymaking that characterized the era of the Imperative. The second view describes, not a public version of the era but rather a refracted reality of it: not false, but undeniably compelling. The Punishment Imperative sought certain societal goals as a matter of formal policy. As designed, it could not help but promote certain social outcomes as a matter of practical reality. It is not possible to fully understand the social importance of the Punishment Imperative without accepting the explanatory validity underlying each of these contrasting views. One reason the Punishment Imperative had such dominance was that it combined a compelling public discourse with a powerful sociopolitical utility.

What can we say about these ideas; what evidence do we have about them? To ask this question is to ask for a kind of verdict: for this grand social experiment, what has been the result?

6

Assessing the Punishment Imperative

The term "experiment," however, carries connotations quite different in the natural sciences than in social developments. It is the rule, indeed almost inevitable, that an experiment in the physical sciences does not disturb the course of the natural events with which it is concerned. Just the opposite is the case with an experiment in current social life. We are told that if an experiment in the New Deal does not turn out well, it will be dropped and something else devised. The implication is that when the experiment is dropped, nothing has happened. But this is just the opposite of the fact; when an experiment is introduced into a set of social relations, these are modified, and modifications persist after the experiment has been withdrawn.

—Anonymous, 1935[1]

Now that we are close to forty years into the grand social experiment in punishment, and especially if (as we believe) it is coming to an end, we should be able to draw some conclusions and extract some lessons learned from it. In the previous chapter, we argued that there were both manifest and latent objectives for the Punishment Imperative—and critiqued the experiment in terms of those objectives. Here we ask what can be said of the overall experiment. We would argue that at least four general conclusions can be drawn: (1) the incarceration rate has been demonstrated to be perhaps surprisingly disconnected from the crime rate, (2) prison expansion has not met its own goals, either manifest or latent, (3) mass incarceration exacerbated, rather than ameliorated, many of the social problems that we remained concerned about at the end of the twentieth century, and (4) mass incarceration has been perhaps one of the best examples of how tightly entwined politics and punishment can become.

The Disconnect between Crime and Punishment

Perhaps no criminological fact is as agreed upon as the fact that we have not been particularly successful in our attempt to incarcerate our way out of crime. When we lock up more people, crime does not necessarily go down. As importantly, crime declines—sometimes quite substantial crime declines—do not seem to translate into decreasing prison use. While imprisonment increased in every year between 1973 and 2009, over that same period crime variably increased, decreased, or stabilized. Figure 2.5 demonstrates the apparent disconnect between crime and imprisonment through tracking the trends in crime and in imprisonment in the United States over the past several decades.

From the mid-1990s on, crime was on the decline regardless of what a place did in terms of incarceration.[2] Places that continued to dramatically increase prison populations experienced decreases in crime, but so did places that did not dramatically increase prison populations. Most empirical research on the relationship between crime and imprisonment suggests that crime (particularly violent crime) can explain some, but certainly nothing like all, of the variation in growth in imprisonment over time and across places.[3] In other words, while crime and imprisonment are clearly not completely disconnected, there is plenty of "unexplained variance." As Todd Clear has previously argued,

> If it is absurd to think that prisons have nothing to do with crime, it is abidingly difficult to determine precisely how prisons affect crime. It may be that locking up a particular prisoner averts crimes that prisoner might have committed had he been free. It might also be that the desire to avoid prison makes some people decide against a temptation to engage in crime. But it cannot be the case that this is the only—indeed, even the main—way prisons are related to crime.[4]

Indeed, the nature of the relationship between crime and imprisonment has proven to be one of the more perplexing to resolve. It is particularly troublesome that although we are in the midst of the longest and most significant crime decline since World War II,[5] we have not yet seen an *equivalent* decline in our rates of imprisonment. Although we have predicted that we are witnessing the beginning of the end for the Punishment Imperative, the mass incarceration that resulted from our grand penal experiment will probably stay with us for some time to come. The cumulative effect of close to forty years of punitive sentencing policy change cannot simply be undone with the declaration that the experiment has ended. As the quotation that opened this chapter makes plain, "when an experiment is introduced into a set of social relations, these are modified, and modifications persist after the experiment has been withdrawn."[6]

Failing on Its Own Terms

The most important lesson we can learn from the Punishment Imperative is that it did not achieve its own manifest aims. There were, at a minimum, two main objectives: to reduce crime and to reduce the fear of crime.

Crime Reduction

Don Stemen recently reviewed empirical studies that have estimated the crime-reduction effect of incarceration.[7] Accounting for study design, Stemen concludes that imprisonment brings at best modest reductions in crime. The most valid studies of the deterrent effect of incarceration[8]— those that control for simultaneity—suggest that a 10 percent increase in the imprisonment rate will bring about somewhere in the range of a 2 to 4 percent reduction in the crime rate.[9] Bruce Western has similarly estimated that the 66 percent increase in imprisonment between 1993 and 2001 reduced the rate of serious crime by 2–5 percent.[10]

In grand terms, the social experiment in mass incarceration has not had much impact on crime. As figure 2.5 shows, the greatest increases in crimes preceded the growth in imprisonment. Most of the crime growth took place in the 1960s, and the first year of the current penal growth was after that time (in 1973). Since that date, crime has gone up twice and down twice, and is today about what it was in 1973. It is hard to argue from these broad trends that the grand penal experiment has had much impact on crime. Indeed, a growing consensus of criminological thought takes this view.[11] On the one hand, there are several criminologists who have long pointed out that the overall impact on crime of this increase in the scale of punishment has been small.[12] Some others, who were at one time more optimistic about the crime-suppression impacts of growing imprisonment,[13] have concluded that to continue the growth will have at best diminishing impact on crime and at worst *accelerating* diminishing returns.[14] Indeed, Raymond Liedka and colleagues conclude that "policy discussion should be informed by the limitation of the fact that prison expansion, beyond a certain point, will no longer serve any reasonable purpose."[15] There is even a growing body of work that suggests that prison population growth itself is criminogenic, creating the very crime that it is trying to prevent—a point to which we will return later in this chapter.[16] But as we argued in chapter 3, the great penal experiment was only partly about crime. It was also about the fear of crime. What about that?

Fear of Crime

We would argue that any decline in public fear of crime has been less about punishment increasing than it is has been about crime decreasing. Although crime has not dropped completely off the public radar, it is no longer one of the issues that Americans identify as a "most important problem" in regular Gallup polls. For more than twenty years, crime consistently ranked quite high among the problems that Americans identified as the "most important problems" facing the country. Indeed, through the 1980s and into the middle part of the 1990s, crime ranked number one among spending priorities but, by 2006, it had been more than five years since crime had made the list of the top five spending priorities.[17] Public support for spending on efforts to "halt the increasing crime rate" also waned in the more recent years and more closely tracked trends in crime than it did trends in imprisonment (see figure 6.1).[18]

Ironically, even as crime reached its lowest point in more than thirty-five years, and although Americans no longer identify crime as a top

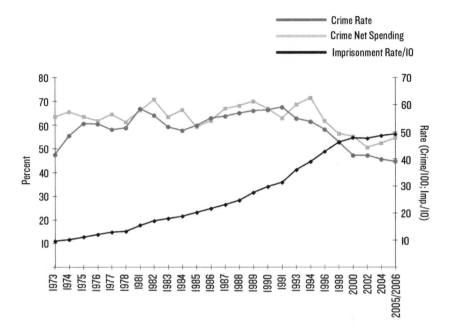

Figure 6.1: Crime, Imprisonment, and Public Support for Spending on Crime Reduction, 1973-2006. Tom Smith, "Trends in National Spending Priorities, 1973-2006" (Chicago: University of Chicago, National Opinion Research Center, 2007).

spending priority, more than 60 percent of Americans still reported in Gallup opinion polls that too little was being spent on "halting the rising crime rate."[19] Perhaps, then, another lesson of the grand penal experiment was that the Punishment Imperative meant there was an enormous elasticity in what Americans were willing to pay for punishment. In 1972, nobody would have thought that we could have afforded this massive expansion in the use of imprisonment—and nobody would have predicted that the American public would be willing to pay for it.

Fueling Social Problems

A third clear conclusion that can be drawn from our grand penal experiment is that it has done nothing to alleviate related social problems. In fact, there are several important ways in which the Punishment

Imperative has exacerbated the very social problems that we were justi-fiably concerned about for the latter half of the twentieth century. Social inequality, racial inequality, and fiscal responsibility—all pressing con-cerns of the late twentieth century—were each exacerbated by an over-reliance on incarceration as a solution to the crime problem. The costs of the Punishment Imperative—both socially and fiscally—have been very high.

Social and Racial Inequality

Incarceration has both direct and indirect effects on social inequality. Indices of inequality suggest that the gap between the haves and have-nots in the United States continues to grow. Nowhere is this effect more pronounced than with regard to young men of color.

As discussed earlier, the experience of incarceration is not equally distributed across the population. Racial and ethnic minorities, particu-larly young black males and increasingly young Hispanic males as well, are vastly overrepresented among the U.S. prison populations. Accord-ing to the most recent Department of Justice figures, at year-end 2010, close to 40 percent of the United States' 1.5 million prisoners were black and more than 20 percent were Hispanic—in other words, more than 60 percent of prison populations were racial or ethnic minorities.[20] Just under one million blacks and Hispanics were serving sentences of more than one year, and more than 7 percent of the black male population between the ages of thirty and thirty-four was currently incarcerated. The imprisonment rate for black men was seven times higher than that for white men.

The contemporary period is not the first in which minorities have borne the brunt of incarceration. Alex Lichtenstein has argued that his-torically there have been two notable surges in the use of imprisonment, and that both disproportionately affected black Americans: the first, a rapid growth in the use of imprisonment across the South, followed the emancipation of slaves in the 1860s, and the second followed the civil rights movement of the 1960s.[21] Lichtenstein points out that although the scale of imprisonment might have reached unprecedented levels in the more recent period, high imprisonment rates, particularly high southern imprisonment rates, also proliferated following the Civil War and Reconstruction. The massive buildup of imprisonment in this earlier period was also felt unevenly, with growth in black rates of imprisonment dramatically outpacing the growth in white rates of imprisonment. Kevin Reitz adds that black-white disparities in incarceration have grown steadily between 1880 and 2000—from 3:1 shortly following emancipation to almost 8:1 in the year 2000.[22]

Many others have noted the not-so-subtle racial undertones of some of the particularly punitive legislation—most notably the crack/cocaine distinction that imposes penalties one hundred times greater in magnitude for the possession of crack cocaine than for the possession of powder cocaine.[23] The evidence for discrimination as a causal determinant of the relationship between race and imprisonment is at best mixed,[24] but whether it was intentional discrimination or not, as Michael Tonry has pointed out, "the rising levels of Black incarceration did not just happen . . . they were the foreseeable effects of deliberate policies."[25]

The impacts of these disparities have been demonstrable. In his masterful analysis of the impact of incarceration policy on the labor market and family prospects, Bruce Western shows that the consequences of incarceration have been felt disproportionately by black men, further alienating them from the labor market, making stable family formation more problematic, and ultimately increasing the economic gap between whites and blacks.[26] Todd Clear has argued that the high rates of incarceration, concentrated in impoverished places, have had a range of negative impacts on those places, including increased rates of sexually transmitted diseases, increased rates of teenage births, and increased rates of serious juvenile delinquency. He concluded that imprisonment was a system "that [fed] upon itself," exacerbating the very social problems that led to the increases in crime that enabled policy shifts toward more reliance on imprisonment in the first place.[27]

Fiscal Flexibility

For those concerned about fiscal responsibility, the social experiment in mass incarceration should be cause for concern because it has certainly not been cheap. Growth in incarceration spending (202 percent) over the past two decades outpaced growth in spending on education (55 percent), higher education (3 percent), and public assistance (which actually decreased by 60 percent).[28] In a way, until very recently, the prison system stood in line first for its budget, and everything else followed. Several years ago, however, Michael Jacobson recognized that this fiscal dominance of the penal system in the budgetary process was beginning to place pressure on political leaders whose constituents were looking for investments in other areas.[29] He argued that crime no longer had the salience as a top-three public worry; the economy, health care, and education were dominating contemporary public concerns. But the money available for these priorities was becoming seriously strained by the revenue requirements of the penal system.

As the national economy moved toward recession in 2001, states also began feeling the fiscal pressure. Facing serious budget shortfalls, states began looking to reduce expenditures and for the first time corrections budgets, which had long enjoyed annual increases, were among those budgets to face cuts in 2002, 2003, and 2004.[30] Across the country states began to rethink their sentencing laws with at least thirty states initiating some form of sentencing reform since 2000 (a point we emphasized in the first chapter and will return to in the final chapter).

Shifting public opinion, particularly around the utility of incarcerating drug offenders given the cost, also drove some of the early policy change. In hindsight, some of this early activity probably signaled the beginning of the end of the Punishment Imperative. Voter dissatisfaction with punitive drug laws led to the passage of Proposition 200 in Arizona in 1996 and of Proposition 36 in California in 2000. The voter-initiated drug-law reforms in California and Arizona each resulted in the diversion of nonviolent drug offenders from prison and represented two early examples of measures the public was willing to take to reduce the pressure that correctional expenditures were exerting on state budgets in the late 1990s. A cost-benefit analysis of California's Substance Abuse and Crime Prevention Act (SACPA, also known as Proposition 36) demonstrated that SACPA saved California $2.50 for every $1 spent and resulted in net savings of more than $173 million in its first year alone.[31] In the years since, states across the country have begun decriminalizing drug possession—most often through voter-approved ballot initiatives. In the most recent 2012 election cycle, for example, voters in both Colorado and Washington chose to *legalize* the use of marijuana. Although Americans had been willing to pay for prison expansion for more than three decades, it seems that the cost of the Punishment Imperative—and the constraints it placed on spending in other areas—ultimately provided the "window of opportunity" necessary for the policy change that we have begun to see occurring across the country.[32]

Punishment and Politics

Although we cannot definitively identify the causes of prison population growth with any precision, it is certainly the case that the social experiment in mass incarceration was driven by increasingly punitive criminal justice policies that ensured that there would be prisoners to fill newly constructed prison cells. One of the more troubling features of the social experiment in mass incarceration is the way in which it has engaged politics. Evidence abounds of the problematic ways in which punishment has engaged politics. Through the 1980s and 1990s, even the slightest indication that a politician might be soft on crime signaled the death knoll for that candidate's election hopes. Demonstrating that one was appropriately tough on crime required supporting "get-tough" policies regardless of their logic, their ability to address the problems they were putatively designed to address, or their cost. Mandatory minimum sentences, habitual offender legislation, and truth-in-sentencing requirements were just a few of the many "get-tough" policies that contributed to the prison buildup.

Just as mass incarceration has engaged politics in problematic ways, politics has engaged the public in perhaps even more disturbing ways.

Politicians tended to play on the public's greatest fears to make the case for greater punishment. Indeed, research demonstrates that crime had long been a bipartisan issue, and, as we have demonstrated, certainly under the Clinton administration as many anticrime measures were offered to the public as under any other. The Reagan administration gave us federal sentencing guidelines and the Anti–Drug Abuse Act of 1986; the first Bush administration gave us mandatory sentencing for drug offenders; the Clinton administration offered the 85 percent–time served truth-in-sentencing requirements for violent offenders. There was no obvious partisan pattern to the pandering. Ironically, the second Bush administration in some ways led the deescalation, offering reentry programs as a part of its Second Chance Act and promoting faith-based rehabilitation programs as well.

But the overall pattern under the Punishment Imperative was that the reforms begotten by the politics of penality created the fuel for the system to grow. Voters in California decided twice—first in 1994 and then again in 2004—that third-time serious and violent felons should face sentences of twenty-five years to life. California voters cast their votes with little understanding of the law, how it would work, or the consequences it would have for corrections, for budgets, or for justice.[33] California's three-strikes law did not impact the California prison system in quite the way that some predicted it might—and it was recently scaled back as the result of a successful 2012 ballot initiative—but that certainly does not mean that three-strikes laws, and other popular punitive policies, did not have serious consequences for prison population growth and for justice.[34] On the one hand, prosecutors, who gained so much in the way of discretion as a result of Punishment Imperative initiatives, had to subvert the law to avoid what they recognized as profoundly unjust outcomes.[35] And, on the other, when the law was not subverted, third-time offenders convicted of relatively minor crimes were serving sentences that were not only exceptionally long (relative to other similarly situated offenders without the strikes) but were also inversely proportional.[36] Under three-strikes-type laws, those who have committed the least serious crimes as their "third-strike" offense experience the most dramatic escalation in punishment. A third-strike offender convicted of aggravated homicide would have probably received a penalty of life without parole (or death in states that retain the death penalty) even without a three-strike provision, but a person convicted of aggravated assault sentenced to 25-to-life under three-strikes laws probably experiences an increase in punishment that is at least two to three times what he would have received. Across the country throughout the 1980s and 1990s, voters endorsed punitive initiatives that met the objectives of the Punishment Imperative but that were often perceived as too rigid by those responsible for meting out justice and were routinely subverted.[37]

Yet the foundation laid by these laws was a cycle of penal growth. New laws increase the policing of our poorest neighborhoods, and more young men are caught up in the penal system as a consequence. The large volume of young black men in the system's clutches serves to reinforce the idea that safety is a problem of race, enabling legislatures to propose ever more draconian measures that are racially disproportionate in their consequences. The neighborhoods where these young men live become places with large numbers of missing men—men who are behind bars—and even larger numbers of men who have cycled through the justice system. These men arrive home from prison with reduced prospects for earnings and family participation, and with increased chances of crime. Their children, too, have increased chances of criminal involvement as a consequence of parental incarceration. Because of the community's high incarceration rates, a range of public problems are exacerbated, from HIV-related health problems to teenage births. Labor markets are weakened, and social networks are damaged. Each of these effects of high incarceration has the tendency to increase crime rates. Higher crime rates lead to more policing and more arrests. The system feeds upon itself and its impacts are not negligible. We review some of those impacts below lest we forget that a social experiment as large and enduring as the Punishment Imperative will have lasting consequences for individuals, for communities, and for crime in those communities.

Incarceration and Communities

The movement of people going into and coming back from prison is thought to put strains on a neighborhood and its residents in the way it affects networks, families, and children.[38] As we have previously emphasized, this process is not evenly distributed across places, but, rather, is highly concentrated, creating specific areas where there are continuously relatively large numbers of people being removed to prison and then later returned. In high-incarceration places, imprisonment—especially of men in the prime parenting age groups—permeates the context, influencing institutional aspects of community life such as labor markets and housing, and interpersonal aspects such as family functioning and parenting.[39] Racial and economic segregation in cities concentrates incarceration in the poorest black neighborhoods. In some urban areas, more than one in six black adult males of the ages twenty to forty-four are in prison,[40] and in sections of Brooklyn, one in seven youth aged 18–24 enters prison or jail each year.[41]

There is a well-established literature on how incarceration affects the individuals who go to prison.[42] Going to prison has a host of negative impacts on the former prisoner. A criminal record operates as a kind of stigma, reducing job prospects, and for black males the interaction of race and criminal record substantially reduces employers' willingness to hire.[43] It reduces postprison lifetime earnings, reducing wages by 30–40 percent.[44] Men who go to prison are about as likely to cohabit after release as those who have not been incarcerated, but they are one-half as likely to marry their partner, even when there is a child involved.[45] Otherwise stable relationships often are dissolved by the nonprison partner once the prison sentence begins.[46] For those who are released from incarceration, chances of separation after release from prison are increased, even when there is a minor child present in the home. It has been estimated that between one-fourth and one-half of all prisoners disrupt a family when they are removed for incarceration, and this helps explain why counties with high incarceration rates have higher-than-expected rates of single-parent families.[47] Among the problems suffered by children during a parent's incarceration are "depression, hyperactivity, aggressive behavior, withdrawal, regression, clinging behavior, sleep problems, eating problems, running away, truancy and poor school grades."[48] Incarceration also affects adult partners of inmates and other family members.[49] These individual-level effects can add up to a prevailing aggregate effect, because the deficits resulting from incarceration are so widely spread in communities where incarceration is concentrated. Parental incarceration is a prime risk factor in delinquency, so it is no surprise that these neighborhoods sustain multigenerational patterns of criminal justice involvement.[50]

The ripple effects of high rates of individual-level incarceration have been substantial. Across time, as different men have cycled through confinement, family after family has been affected by imprisonment. Dina Rose and her colleagues have reported, for example, that in some Tallahassee neighborhoods, almost every family has a family member who has been imprisoned within a five-year period.[51] Donald Braman's study of a District of Columbia neighborhood, Adrian LeBlanc's study of the South Bronx, and Sudhir Venkatesh's study of New York City housing projects each reported similarly high, nearly ubiquitous, family-level experiences with incarceration of a loved one.[52] As scholars continued to investigate the collateral consequences of mass incarceration, an important literature emerged on the way incarceration affects marriage, families, and children in various deleterious ways.[53]

Impact on Communities

This rapidly growing literature has only just begun to demonstrate the importance of incarceration as a dynamic affecting a range of community-level attributes, and the cumulative impact of this concentrated incarceration in communities is only beginning to be understood. The impact of the flow of offenders into prisons and back out to neighborhoods on crime in those neighborhoods has been of particular interest. Very recent work has tried to investigate the impact of level of prison cycling—the removal of people for incarceration and their eventual return—on those places, with a specific focus on the relationship between incarceration and crime. This work is rooted in the social science tradition that views crime not only as an individual-level phenomenon but also an ecological one. In their seminal work on social disorganization, Clifford Shaw and Henry McKay pointed out that social processes such as mobility can affect a place's propensity for crime; this point was part of their larger observation that characteristics of communities have effects that are separate from the simple aggregate of the characteristics of the individuals who live there.[54] Recent work has shown that contextual poverty, unemployment, and demographic characteristics are often correlated with the level of crime.[55] This body of work all derives from the social fact that incarceration concentrates in communities having characteristics associated with social disadvantage.

Communities and Concentrated Incarceration

Studies of the impact of incarceration on communities have taken two main approaches. The first looks at the effect of aggregation of individual and family-level effects that may produce community-level correlations. The second posits that there are separate effects that operate at the community level and that these may in turn influence individual-level behavior.

Community or ecological effects occur when concentrated incarceration changes the social environment of a community for everyone, not just those who are directly touched by the incarceration cycle. Ecological effects stem from the way incarceration alters the role young men play in ecological-level dynamics, such as labor markets, and promotes juvenile delinquency.[56] In high-incarceration places, researchers have found that the social and personal relationships are altered in important ways. The absence of young men due to incarceration can also alter social networks that already tend to be thin, with far more strong ties than weak ones, increasing community reliance on the state for social support.[57] Incarceration also disrupts patterns of sexual conduct, especially for girls, in ways that explain the higher-than-expected rate of sexually transmitted diseases and teenage births in high-incarceration communities.[58] Still more work has demonstrated that mass incarceration has significantly increased the rate of poverty for those not incarcerated.[59]

Building on these observations, researchers and theorists suggest that highly concentrated incarceration would negatively impact public safety in places.[60] While some posited crime-enhancing effects that flow through relationships between the men who cycle through the prison and back into the neighborhood and those who live in the neighborhood,[61] others built on the social disorganization tradition to show how high levels of incarceration, concentrated in poor places, would be expected to produce a "tipping point" at which the incarceration would cause crime to go up rather than down.[62] Although the dynamics (and perhaps the precise nature) of the relationship among crime, incarceration, and communities are still contested, there are few who would deny that incarceration has had demonstrable impacts on the communities hardest hit by the Punishment Imperative.

A Summary Assessment of the Punishment Imperative

We have characterized the Punishment Imperative as a grand social experiment, noting the ways in which this is a useful metaphor, even if it is not entirely apt. We used this point of view because it offers a doorway to an overarching review of the Imperative—a set of "findings," if you will. As with any complex social phenomenon, the results are not simple, but they are more or less straightforward. Each of these summaries has been explained in detail in previous sections of the book, with numerous citations. Here we remind the reader of what the Punishment Imperative has wrought.

Reducing Crime

Crime has indeed gone down now, for a decade or more. The crime drop encouraged the advocates for the penal model, but it is a largely spurious association. The body of research about the relationship between incarceration and crime is voluminous and complicated, but the overall implications of this research are as follows.

- Longer prison sentences do not deter people who receive them from crime; there is almost no relationship between the length of a prison stay and the likelihood of recidivism.
- Going to prison does not deter; people who receive probation are no more likely (and may be slightly less likely) to recidivate.
- Incapacitation effects of prison are small primarily due to replacement.
- Rehabilitation programs offered in prison are less effective than when they are offered in the community.
- The deterrent power of the increased risk of imprisonment is undermined by the delay between arrest and sentencing and by a process that many people think is unfair.

The big picture of incarceration and crime is consistent with these points. While prison populations increased between 1972 and the early 1990s, and especially during the steepest increases in the 1980s, crime rose. When the rate of prison growth began to decline, crime began to drop. So while scholars acknowledge that prison growth has some suppressive effect on crime, there is a growing consensus that the effect of imprisonment is relatively small and is overwhelmed by other factors that have a much more significant impact on crime rates. The Punishment Imperative has contributed little to reductions in fear of crime. For most of the period when incarceration rates rose, fear of crime remained high, regardless of fluctuations in crime. Recent polls find that crime has dropped from its place high on the list of public concerns, replaced by economic concerns and international terrorism. It appears that fear of crime tracks more closely to other factors having little to do with punishment rates.

Increasing Solidarity with Victims of Crime

A vibrant victims' movement remains a salient aspect of penal code reform, especially as signified by "name" laws that, as a consequence of highly publicized crimes, codify restrictions on the convicted, their sentencing, or their parole eligibility. Victim participation at various stages of the criminal justice system is now standard practice. While there is no question that victims routinely feel mistreated in the justice system, it is equally apparent that victims have a much higher profile today than they did forty years ago.

It is not at all clear that the Punishment Imperative has had anything to do with this. There is no study showing that victims cite punishment today as a more satisfactory aspect of the justice system than they did, say, forty years ago. Indeed, restorative justice reform is predicated on the fact that many victims *still* feel a sense of letdown and emptiness after the sentencing is over. The increases in punishment were clearly *responsive* to victim concerns, but they just as clearly did not resolve them.

Controlling the "Dangerous"

According to the more critical view, controlling the dangerous was a latent goal of the Punishment Imperative. The Punishment Imperative was designed to make sure that the class of people who most make us worry about our safety are under surveillance and control.

It has not turned out well. Not because control did not happen. It did. The problems have been all the collateral consequences of "controlling the dangerous." People who go to prison for the most part come out, and while they are locked up others take their role in crimes in the community. Many engage in a lifetime of cycling in and out of the prison system. Instead of a standing rate of incapacitation, prison represents a standing "time out" for a large swath of poor, mostly minority communities. In these places, a large number of men (and many women) are locked up on any given day, but *who* is behind bars changes from day to day.

If the crime-control impact is small, the community-level impact is not. Studies show that the expanding prison system has contributed to each of the following: (1) intergenerational criminality, (2) broken families, (3) problems in school, (4) sexually transmitted diseases, (5) teenaged births, (6) anticonventional attitudes, (7) depleted labor markets,

(8) racial inequality, (9) and crime. This pattern of collateral consequences has helped to solidify the disadvantage of people who live in high-incarceration neighborhoods, creating and expanding a quasi-permanent class of people who occupy the status of "dangerous."

Race

Without a doubt, the most serious consequences of the Punishment Imperative have been the way it exacerbated racial inequalities and fueled racial injustice. The fivefold increase in the size of the penal system, especially the number of people of color behind bars, has been an intervention into racial stratification of enormous magnitude. Black boys born today have a nearly one-in-three chance of ending up in prison by the time they become men. Black children are increasingly being raised in families with regular personal connections to the U.S. prison system. Economic inequality between African Americans and other racial/ethnic groups in the United States has been exacerbated by the consequences of the way the growing U.S. penal system has disproportionately affected them. After demonstrating the ways in which mass imprisonment has damaged black families and weakened their economic opportunity, Harvard sociologist Bruce Western concludes, "Pervasive incarceration and its effects on economic opportunity and family life have given the penal system a central role in the lives of the urban poor."[63]

Several scholars have noted that the growth of the U.S. prison system has been a driver of racial division in the United States. Notably, legal scholar Michael Tonry has written eloquently and extensively about this issue.[64] The thrust of his work is simple: anyone could have easily foreseen that the drug laws passed in the 1980s and 1990s would have disproportionate impact on people of color. If they did not know, then they were willfully blind to the obvious; if they did know, then they were willing to trade enormous racial inequities to advance their punitive agenda.

Throughout this book we have chronicled the collateral consequences of our contemporary penal policy for people of color. The list of effects is shocking to the mind. Among the myriad social problems that have been demonstrated to arise from the expansion of the prison system are broken families, weakened parental relationships with children, loss of earnings, economic damage to communities, reduced personal health, shorter life expectancies for youth, and teenage births. To top it off, there is growing evidence that the concentrated growth of incarceration has contributed to higher crime rates in the neighborhoods that send so many people to prison, only to receive them back a short time later. It is entirely plausible that none of the policies of the Punishment Imperative was designed to produce these results. But the concentration of the grand penal experiment among poor males, especially minority-group members, means that the collateral consequences they suffer from the expanded justice system are a main product of the generation-long changes in that system. The bottom line is that this group, the country's most vulnerable citizens, suffer the consequences of both crime itself and the social responses to crime.

Michelle Alexander has recently referred to this as "The New Jim Crow."[65] Her central claim is that "something akin to a racial caste system currently exists in the United States" in which people with criminal records "have scarcely more rights, and arguably less respect, than a black man living in Alabama under Jim Crow."[66] The substantive analysis she offers—the war on drugs, collateral consequences of conviction, and sociopolitical consequences of the growth of the prison system—has been made by other writers. What sets her work apart is the passion in her analysis and the sharpness of her eye. In her view,

> This is, in brief, how the system works. The War on Drugs is the vehicle through which extraordinary numbers of black men are forced into the cage. . . . Vast numbers of people are swept into the criminal justice system by the police, who conduct drug operations primarily in poor communities of color. . . . Because there is no meaningful check on the exercise of police discretion, racial biases are guaranteed free rein. In fact, police are allowed to rely on race as a factor in selecting whom to stop and frisk . . . effectively guaranteeing that those who are swept into the system are primarily black and brown. . . . Prosecutors are free to "load

up" defendants with extra charges, and their decisions cannot be challenged for racial bias. Once convicted . . . drug offenders spend more time under the criminal justice system's formal control . . . than drug offenders anywhere else in the world. . . . The final stage has been dubbed by some advocates as the period of invisible punishment. . . . [T]he unique set of criminal sanctions that are imposed on individuals after they step outside the prison gates . . . operate collectively to ensure that the vast majority of convicted offenders will never integrate into mainstream, white society . . . [T]hey will eventually return to prison and then be released again, caught in a closed circuit of perpetual marginality.[67]

That we, wittingly or not, designed a system that was intentionally tough on people who engaged in crime is of no surprise to anyone. That it has been so enormously damaging to generations of poor black men should not shock us at all.

Summary

Like other grand social experiments, the Punishment Imperative produced a wide range of results. There were so many policy changes, great and small, over such a long period of time, that it is not possible to say in summary fashion that change X produced result Y. With no control group, it is not easy to say, in the scientific sense, that this new policy caused that eventual result.

Furthermore, so much of what happened as the Punishment Imperative held sway was both bold and nuanced. For example, community supervision policies that increased the pressure on probationers and parolees, through regular drug testing, the proliferation of technical conditions, and an emphasis on tough enforcement had the surface effect of increasing the rate at which people who were released from prison would go back, whether or not they were arrested for a new crime. But it also had the more subtle effect of distorting the role of the probation or parole officer. These roles had been invented as ways of making reintegration into the community easier, of providing official support for the social adjustment of people who had criminal histories. Early theories of probation and parole supervision actually saw these roles as *community advocates* for those under correctional supervision. The get-tough movement changed that profoundly. These days, people in these jobs mostly function as community surveillance workers.

When looked at in the broadest sense, the Punishment Imperative had this main result: the criminal justice system now operates as a self-sustaining cycle of gathering increasing numbers of poor people, mostly men and mostly black, into its clutches, profoundly damaging their life chances, and returning them to communities bereft of the capacity to absorb them. It has been politically cancerous, privileging rhetoric that baits the more base public emotions rather than encouraging sound policymaking and strategic thinking. It has been a vast fiscal dark hole, guaranteeing that for generations public money must be moved from public goods such as schools, health care, and infrastructure to instead support and maintain a quasi-permanent, separate community of the incarcerated and controlled. And it has been empirically wrong, doing shockingly little about the crime problem it was originally designed to address.

This summary description of the results of the experiment makes it seem that it has been a complete failure. Yet the summary also calls to mind the analysis in the preceding chapter. There were many people who sincerely and optimistically believed that growing the punishment system would lead us out of the crucible of crime. But there are now others who, persuasively, point to another function, the control of a mass of marginal young men, more black than any other color. On that criterion, the social experiment may be seen as far less of a complete failure.

There are indications that policymakers now know much of what has been summarized here, and it seems they have started asking themselves, "Is this a policy experiment we wish to continue?" As we argued in the opening chapter, intellectual leaders and elected officials alike have already begun to finds ways of reversing the policies of the last forty years. In the final chapter, we explore mechanisms by which the Punishment Imperative may be more rapidly brought to its conclusion.

7

Dismantling the Punishment Imperative

In our opening chapter, we argued that the Punishment Imperative, dominant for more than a generation, has now run its course. If we are right, then we are still in the very earliest days of this change. Yet if we are right, it will be because an uncoordinated set of forces distributed around the country has reached an unofficial conclusion that the time has come to deescalate the penal system. There are certainly many people making this argument today—on the left, on the right, and in the center. For reasons that often differ, today's debates have much less to do with how to get tougher and much more to do with how to stop throwing money at the penal system. The brief look at reform around the country that we provided at the beginning of this book offers an impressive list of states that are enacting policies intended to reduce the size of their prison populations.

From this we can draw two conclusions. The first conclusion is obvious: the tide has turned, and the energy for penal reform is on the side of something new; the Punishment Imperative is no longer the driving force for all correctional policy talk. The second conclusion is much more subtle: a great deal of this current reform effort is unlikely to have much effect on prison populations. Reformers are often naïve, thinking that small adjustments in correctional programs will result in large changes in imprisonment. They are also cautious in this new agenda, and want to take actions that will not directly confront the Punishment Imperative, so they often talk about strategies that do not sound like releasing people from prison or reducing their surveillance. In making these observations, we think we are seeing the very early days of the new paradigm. People seem to have crossed the first threshold—reducing imprisonment is now a desirable aim. The practical question is, what will it take to do something about the problem of mass incarceration?

Reducing the Prison Population: The Iron Law

The answer to this question is at once simple and daunting. It is simple, because of the "Iron Law of Prison Populations."[1] The Iron Law holds that prison populations are entirely produced by just two statistics: *flow*, how many people go to prison, and *LOS*, their length of stay. The corollary, then, is that to reduce prison populations one must reduce either the number of people who go to prison, how long they stay, or (for maximum effect) both.[2]

There are two daunting aspects of this simple idea. One is that the political and tactical foundation for reducing either of these two numbers is quiescent. As we write, around the nation states are struggling with their prison populations, looking for ways to control costs. As elected leaders cautiously propose different mechanisms to control prison costs, they undergo close scrutiny for any indication that these mechanisms—and by extension, the politicians endorsing them—will put the public at risk. Demonization is even now a constant risk for any public servant who seeks reasonable means to control prison costs.

The second daunting problem arises from the first: many of the most popular prison-cost proposals do not have much capacity to control costs. There is a softer, programmatic means to confront prison costs, based on the idea that "rehabilitation programs" will reduce recidivism rates. Advocates of this approach argue that research has demonstrated that rehabilitation programs can reduce recidivism rates by 20 percent or more. They say that the secret to controlling prison costs is to invest in treatment programs in prison and during reentry from prison, which will in turn lead to reduction in the number of people released from prison who return to it.

This is an appealing idea, for it enables its proponents to propose to reduce prison populations without proposing either to let some people out of prison or to divert others from incarceration. The reduction in prison intake coming from greater rehabilitation will lead to a reduction in prison costs as success rates rise.

But it is exceedingly unlikely that this strategy will have much impact on prison costs, for two reasons. Others have commented on the limits of rehabilitation programs for reducing the prison system,[3] and here we summarize their observations.

First of all, the research literature in support of rehabilitation programs includes a very strong theme that many programs do not work.[4] Those programs that do succeed—those that follow certain criteria for "what works"[5]—can be expected to attain recidivism reduction rates of upwards of 20–30 percent. But this result comes about for a relatively small subset of all people who go through the corrections system: those who are high risk and have a "criminogenic need," that is, a need that can be changed through a treatment program; and those for whom a treatment program is available. A large number of people do not fit either category. Joan Petersilia, for example, has estimated that although 40 percent of people in the California prison system have a need that could be addressed through treatment, only about 10 percent actually receive the treatment they need.[6] Faye Taxman and her colleagues have similarly estimated that only about 11 percent of the people under correctional authority get the program services they need, and only about 8 percent are in such a program at any given time.[7] In other words, under current programmatic levels, only about 10 percent of those who need treatment can receive it. Unless there is a wholesale expansion of treatment programs—say on the order of a five- to tenfold increase—the prospects for reducing imprisonment through treatment are dim.

Second, even if we could expect more from proven treatment programs—even if we could bring them to scale and if there were *an appropriate treatment program for every client of the corrections system*—the basic math does not suggest that this approach has much promise. Let us say that a given prison system has a prison recidivism rate of 40 percent; that is, two of five who leave prison return. Let us further assume, for ease of math, that 50 percent of the prison entry cohort comes as parole failures. If a prison or reentry treatment program had an impact of 25 percent, that means it would reduce the failure rate from 40 percent to 30 percent. We can all agree that this is a very good outcome and is one that we would very much like to achieve, benefiting everybody. But it means that the prison entry cohort, all else being equal, would be reduced by 5 percent each year.

This seems like a big number, but it is a highest-possible-impact estimate. To the extent that some programs are weak, the effect on entry rates is diminished. To the extent that many parole failures serve short terms, the effect on stock populations is further diminished. To the extent that entry cohorts include fewer parole failures, the effect is diminished even more. So that by the time all of the "in practice" caveats are added to the situation, what starts out as a best-case 5 percent annual reduction in prison intake turns out to be a mere fraction of that effect. It is a small enough effect that it could easily be overwhelmed by other factors having to do with changes in sentencing laws or practices, or crime rates. And this is why a program-based prison-reduction strategy will take a very long time to work.

In fact, to have significant impact on prison populations, the main culprits behind the growth of incarceration in the United States must be confronted head-on. Length of stay has doubled since 1972, and the rate of felony sentencing to incarceration has changed from 25 percent in 1972 to 75 percent today.[8] Various strategies for reducing prison populations are now under consideration.[9] We think three deserve to be especially highlighted because they will be central to any meaningful strategy to reduce mass incarceration and overcome the worst excesses of the Punishment Imperative. These three agenda items are (1) repealing mandatory penalties, (2) reducing length of stay, and (3) reducing rates of recidivism.

Agenda One: Repeal Mandatory Sentences, Especially for Drugs

A central engine for incarceration growth has been mandatory sentencing, especially for drug-related crime. If we are to make headway in reducing mass incarceration, mandatory sentencing must be eliminated, especially for drug crimes.

Beginning in the mid-1970s and continuing through the 1980s and 1990s, mandatory sentencing provisions emerged as among the most popular of the sentencing reforms. By 2002, all fifty states and the federal government had enacted mandatory sentencing provisions for one or more offenses. These mandatory sentence provisions typically attach to violent, sexual, drug, and weapons offenses, and to habitual offending.[10] Despite their popularity, there is widespread agreement around the negative consequences of mandatory sentencing. These consequences include growing prison populations,[11] the transfer of discretion from judges to politicians,[12] increased disparity,[13] and compromised proportionality in sentencing.[14] While all four of these consequences call into question the utility of these provisions in their effects, the latter three additionally raise fundamental questions for justice.

Just as there is widespread agreement around the negative consequences related to mandatory sentencing, there is also broad-based support for their repeal. Indeed, support for the repeal of mandatory sentencing provisions can be found across the spectrum. Scholars have long questioned the wisdom and lamented the outcomes of these provisions. National organizations and several national commissions, including the U.S. Sentencing Commission, the National Criminal Justice Commission, and the Justice Kennedy Commission, have called for the repeal of mandatory sentencing. Although the calls for repeal have been particularly pronounced in the area of drug law reform, these entities support sentencing law reform—and mandatory sentencing repeal—more broadly.

Mandatory minimum sentences, which were purportedly enacted to serve as deterrents, produce equality in sentencing, circumvent discretion, and reduce disparity, have been attacked as failing on each of these grounds. Each of these is discussed in turn.

Because mandatory sentences impose more certain and more severe penalties for certain specified offenses, mandatory sentences were expected to deter commission of the offenses targeted. With regard to the deterrent effect of mandatory penalties, a number of empirical works have assessed mandatory sentence provisions in practice. Some of these include the U.S. Sentencing Commission Report, *Mandatory Penalties in the Federal Criminal Justice System*,[15] a study of New York's Rockefeller Drug laws,[16] two studies of Massachusetts' mandatory one-year prison term for the possession of an unlicensed firearm,[17] one study of Michigan's mandatory two-year prison term for the use of a firearm during the commission of a felony,[18] and a study of Oregon's Measure 11.[19] All five of the cited empirical studies suggest that, even if deterrence could be realized, the deterrent effects of mandatory sentences are likely to be marginal. The deterrent effect of mandatory sentencing is minimized because the laws themselves tend to be seen as too harsh by many of the central actors in the criminal justice system who are responsible for enforcing them, and these actors, from the police to the prosecutors and the judges, often go out of their way to circumvent the laws and avoid imposing the mandatory penalty.

Mandatory sentencing schemes also raise concerns around equality. The equality principle in sentencing requires not only that similar cases be treated similarly but also that different cases be treated differently. As legal scholar Michael Tonry has argued, mandatory sentences focus entirely on treating similar crimes similarly "but at the cost of ignoring differences in [offenders'] lives and circumstances that many judges (and others) believe ethically relevant to thinking about just punishments."[20] Mandatory sentencing laws leave no room either for an assessment of individual culpability beyond prior offense history or for the tailoring of a sentence to fit that culpability. So, while these laws achieve equality in one sense (offense-based), they violate the equality principle in another (offender-based).

Nor have mandatory sentences necessarily reduced discretion. Mandatory sentences have simply transferred discretion from judges, who once determined appropriate punishment, to the legislature, which enacts these penalties (often in conflict with the recommendations of the state's sentencing commission), and most importantly to the prosecutors, who have complete and unchecked discretion in the charging of offenses and plea-bargaining of cases.[21] It can also be argued that these laws have done more to create disparity than to eliminate it. Mandatory sentences result in disparate punishment because prosecutors, judges, or juries perceive them to be unjust and circumvent them. Prosecutors circumvent when they make their charging decisions and judges/ juries when they refuse to convict on the charge for which an unjust mandatory penalty is stipulated. Michael Tonry concludes that "patterns of circumvention are generally ad hoc and idiosyncratic with the result that sentencing disparities are often extreme: among like situated offenders, some will be sentenced to the ten- or twenty-year minimum sentence and others, benefiting from circumventions, will receive much less severe sentences."[22]

While much of the disparity associated with mandatory minimums comes from various methods of circumventing the laws, in some cases disparities are written right into the law. Despite recent legislative revisions, the distinction in mandatory minimum penalties for possession of crack versus powder cocaine has been among the most criticized of sentencing policies.[23]

Most scholars now consider mandatory minimum penalties unjust and unfair. Conservative criminologist John J. DiIulio, who at one time would have favored such a harsh approach to the control of crime, has decried mandatory drug penalties, arguing that "to continue to imprison drug-only offenders mandatorily is to hamstring further a justice system that controls crime in a daily war of inches, not miles."[24] Franklin Zimring argued more generally that "the mandatory term is a huge expansion of punishment, rendering excessive outcomes in many cases to ensure sufficiency of punishment in a very few that might otherwise escape their just deserts."[25] Members of the judiciary, including former and current Supreme Court justices, have come to agree. Supreme Court Justice Anthony Kennedy has spoken out against mandatory minimum penalties in a number of public forums. During an address to the American Bar Association (ABA), for example, Justice Kennedy proclaimed that he "[accepts] neither the wisdom, the justice nor the necessity of mandatory minimums. In all too many cases they are unjust" and added that "our resources are misspent, our punishments too severe, our sentences too long."[26] Toward the end of his provocative address, Justice Kennedy challenged the ABA "to study these matters, and to help start a new public discussion about the prison system." In response to that challenge, the ABA formed the Justice Kennedy Commission and issued a report in which they urged "states, territories and the federal government to ensure that sentencing systems provide appropriate punishment without over-reliance on incarceration."[27] The principle resolution noted that "lengthy periods of incarceration should be reserved for offenders who pose the greatest danger to the community and who commit the most serious offenses, and alternatives to incarceration should be available for offenders who pose minimal risk to the community and appear likely to benefit from rehabilitation efforts."[28] The first and most prominent recommendation in the Justice Kennedy Commission Report: repeal mandatory minimum sentences.

Justice Kennedy was not alone in his condemnation of mandatory sentences. The late Chief Justice William Rehnquist also questioned the need for mandatory sentencing, arguing that it "frustrate[s] the careful calibration of sentences":

These mandatory minimum sentences are perhaps a good example of the law of unintended consequences. There is a respectable body of opinion which believes that these mandatory minimums impose unduly harsh punishment for first-time offenders—particularly for "mules" who played only a minor role in a drug distribution scheme. Be that as it may, the mandatory minimums have also led to an inordinate increase in the federal prison population and will require huge expenditures to build new prison space. . . . Mandatory minimums . . . are frequently the result of floor amendments to demonstrate emphatically that legislators want to "get tough on crime." Just as frequently they do not involve any careful consideration of the effect they might have on the sentencing guidelines as a whole. Indeed, it seems to me that one of the best arguments against any more mandatory minimums, and perhaps against some of those that we already have, is that they frustrate the careful calibration of sentences, from one end of the spectrum to the other, which the sentencing guidelines were intended to accomplish.[29]

There have been successes in the fight against mandatory sentencing—some particularly active advocacy groups like Families Against Mandatory Minimums (FAMM) have commissioned reports to document the failures of mandatory sentencing and the successes in the fight for smart sentencing reform.[30] Facing budget shortfalls and prison crises of varying magnitudes, state legislatures have begun to rethink their mandatory sentencing policies. A number of states have scaled back or eliminated mandatory sentencing provisions. In 2001, legislatures in Indiana, Connecticut, and Louisiana passed legislation that removed or reduced mandatory penalties for drug offending. Although most of these "smart on crime" choices have been incremental, in 2003, Michigan repealed almost all of its mandatory sentences for drug offenses, replacing those sentences with structured sentencing under guidelines.[31] More recently, between 2009 and 2010, New York, Rhode Island, and South Carolina repealed most of their mandatory minimum drug sentences, and Massachusetts relaxed parole eligibility restrictions for drug offenders.[32]

It seems that state legislatures are beginning to recognize that the concerns that mandatory sentencing provisions were intended to address (disparity, abuse of discretion, etc.) can be achieved through other, less problematic sentencing initiatives. Structured sentencing, usually achieved through the enactment of guidelines, is now widely viewed as a preferred approach for dealing with issues of discretion, disparity, and proportionality.[33] In contrast to mandatory sentencing provisions, structured sentencing systems guide, but do not eliminate, judicial discretion.

Agenda Two: Reduce Length-of-Stay (LOS)

There are two kinds of strategies focused on length of stay: programs that release prisoners before their maximum length of stay and sentencing changes that reduce sentences across the board. In the discussion below, we repeatedly use the modifier "about" and "nearly" to describe these effects on prison populations, because we are using the "average" length of stay to estimate the changes. It turns out that in the case of prison populations, "average" lengths of stay are misleading. In fact, most prison populations are comprised of a sizeable number of relatively short stays and a smaller (but quite important) number of longer stays. This means there are two kinds of "averages" of interest, arithmetic averages and medians. For most purposes, medians provide better estimates of impacts, but they mean that calculating the systemic impact of changes is not straightforward.

In the discussion below, we act as though the calculations are arithmetic means, and describe the effects accordingly. But a more technically accurate measure for actual forecasts would be disaggregated sentence groups and median time served. That would require actual data about prison sentence distributions for a given prison system that is beyond the scope of this chapter.

There is one additional introductory point: the presence of large numbers of people serving ultra-long sentences makes calculating medians and means for time served problematic. We do not actually know these numbers until the people serving ultra-long sentences (who generally are never released) die.

Longer-stay prisoners also create a problem for length-of-stay reduction strategies when they are a main source of growth (as they are in most state prison populations). This point can be illustrated by reference to the most extreme long-termers: those who have received a sentence of life without parole. A single life-without-parole sentence for a 25-year-old (who will live to sixty-five) turns out to be a forty-year length of stay. That person represents the equivalent of a two-year time-served sentence every other year for two decades. Those two-year sentences can be altered at the margin without affecting very much the average population over that forty-year period. If one more life-without-parole sentence is added to the mix, it makes the adjustments in the shorter sentences all the less meaningful. Long sentences create a permanent prison population base that becomes increasingly impervious to changes in the short-termers.

Release Strategies

METHOD NO. 1: PAROLE

For states with indeterminate sentencing structures where parole boards make the release decisions, rates of parole release represent one of the most rapid levers that can be used to reduce length of stay (LOS). Each state represents a different statutory challenge in speeding up parole, but most states have been reluctant to release people at their first parole eligibility. A state that routinely denies parole at the initial hearing for nearly all cases and sets a new hearing a year later would reduce LOS for parole-eligible cases by at least a year, overall, if it eliminated this practice. This would result in an immediate and permanent sizeable reduction in the prison population.

This is the method that is being used by states when they focus on improved prisoner reentry, and it pays dividends, over time, when system-wide improvements take place. When improved parole practices include education and training of parole board members, a greater array of community-based options for their consideration on a case-by-case basis but uniformly available across the state, particularly in urban areas, and a concerted effort by the agency that supervises parole to improve transition planning before release and case management afterwards, parole approval rates will go up. When the rates go up, more prisoners are released. With improved transition plans and improved supervision techniques, more former prisoners will succeed with fewer returns for new crimes and fewer returns for technical violations.

While there are practical operational examples of this in many states, there has never been a concerted effort to determine which of the many aspects of improved prisoner reentry are more or less responsible for the improved outcomes.

Michigan's Prisoner Reentry Initiative (MPRI) can be used as an example. After spending years on improving the assessment tools that the parole board used to help make release decisions (use of the COMPAS for risk and need assessment, the VASOR for sex offenders,[34] and other instruments for risk assessment of the mentally ill and chronic co-occurring disordered prisoners) and implementing statewide options for community supervision and treatment, the MPRI increased the parole approval rate from 48 percent in 2002 to 62 percent in 2009, with over 70 percent of prisoners receiving a parole approval at their first parole hearing.[35] This resulted in the number of persons placed on parole increasing from about 10,700 in 2002 to over 13,500 in 2009—a 26 percent increase in the number of prisoner paroled—and, over the course of those seven years, a total increase of over 6,200 prisoners released using 2002 as the baseline. (In 2000 only 9,133 prisoners were released, so if that year was used as the baseline the changes would be even more dramatic.)

As previously stated, the parole rate and the parole population increased, the number of technical violations decreased, and the rate of parolees convicted of new crimes and sentenced to prison stayed about the same. The end result was that after working with over twenty-two thousand prisoners, the MPRI achieved a 33 percent improvement in parolee success in the community, as evidenced by fewer revocations back to prison. All told, nearly three thousand fewer former prisoners returned to prison from 2002 through 2009. An evaluation is being planned to determine to what extent different aspects of the MPRI were more or less responsible for this dramatic shift.[36]

METHOD NO. 2: SPECIAL EARLY RELEASE
Early release programs used as temporary measures to ease correctional population pressures cannot make any long-term reductions in prison

costs. Prison populations are produced by a set of decision dynamics external to the prison system. If a cohort is released early, but nothing else changes, then the pressures producing the prison population reconstitute it. That is, if the cohort is released an average of three months early, the population returns to what it would have been in about three months. These types of policies, however, are eschewed by politicians and are often controversial, if not devastating.

Across-the-board release policies do better—both operationally and politically. For example, a new good-time provision that adds a day a week of earned credit off the maximum term will result in systemic earlier releases. If everyone earned all that additional good time, and nothing else changed, the prison population would reach a new stability at about 85 percent of its earlier level. That does not mean the population will drop to a new level. If the population had been increasing at a rate of 4 percent a year, the effect of early release on the stock population will be replaced by growth in about the third year. If the average length of stay is about three years, and the underlying growth rate is 4 percent, the populations will be roughly stable for three years, then return to growth.

Because of this, several states have experimented with across-the-board LOS strategies to reduce prison populations. One mechanism is to increase the amount of "good-time" (or earned release time) a person can earn. This can be a promising (and low-profile) strategy. For example, an increase of good time of five days per months could reduce overall LOS quite dramatically; for example, a state with an average LOS of thirty months would drop up to five months off that average. Interestingly and quite notably, Michigan did not employ any "early release" strategies, not only because they weren't supported by the politicians who run state government but also because they weren't needed. Focusing on prisoners eligible for parole by implementing the various measures that have been mentioned, coupled with fewer new court commits and improved prison operations, were successful enough strategies to reduce the population by 12 percent in Michigan.

Sentencing Change Strategies

METHOD NO. 1: TARGETED SENTENCE REDUCTION

Using a policy approach to make across-the-board sentencing reductions can also result in a quite dramatic impact. One of the main engines of prison population growth has been the federal government's "truth in sentencing" program (enacted under President Clinton) that gave states financial incentives to meet a goal of 85 percent time served for "serious and violent" felons. By the time the incentives were revoked, states had already changed their sentencing laws to correspond to the federal expectation and the laws remain on the books. Several states moved to an 85 percent rule while a few went to 100 percent. These policies have, of course, a broad and long-term impact on increasing prison populations and are in some states largely responsible for population growth. There has never been a study that compares the incentives (cash in) to the costs (cash out) while estimating the impact on crime. Given what we know about such things, it is probably the case that this federal policy has cost millions if not billions without any appreciable impact on crime. And given the politics of imprisonment, state legislatures have been extremely reluctant to change these laws back.

Evidence from the states suggests that the impact of changes to truth-in-sentencing laws can be vast. By redefining what constitutes the label "serious and violent," states can realize substantial potential reductions in LOS for large numbers of people. In Mississippi, for example, a change in release eligibility for a large number of nonviolent offenders from 85 percent of the maximum term to about 25 percent resulted in substantial cost savings to the state (with no subsequent increase in recidivism among parolees released much earlier under the new law). The evidence from Mississippi suggests that even incremental changes in truth-in-sentencing laws could have substantial impacts on the size of prison populations.

METHOD NO. 2: OFFENSE-SPECIFIC STATUTORY CHANGES

Changes in sentencing have much potential to alter the underlying prison population. For a prison population that has an average LOS of thirty months, an across-the-board reduction in prison LOS of 10 percent (three months) would reduce the prison population by 10 percent in about thirty months, similarly to the "good time" example above.

But legislatures almost never alter sentencing in this way. (They alter other government services in an across-the-board manner, such as school and pensions, but not prisons.) Instead, specific offense groups are targeted. The impact of these changes is proportional to the size of the offense group in the prison population. Roughly speaking, if the sentence reduction above is applied to, say, people serving time for drug possession, and they constitute 10 percent of the prison population but serve twenty months, then the impact will be an average of about .2 months across the population. In the example cited above, with average length of stay of thirty months for the prison system, the average will drop to 29.8 months, a drop that will be almost unnoticeable in the face of the existing prison population hydraulics.

METHOD NO. 3: RECIDIVISM STATUTES

One significant source of much recent prison growth has been the predominance of recidivism statutes. Here, there is much variation from state to state, but the general scenario is that a person who is convicted of a second serious felony within a particular window of time will have an automatic sentence enhancement of a particular level.

The effect of eliminating these enhancements is straightforward: people's sentences return to the base for the original crime. Calculating the impact of this change on prison populations is a bit more complex, because it cannot be done without knowledge of the mix of people serving time under recidivism statutes. To illustrate, let us assume a simple prison entry cohort of one thousand people. Twenty (2 percent) are serving life without parole and will stay in the prison until they die (an average of forty years). One hundred and ninety (19 percent) are serving short sentences, with a length of stay of one year. Six hundred (60 percent) are serving "normal" sentences with an average length of stay of two years. And two hundred (20 percent) are serving "recidivist" sentences that are doubled, an average of four years. This entry cohort will serve 2,980 years (a hefty if realistic thirty months per person). If the recidivist statute is eliminated, the group will instead serve 2,580 years (a bit over two years per person, a significant reduction of 14 percent). Most people would think of this as a meaningful reduction in the prison population.

Agenda Three: Reduce Recidivism

Sentencing reform is a heavy lift. As an alternative, many policymakers have tried to mount new efforts to reduce recidivism, especially technical revocation. Approaches that promise to reduce recidivism rates are politically quite attractive, because they reduce risk rather than increase it. They also avoid the politically threatening problem of "early" prison releases, which can come back to haunt a politician who promotes them. In a very real way, everyone benefits when recidivism rates drop.

One of the most prominent current models is project HOPE, in Hawaii.[37] The HOPE model imposes routine drug testing carried out through randomly scheduled office visits as a condition of probation. It then enforces those conditions using short-term jail stays when people either fail to make their appointments or turn in dirty urine samples. Sanctions are imposed immediately—jail terms start typically the same day as the dirty urine or missed office visit. If failures continue, jail stays gradually lengthen until probation is finally revoked and the person is sent to prison. Follow-up studies using random assignment to HOPE or regular probation show that HOPE clients spend 50 percent less time in jail and fail about one-third less, as well. The results of the HOPE model have led Kleiman to claim that it is possible to have both "less crime and less punishment."[38]

The Council of State Governments (CSG) Justice Center has initiated a series of projects that target recidivism rates, especially technical failure. Their work began in Connecticut, where they focused a legislative agenda on probation and parole. In the end, their work was estimated to save $30 million in imprisonment costs when "probation violations dropped from 400 in July 2003 to 200 in September 2005 [and t]he decrease in the prison population over a two-year period was steeper than that seen in almost any other state while the crime rate continued to drop. Almost $13 million of the nearly $30 million saved was reinvested in community-based pilot projects."[39]

Following its pilot effort in Connecticut, which started in 2005, additional states demonstrated interest in working on justice reinvestment with the CSG Justice Center. With funding support from the U.S. Department of Justice, the Pew Center on the States, the Open Society Institute, other private foundations, and states themselves, the CSG Justice Center began working intensively in Kansas and Texas. Results in these states mirrored those in Connecticut. By 2010, the CSG Justice Center had worked in over ten states, and it currently has active projects in fifteen states.[40] Employing a similar strategy, the Urban Institute has been working with local governments on jail-oriented justice reinvestment projects.[41]

A focus on reducing failure rates of people poses two problems. First, there is a ceiling on how much the incarceration rate can be affected by reductions in recidivism. Let's say, for example, that in a given jurisdiction, 40 percent of all people released from prison are back within their first year, and they serve an average of a year before they are again released. Let us also say that a justice reinvestment program reduces rates of return to prison by a sizeable rate, again say 40 percent. This means that the overall impact of the strategy will affect 16 percent of all releases. In a high-incarceration neighborhood that receives one hundred people returning from prison in a year, twenty-four will go back instead of forty. If a year of incarceration costs an average of $40,000, the sixteen people who do not go to prison will "save" $640,000. These are not real savings, of course, because diverting sixteen people from prison does not enable the corrections system to close a prison, so its budget remains essentially unaffected. Working under these assumptions, the program will have to affect one thousand people in reentry in order to generate "savings" of 160 prison years—a much more considerable figure of $6.4 million.

But these figures are also based on very friendly assumptions. If the justice reinvestment program is aimed at reducing technical revocation rates, as many are, and the technical return-to-prison rate is 20 percent, the effect is halved. If the impact of the program on recidivism rates is a much more reasonable 20 percent reduction, the effect is halved again. If the average stay in prison for a technical revocation is not a year, but is six months, the effect is halved again. Under the alternative assumptions—20 percent return rate, 20 percent reduction in return rate, and six-month stay—to achieve a reduction of 160 prison years will require a program that reaches four thousand people in reentry. If the program costs $1,600 per person for the services it provides, it eats up all the "savings." Under these numbers, it would be a more or less break-even venture.

Despite these limitations, efforts to control prison populations by reducing revocations have proven quite popular, and the Council of State Governments touts several success stories using this method. Of course, one of the key advantages of the CSG approach is that it begins by gathering data on rates of recidivism and program participation, and from these data estimates are made of savings to be generated by various strategies. The data typically lead to a potpourri of recommendations, only some of which involve working to reduce failure rates. Taken together, these strategies have produced sizeable estimates of total savings.[42]

We would be remiss if we did not mention a final area of reforms that would substantially reduce recidivism rates: eliminating collateral consequences of conviction and incarceration. As we have described in chapter 4, those people convicted of felony offenses, especially those returning from prison, face a stunning array of civil and legal impediments to return to full citizenship.[43] Very few of these restrictions have substantive connection to legitimate correctional objectives beyond being punitive. In ratcheting up the punitive pressure, many of these restrictions are counterproductive to public safety and others are simply irrelevant. To the extent that a given collateral consequence of a felony conviction has no demonstrable relationship to public safety, it should be eliminated.

Our list of three priorities is offered in order of expected effect size. Eliminating mandatory penalties will reduce the number of people who go to prison, offering an immediate reduction in imprisonment; reducing length of stay will result in an additional, gradual reduction in prison numbers; and in the long term, reduced rates of recidivism will in turn affect the prison cycling rates. There is, today, an increasingly popular strategy for putting those policies into place and taking advantage of the savings they produce. It is known as justice reinvestment. We conclude with a discussion of this as a new overarching prison population control strategy.

Justice Reinvestment: Focusing on Incentives

Justice reinvestment is an alternative to broad-based sentencing reform and the recent emphasis on revocation. "Justice reinvestment" is a relatively new term; Susan Tucker and Eric Cadora coined it in a policy paper published by the Open Society Institute, in which they said,

> The goal of justice reinvestment is to redirect some portion of the $54 billion America now spends on prisons to rebuilding the human resources and physical infrastructure—the schools, healthcare facilities, parks, and public spaces—of neighborhoods devastated by high levels of incarceration.[44]

Despite the fact that this original publication had but a small distribution, the idea of justice reinvestment has caught on quickly, very much by word of mouth, gaining popularity at a rapid pace. By far, the most proximate catalyst for the emergence of justice reinvestment has been the fiscal crisis. Over the past decade, a combination of political shifts, accumulating empirical evidence, and fiscal pressures has come together to make downsizing prisons a feasible idea, politically and tactically. But the current fiscal crisis gives impetus to the desire to use prison funds elsewhere.[45]

Justice reinvestment, then, is an idea that resonates with several contemporary realities. It promises to reduce the size of the prison population, thereby reducing the costs of incarceration. The savings are to be diverted to support communities that contribute the most people to the prison system, in order to interrupt the prison-community cycle. The theoretical foundation for justice reinvestment includes the broad literature of community development.[46] The practical foundation is a wide range of experiences, documented by various advocates and policy groups.[47]

While there is considerable momentum for justice reinvestment, there can be no doubt that it is an idea in its infancy. Only a handful of projects have been mounted, and no strong empirical base yet exists about the strategy. But even so, given the activity to date, justice reinvestment is an idea to reckon with.

Reinvesting in Government

A central problem with current justice reinvestment strategies is that they have often resulted in redirecting government funds from corrections to other government-based social services.[48] The rationale is that through these services, failure rates are reduced and costs averted. There is nothing wrong with this, but the original rationale for justice reinvestment, quoted above, was to use prison savings for "rebuilding the human resources and physical infrastructure—the schools, health-care facilities, parks, and public spaces—of neighborhoods devastated by high levels of incarceration." This may imply a role for government services, but it is certainly not a service-delivery agenda. It calls instead for a community-development agenda.

There are good reasons why much of the justice reinvestment activity to date has focused on upgrading services for people who have been convicted of crimes. Drug and alcohol addiction are dominant themes in the lives of many who end up in prison or jail, and few of them can remain substance-free without some form of treatment. Many are homeless. Likewise, poor educational backgrounds and limited job readiness are endemic in this group. Obtaining housing, finding good work, and advancing one's education are important potential pathways out of the prison cycle.[49]

It is also true that a transfer of funds from one government sector to another is far less complicated than transfer to the private sector. Services for people who are under correctional supervision, either in prison or in the community, fall woefully short of need—it has been estimated that between 10 and 15 percent of those who go through the system have their most pressing needs met by current programs.[50] Expanding those services is surely a high priority.

Yet there is something left wanting about the movement of correctional funds to social service budgets. The people who work for social services are not necessarily the citizens who live in high-incarceration communities. While the services they provide may end up improving the social adjustment prospects for those who live in high-incarceration communities, the salaries spent employing those service providers end up being spent outside those troubled places.

The promise of justice reinvestment is at its most profound when it contains the core idea that money now spent incarcerating people will instead be used to develop the social stability of the very communities from which those people came. This is a very tall order. In their original essay, coining the phrase, Tucker and Cadora envisioned a kind of "urban justice corps," in which young people who otherwise would be behind bars are instead working to rebuild their communities. As the authors put it,

Local government would develop a diversified investment strategy with a portfolio of risk reducing initiatives. The idea of a civic justice corps is to mobilize people returning home from prison as agents of community restoration. They would join with other community residents to rehabilitate housing and schools, redesign and rebuild parks and playgrounds, and redevelop and rebuild the physical infrastructure and social fabric of their own neighborhoods. But the civic justice corps is only one possible investment in a public safety portfolio. Other investments might include a locally run community loan pool to make micro-loans to create jobs or family development loans for education, debt consolidation, or home ownership and rehabilitation, transportation micro-enterprises for residents commuting outside the neighborhood, a one-stop shop for job counseling and placement services, or geographically targeted hiring incentives for employers.[51]

This is a model of a different kind of justice reinvestment, one that has as its direct target the infrastructure of troubled communities. It organizes private and parochial forms of social control, not public control.[52] Most of all, it places heavy reliance on the private and semiprivate sectors for their involvement in community life.

The Problem of Incentives

As a result of growing public scrutiny and declining public revenues, criminal justice is under increasing pressure to become more efficient. This pressure emanates from various sources—nonjustice service providers who see their budgets diminishing as criminal justice agencies eat up a growing part of a diminishing pie, citizen groups who are dissatisfied with recurring problems in correctional services, and political leaders whose hands are increasingly tied by growing justice demand. A consequence of this situation is that justice officials and community leaders alike seek greater efficiency from criminal justice policy.

The inherent problem for criminal justice leadership is that the search for greater efficiency implies a capacity for risk taking that has structural limitations for criminal justice and the community alike. The fact is that criminal justice incentives do not promote efficient decisions. Here are some examples:

- Judges have no financial incentive to keep convicted felons locally; they have political (and in some cases, financial) incentives to transfer the costs of convicted felons to the state level.
- High-incarceration communities have little financial or developmental incentive to maintain convicted felons locally (absorbing the costs they impose). There is an incentive to have felons removed for brief periods and transferred to the cost centers of prison, operated elsewhere in the state and paid for by other communities' tax dollars.

- Politicians have very limited political incentive to support alternatives to prison. In economically troubled areas, there is an incentive to build new facilities and send felons to them to be supervised so that costs will be transferred to income in those areas. There is a fiscal incentive to hold down the costs of prison, but politicians who support policies that do this seldom represent constituencies that directly benefit from the reduction in prison costs.

There are also ways in which the incentive structure actually inhibits innovation and sensible risk taking, by imposing costs on risk takers without allowing them to benefit from the savings of their decisions, while at the same time failing to discipline the risk averse by imposing costs for inefficiency:

- Judges who retain convicted felons in the community because they predict they will do well there receive no fiscal or programmatic benefits from taking this risk, even though they are well aware of the way they will experience the costs—in the form of public and system (prosecutorial) disapproval—should their prediction turn out to be wrong.
- Judges who send convicted felons to the state prison system, at a cost to taxpayers ten times higher than that of a local alternative program, feel no fiscal consequences for this decision, regardless of how the decision turns out in the long run.
- Prosecutors who are elected on the basis of their "toughness" on crime face potentially powerful political costs should they support a reduced reliance on imprisonment.
- Prosecutors who send a large number of people to prison face no direct budgetary consequences for these costs; they are borne by others.
- Citizen groups who create strong local programs to serve as sentencing alternatives save money for taxpayers who live elsewhere, but absorb all the public-safety and program-effectiveness risks of "doing the right thing" with fellow citizens of the neighborhood.
- Citizen groups who oppose strong local alternatives for people who have been convicted of crimes transfer both the risks and the costs of those people to the other places where they go—prisons and neighborhoods.

- Probation and parole officers who are quick to revoke a parolee on the basis of the slightest misstep save themselves from the risk of greater failure, while imposing the costs of return to prison on other taxpayers and systems.
- Probation and parole officers who treat return to prison as a last resort do not see any of the savings they generate in taxpayer costs, but they embrace considerable professional risk in doing so.

More examples could be given, but these obvious ones highlight the key problem. The incentive structure in the criminal justice system does not link risk taking and rewards; nor does it link risk-transfer decisions to the costs of these decisions. The incentive structure in criminal justice is inherently conservative, stifling innovation by punishing efficient decisions when they are risky while rewarding expensive decisions in which decision makers pass their costs on to others. It would be inconceivable for the private sector to operate under such a stifling set of disincentives for efficiency and innovation, yet we sustain this structure in criminal justice.

There are, of course, good reasons to be conservative in criminal justice risk taking. Especially, we want to avoid decisions that lead to new crimes, because the costs of these crimes are borne by their victims. Yet it is to our detriment that we perpetuate a system in which costs and benefits are delinked. Among other things, a range of new practices with minimal implications for public safety may exist that never are tried out, simply because the incentive structure makes it difficult.

Reorienting Incentives

Attempts to create new systems of financial incentives for using non-prison penalties have a bit of a history in criminal justice. The most widely known strategy was the California Probation Subsidy Program, which reimbursed California counties for using probation instead of prison, and had the express purposes of reducing incarceration rates and saving money. The probation subsidy was evaluated by Edwin Lemert and Forrest Dill.[53] The results were troubling. They found that many of the people retained on probation served jail sentences locally instead of going to state prison, and when the cost of the subsidy was factored in, nether savings nor reduced incarceration were realized.

Despite these disappointing results, state policymakers have continued to seek to create fiscal incentives for local correctional officials to keep people convicted of crimes in local correctional systems, instead of sending them to state prison. Three-quarters of the states have some sort of fiscal arrangement to promote this form of community-based corrections.[54]

While there have been numerous studies of various individual programs working under community corrections incentives systems, there have been scant few studies of the underlying impact of incentives-based correctional strategies. Policymakers widely believe them to be effective at reducing correctional costs and increasing correctional effectiveness, but this confidence is based on a weak empirical foundation. While there is little doubt that "evidence-based" strategies, provided in community settings, have enormous promise, whether this has translated into a potpourri of effective local programs in practice is an open question.

Equally important, subsidy-oriented incentive systems have tended to grow local social service initiatives, such as treatment beds, but they generally do not relate to the private sector economy nor the community infrastructure. For the most part, the evidence-based movement in corrections has engaged the government sector in the design and execution of programs. It has left largely untapped the private sector as a catalyst for controlling prison costs.

Incentives and the Private Sector

What would happen if the criminal justice incentive structure more closely linked the benefits of innovation to the costs for private-sector innovators? What if those who innovated in efficient ways that reduced the costs taxpayers incur for criminal justice reaped some of the benefits of those efficiencies? What if we sought to seed local risk taking and innovation with a share of the return, when those innovations reduce costs for all?

What is needed is a new set of financial incentives that would create reasons for communities to welcome felons to be kept locally, reinforce (and support) local service capacities, and provide a mechanism for community infrastructure development.

There are two main impediments to changing the incentive structure along the lines described above. When exposed to the problem of the incentives-risks misfit in criminal justice, people inevitably ask, "How would a different approach work, and where is it being tried?" This common response highlights the two main problems that must be confronted. First, while there are several examples of initiatives that have tried to address the problem of incentives, there is no obvious and proven system for doing so; changing the incentives structure requires that new ideas be developed that create arrangements particular to the jurisdiction in question. Second (and following the first point) people lack experience in how such an alternative system of arrangements would work.

This suggests that there is an overriding need for new models of risk-incentive fit that are "on-the-ground" models, offering program designs and policy structures that have obvious fit to real circumstances of communities and crime. Such models will not be created as abstract ideas by outsiders, but rather will be developed and tailored by the very same people who would be called upon to operate them. The core idea is that local solutions have to be built by local actors. For this to happen, there is a need for people to experience these alternatives in a way that inspires confidence that they could be used successfully in their own criminal justice contexts. Such models, to be viable, would operate according to seven principles:

- *Principle 1:* No benefits follow when the decision leads to more crime. The paramount concern that drives prison-dependent polices is to avoid crime. Alternative funding mechanisms, to be viable, must not result in more crime, and so the rewards for risk taking must be structured in such a way that they disappear when they lead to more crime.
- *Principle 2:* The crime victim gets a voice. A second driver for prison reliance is concern about the victim. This concern has to be addressed, either in

direct victim consultation or in symbolic consultation through participation of victims groups in an advisory capacity.

- *Principle 3:* New strategies must be truly cost efficient, and the amount of money transferred to the risk taker must be related to the amount of money truly "saved." Social control nets must not be widened. Money transferred from one source to another must reflect actual savings by that source of the transfer.[55]

- *Principle 4:* Nothing happens without both system and community oversight. Victims are not the only important constituent group. Both the justice system and the community must have confidence that the new strategies being adopted are wise and effective. This suggests a kind of oversight that is both consultative and evaluative.

- *Principle 5:* The taxpayers get a cut of the action. Some of the money saved by new structures must go back into the general coffers. For the general public, this cannot be a zero-sum game, and public risks must be compensated by public benefits.

- *Principle 6:* A dollar must recycle itself in target communities. One of the central problems about community investments is that dollars to innovate in communities do not stay there very long. People who receive pay for being involved in the community-change efforts spend their money outside of the community, and so the total local wealth created by the investment is small. In contrast, money that changes hands several times within that community represents magnified wealth for that community.

- *Principle 7:* Program providers must be accountable for their results. New strategies must be evaluated, and strategic justice reinvestment work must be evidence-based. Inherent within the idea of public safety is a broad expectation that newly funded programs meet accepted criteria for the work they do, so that new programs are housed in proven strategies and are themselves subject to evaluation.

This outline of a "justice reinvestment" mode is an ideal type. As far as we are aware, nowhere is what we have described here being tried in its entirety. But the ideas here are beginning to form the foundation for a new conversation about correctional priorities, and they are also becoming a kind of familiar framework for innovation.

That is not to say that justice reinvestment efforts have been moving forward without resistance or controversy. Recently, a group of proponents of justice reinvestment as an ideal reviewed the current efforts underway in the justice reinvestment arena, and wrote quite critically about the prospects of these efforts for achieving meaningful reductions in prison populations.[56] It is not surprising that these early efforts to structure these major redirections in penal strategy will struggle to get it right. If our viewpoint is correct, and we are in the early days of a new way of looking at the penal system (one not wholly captive to the Punishment Imperative) then it is certainly to be expected that this new thinking will come in fits and starts. Justice reinvestment itself may come and go as an idea, but the insights contained within the strategy will serve to guide the next generation of creative penal thinking.

Concluding Thoughts

We recognize that our prediction that the Punishment Imperative is over and the end of the era of mass incarceration is near will be received with some disbelief. We are particularly cognizant of how quickly good faith efforts to address the problem of mass incarceration through policies intended to divert offenders from prison to communities can be derailed. This is certainly a valid critique of justice reinvestment. Too, there are obvious perils to such approaches, and we have already seen problems associated with negative publicity in at least four states.[57] We recognize that a key to sustaining meaningful reductions in prison populations over time will be controlling crime. In recent years, at least nineteen states have managed to reduce both prison populations and crime,[58] but any increases in crime that temporally follow significant reductions in the use of incarceration will inevitably provoke anxieties about the wisdom of these new crime and sentencing policies.[59] Correctional researchers should now be designing the research that can parse some of the differential effects of prison reduction schemes across places so that we can adequately respond when policymakers and practitioners ask how best to handle the release or diversion of offenders from prison.

We therefore conclude with these final thoughts. For close to forty years now, policymakers have passed a constant barrage of policies that, unless repealed, virtually ensure further prison population growth. The myriad problems arising from these policies were not an accident; there should be no surprises here. In the early, heady days of the incarceration boom, there were plenty of social scientists who predicted that increased incarceration was a necessary condition for falling crime.[60] There are not very many people left in this camp. Michael Tonry has argued persuasively that every social scientist should have known of the racially and economically disproportionate effects that would follow from policies of mass incarceration, and there was a solid body of social science evidence to suggest that the crime-control results of mass incarceration would be minimal.[61] Now we also know that the current level of incarceration is unsustainable, if we do not want to exacerbate the undesirable consequences of mass incarceration.

In saying this, we do not mean to ignore the social scientists and intellectuals who, along the way, argued for the merits of the Punishment Imperative. There were many of these, some of whom based their work on empirical studies and others of whom made strong logical claims.[62] A main feature of the Punishment Imperative, as we have argued, was that it claimed a certain scientific and intellectual foundation. It turns out that the empirical claims were largely wrong, and the intellectual case was flawed, not by what it said but by what it left out.

There are, going forward, two potential story lines. One is "more of the same." In 2007, James Austin and his colleagues projected that under steady state policies, the size of the prison population would continue to grow, adding more than 192,000 more prisoners by the year 2011.[63] Significantly, they did not have to make an assumption about crime in order to see that increase—if crime had gone up, their estimate might have turned out to be low. If the recent (relatively slight) drops in prison populations are just an anomaly[64] and prison populations resume their decades-long pattern of increase, then shocking statistics, such as the 32 percent chance that a black male born in 2001 would go to prison during his lifetime, will be nostalgia for future generations.[65] This is an almost unconscionable story line, but there are no reasons, absent fairly substantial policy action, to think it won't happen.

The second story line is even more remarkable, yet is the one we think we now see emerging. In this story line, a weary public becomes alarmed by mass incarceration, and a political will develops to change its course. In this scenario, we begin to learn the lessons of the grand, forty-year penal experiment and change directions. Even if we reverse course and move away from the Punishment Imperative, that grand social experiment close to four decades in the making has profoundly affected social relations. Undoing the damage that has been done would take more than the repeal of a few of the more draconian policy initiatives; it would require—we say with full awareness of the irony—a new grand social experiment in our penal system.

In this book, we have argued that there is increasing energy for a new story about punishment in America. The old regime of the past, the Punishment Imperative, has, we think, run its course. It will never be completely gone, of course. Fundamental beliefs in the value of punishment, and the needs for ever more of it, have always been with us and will continue to be. It is just, we think, that this view will no longer be dominant in the American scene. The last forty years have run their course, and a new agenda is about to arise.

NOTES

NOTES TO CHAPTER 1

1. Jim Webb, "Why We Must Fix Our Prisons," *Nation* (updated March 29), http://www.parade.com/news/2009/03/why-we-must-fix-our-prisons.html, accessed November 29, 2009.

2. Alfred Blumstein and Jacqueline Cohen, "A Theory of the Stability of Punishment," *Journal of Criminal Law, Criminology, and Police Science*, 63 (1973), 198–207, Alfred Blumstein, Jacqueline Cohen, and Daniel Nagin, "The Dynamics of a Homeostatic Punishment Process," *Journal of Criminal Law and Criminology*, 67 (1977), 317–34, Alfred Blumstein and S. Moitra, "An Analysis of the Time-Series of the Imprisonment Rate in the States of the United States: A Further Test of the Stability of Punishment Hypothesis," *Journal of Criminal Law and Criminology*, 70 (1979), 376–90.

3. We originally made an early version of this argument in Natasha A. Frost and Todd R. Clear, "Understanding Mass Incarceration as a Grand Social Experiment," *Studies in Law, Politics, and Society*, 47 (2009), 159–91.

4. Pew Center on the States, "State Population Declines for the First Time in 38 Years" (Washington, DC: Pew Charitable Trusts, 2010).

5. David Garland, "The Peculiar Forms of American Capital Punishment," *Social Research: An International Quarterly of the Social Sciences*, 74/2 (2007), 435–64, David Garland, *Peculiar Institution: America's Death Penalty in an Age of Abolition* (Cambridge, MA: Harvard University Press, 2010), Michael Tonry, "Looking Back to See the Future of Punishment in America," *Social Research: An International Quarterly of the Social Sciences*, 74/2 (2007), 353–78, Michael Tonry, "Explanations of American Punishment Policies," *Punishment & Society*, 11/3 (2009), 377–94, James Q. Whitman, *Harsh Justice: Criminal Punishment and the Widening Divide between America and Europe* (New York: Oxford University Press, 2003), viii, 311 , [10] of plates, James Q. Whitman, "What Happened to Tocqueville's America?" *Social Research: An International Quarterly of the Social Sciences*, 74/2 (2007), 251–68.

6. Three academic journals, *Daedalus* in 2010 and *Criminology & Public Policy* and *The Prison Journal* in 2011, have devoted entire issues to the problem of mass

incarceration, and each included several articles written by prominent scholars offering strategies for reducing prison populations and moving away from our dependence on incarceration. See, for example, Alfred Blumstein, "Approaches to Reducing Both Imprisonment and Crime," *Criminology & Public Policy*, 10/1 (2011), 93–102, Alfred Blumstein, "Bringing Down the U.S. Prison Population," *Prison Journal*, 91/3 suppl. (September 1, 2011), 12S–26S, Todd R. Clear and Dennis Schrantz, "Strategies for Reducing Prison Populations," *Prison Journal*, 91/3 suppl. (September 1, 2011), 138S–59S, Don Stemen, "Reconsidering Incarceration: New Directions for Reducing Crime" (New York: VERA Institute of Justice, 2007), Marie Gottschalk, "Cell Blocks and Red Ink: Mass Incarceration, the Great Recession, and Penal Reform," *Daedalus*, 139/3 (2010), 62–73.

7. Terry Carter, "Prison Break: Budget Crises Drive Reform, but Private Jails Press On," *ABA Journal*, October (2012), 44–51, Steven Gray, "Why Mississippi Is Reversing Its Prison Policy," *Time*, June 10, 2011.

8. Compare, for example, the Second Chance Act of 2008 with the Violent Crime Control and Law Enforcement Act of 1994.

9. Blumstein, "Approaches to Reducing Both Imprisonment and Crime," Clear and Schrantz, "Strategies for Reducing Prison Populations," Steven N. Durlauf and Daniel S. Nagin, "Imprisonment and Crime: Can Both Be Reduced?" *Criminology & Public Policy*, 10/1 (2011), 13–54, Mark A. R. Kleiman, *When Brute Force Fails: How to Have Less Crime and Less Punishment* (Princeton, NJ: Princeton University Press, 2009), Lawrence W. Sherman and Heather Strang, "Restorative Justice: The Evidence" (London: Smith Institute, 2007).

10. Gray, "Why Mississippi Is Reversing Its Prison Policy."

11. Nicole D. Porter, "On the Chopping Block: State Prison Closings" (Washington, DC: Sentencing Project, 2011).

12. Todd R. Clear and James Austin, "Reducing Mass Incarceration: Implications of the Iron Law of Prison Populations," *Harvard Law and Policy Review*, 3 (2009), 307–24. See also Natasha A. Frost and Todd R. Clear, "New Directions in Correctional Research," *Justice Quarterly*, 29/5 (2012), 619–49.

13. Porter, "On the Chopping Block: State Prison Closings."

14. Thomas Caplan, "Cuomo Administration Is Closing 7 Prisons: 2 Are in the City," *New York Times*, July 1, 2011.

15. Charlie Savage, "Trend to Lighten Sentences Catches on in Conservative States," *New York Times*, August 13, 2011.

16. Gray, "Why Mississippi Is Reversing Its Prison Policy," Pew Center on the States, "2012 Georgia Public Safety Reform: Legislation to Reduce Recidivism and Cut Corrections Costs" (Washington, DC: Pew Charitable Trusts, 2012).

17. Marie Gottschalk, "Dollars, Sense, and Penal Reform: Social Movements and the Future of the Carceral State," *Social Research: An International Quarterly of the Social Sciences*, 74/2 (2007), 669–94, Marie Gottschalk, "Money and Mass Incarceration: The Bad, the Mad, and Penal Reform," *Criminology & Public Policy*, 8/1

(2009), 97–109, Marie Gottschalk, "Cell Blocks and Red Ink: Mass Incarceration, the Great Recession, and Penal Reform," *Daedalus*, 139/3 (2010), 62–73, Michael Jacobson, *Downsizing Prisons: How to Reduce Crime and End Mass Incarceration* (New York: New York University Press, 2005), Steven Raphael and Michael A. Stoll (eds.), *Do Prisons Make Us Safer? The Benefits and Costs of the Prison Boom* (Washington, DC: Russell Sage Foundation, 2009).

18. Pew Center on the States, "2012 Georgia Public Safety Reform: Legislation to Reduce Recidivism and Cut Corrections Costs."

19. Special Council on Criminal Justice Reform for Georgians, "Report of the Special Council on Criminal Justice Reform for Georgians" (Atlanta: Georgia General Assembly, 2011).

20. Ibid., 1. See also Special Council on Criminal Justice Reform for Georgians, "Report of the Special Council on Criminal Justice Reform for Georgians" (Atlanta: Georgia General Assembly, 2011).

21. Malcolm C. Young, "Getting Prison Numbers Down—for Good," http://www.thecrimereport.org/news/inside-criminal-justice/2012-01-getting-prison-numbers-downfor-good, accessed January 6, 2012.

22. Available at http://www.justicecenter.csg.org, accessed December 29, 2011. Senator Jim Webb (of Virginia) continues to introduce the National Criminal Justice Commission Act, which, if passed, would establish a commission to perform a comprehensive review of the criminal justice system. Although the bill passed in the House of Representatives in 2010, it has repeatedly stalled in the U.S. Senate. See Senator Webb's website for the current status of the bill: http://www.webb.senate.gov/issuesandlegislation/criminaljusticeandlawenforcement/Criminal_Justice_Banner.cfm, accessed October 4, 2012.

23. Right on Crime, Statement of Principles (2010), Austin: Texas Public Policy Foundation. Available online: www.rightoncrime.com, accessed December 29, 2011.

24. Ibid.

25. Kleiman, *When Brute Force Fails: How to Have Less Crime and Less Punishment*. See also Mark A. R. Kleiman, "Toward Fewer Prisoners and Less Crime," *Daedalus*, 139/3 (2010), 115–23.

26. Michael Jacobson argued several years ago—prior to the most recent recession—that we would almost certainly see a fiscally driven downsizing of prisons in the coming years. Jacobson, *Downsizing Prisons: How to Reduce Crime and End Mass Incarceration*.

27. Franklin E. Zimring, *The Great American Crime Decline* (Studies in Crime and Public Policy) (New York: Oxford University Press, 2007), xiv, 258.

28. Richard A. Oppel, "Steady Decline in Major Crime Baffles Experts," *New York Times*, May 24, 2011, A17.

29. Jason Kandel, "LA Continues 9-Year Crime Drop," http://www.nbclosangeles.com/news/local/LA-Crime-Drops-Again-136756023.html, accessed January 8, 2012.

30. Tamara Audi and Gary Fields, "L.A. Is Latest City to See Crime Drop," *Wall Street Journal,* January 8, 2010, A9.

31. In the most recent Gallup poll, conducted in March of 2011, crime was eighth on the list of problems Americans were concerned about, falling behind the economy (ranked number 1), federal spending and the deficit (2), health care (3), unemployment (4), social security (5), size of federal government (6), and availability of energy (7). For more detail, see Lydia Saad, "Americans' Worries about Economy, Budget Top Other Issues: Worry about Energy Up since 2010, Flat for Other Issues," http://www.gallup.com/poll/146708/Americans-Worries-Economy-Budget-Top-Issues.aspx, accessed December 30, 2011.

32. It is important to note that not all of these initiatives have met with sweeping success. In some states, the reforms have been met with quite vociferous public protest and policymakers have, perhaps quite predictably, yielded to political pressure and pulled back on reforms. Young, "Getting Prison Numbers Down—for Good."

33. Massachusetts offers the perfect recent example of this. In December 2010, a Woburn police officer, John Maguire, was shot and killed during a robbery by Domenic Cinelli. Cinelli was a parolee who had been sentenced to life but released two years earlier despite his violent criminal history. Perhaps not surprisingly there was immediate and substantial public outcry over Cinelli's early release. Responding in part to public pressure, Governor Deval Patrick launched a formal inquiry and within weeks of Officer Maguire's tragic death, the chairman of the Parole Board, the other Parole Board members who deliberated on the Cinelli case, and the former executive director of the Parole Board, who had since moved on to a new position within the Department of Corrections, had all resigned. There was immediate talk of completely abolishing discretionary parole release in Massachusetts, and although the state parole agency ultimately survived the fallout, there has been a substantial dropoff in the parole release rate in the years since. Moreover, the fallout did not end with the publication of the report. Ongoing concern about violent recidivists in the wake of the Cinelli shooting has led to the recent passage of a three-strikes law in Massachusetts. See the Commonwealth of Massachusetts Executive Office of Public Safety and Security, "Official Review of the Cinelli Case for the Office of the Governor" (Boston: Executive Office of Public Safety and Security, January 12, 2011).

34. Brian Bennett, "Fact Check: Romney Says It's Illegal to Have Automatic Weapons," *Los Angeles Times,* October 16, 2012.

35. In the most recent Gallup polls (June–Sept. 2012), only 0.5–1 percent of Americans identified crime and violence as the "most important problem facing this country today." Gallup Inc., "Most Important Problem," http://www.gallup.com/poll/1675/most-important-problem.aspx, accessed November 28, 2012.

36. Jonathan Simon, *Governing through Crime: How the War on Crime Transformed American Democracy and Created a Culture of Fear* (Studies in Crime and Public Policy) (New York: Oxford University Press, 2007), viii, 330.

37. Franklin E. Zimring, *The Great American Crime Decline* (New York: Oxford University Press, 2007), xiv, 258.

38. Michelle Alexander, *The New Jim Crow: Mass Incarceration in the Age of Colorblindness* (New York: New Press, 2010).

39. Natasha A. Frost, "Reentry as a Process Rather Than a Moment," in Karim Ismaili (ed.), *U.S. Criminal Justice Policy: A Contemporary Reader* (Sudbury, MA: Jones and Bartlett Learning, 2011), 159–82.

40. Alfred Blumstein and Kiminori Nakamura, "Redemption in the Presence of Widespread Criminal Background Checks," *Criminology,* 47/2 (2009), 327–60, Shadd Maruna and Anna King, "Once a Criminal, Always a Criminal? 'Redeemability' and the Psychology of Punitive Public Attitudes," *European Journal of Criminal Policy and Research,* 15/7–24 (2009), Shadd Maruna, "Reentry as a Rite of Passage," *Punishment & Society,* 13/1 (2011), 3–27.

41. Joan Petersilia, *When Prisoners Come Home: Parole and Prisoner Reentry* (New York: Oxford University Press, 2003), Jeremy Travis, *But They All Come Back: Facing the Challenges of Prisoner Reentry* (Washington, DC: Urban Institute Press, 2005), xxvii, 391, Jeremy Travis and Christy Ann Visher (eds.), *Prisoner Reentry and Crime in America* (New York: Cambridge University Press, 2005), ix, 264.

NOTES TO CHAPTER 2

1. Paige M. Harrison and Jennifer C. Karberg, "Prison and Jail Inmates at Midyear 2002" (Washington, DC: Bureau of Justice Statistics, 2003).

2. Pew Center on the States, "1 in 100: Behind Bars in America 2008" (Washington, DC: Pew Charitable Trusts, 2008).

3. Thomas P. Bonczar, "Prevalence of Imprisonment in the U.S. Population, 1974–2001" (Washington, DC: Bureau of Justice Statistics, 2003).

4. Ibid.

5. Roy Walmsley, "World Prison Population, 8th Edition" (London: International Centre for Prison Studies, 2009).

6. See though Roger Matthews, "The Myth of Punitiveness," *Theoretical Criminology,* 9/2 (2005), 175–201.

7. Walmsley, "World Prison Population, 8th Edition."

8. William J. Chambliss, *Power, Politics, and Crime* (Boulder, CO: Westview, 2001), xiv, 173.

9. Adam Liptak, "Inmate Count in U.S. Dwarfs Other Nations," *New York Times,* April 23, 2008, A1.

10. Walmsley, "World Prison Population, 8th Edition."

11. Paul Guerino, Paige M. Harrison, and William J. Sabol, "Prisoners in 2010" (Washington, DC: Bureau of Justice Statistics, 2011).

12. Lauren Glaze, "Correctional Populations in the United States, 2010" (Washington, DC: Bureau of Justice Statistics, 2011), Heather C. West and William J. Sabol, "Prisoners in 2007" (Washington, DC: Bureau of Justice Statistics, 2008).

13. Lauren Glaze and Thomas P. Bonczar, "Probation and Parole in the United States, 2010" (Washington, DC: Bureau of Justice Statistics, 2011).

14. Ibid.

15. Pew Center on the States, "One in 31: The Long Reach of Corrections" (Washington, DC: Pew Charitable Trusts, 2009).

16. Glaze, "Correctional Populations in the United States, 2010."

17. Lauren E. Glaze and Thomas P. Bonczar, "Probation and Parole in the United States: 2007 Statistical Tables" (Washington, DC: Bureau of Justice Statistics, 2009).

18. Bureau of Justice Statistics, "Justice Expenditure and Employment Extracts" (Washington, DC: Bureau of Justice Statistics, 2008).

19. Ibid.

20. Pew Center on the States, "One in 31: The Long Reach of Corrections."

21. Ibid., 2.

22. Todd R. Clear and James Austin, "Reducing Mass Incarceration: Implications of the Iron Law of Prison Populations," *Harvard Law and Policy Review*, 3 (2009), 307–24.

23. Thomas P. Bonczar, "Table 8. State Prison Releases, 2003: Time Served in Prison, by Offense and Release Type" (Washington, DC: Bureau of Justice Statistics, 2007).

24. Thomas P. Bonczar, "Table 1. State Prison Admissions, 2003: Offense, by Type of Admission" (Washington, DC: Bureau of Justice Statistics, 2007).

25. William J. Sabol, Heather C. West, and Matthew Cooper, "Prisoners in 2008" (Washington, DC: Bureau of Justice Statistics, 2009).

26. Norval Morris and Michael H. Tonry, *Between Prison and Probation: Intermediate Punishments in a Rational Sentencing System* (New York: Oxford University Press, 1990), 283.

27. Stanley Cohen, *Visions of Social Control: Crime, Punishment, and Classification* (New York: Polity Press, 1985), x, 325.

28. Katherine Beckett and Steve Herbert, *Banished: The New Social Control in Urban America* (New York: Oxford University Press, 2010).

29. Diana Gordon, *The Justice Juggernaut: Fighting Street Crime, Controlling Citizens* (New Brunswick, NJ: Rutgers University Press, 1990).

30. Beckett and Herbert, *Banished: The New Social Control in Urban America*.

31. Joan Petersilia, "Understanding California Corrections: A Policy Research Program Report" (Berkeley: California Policy Research Center, 2006).

32. Guerino, Harrison, and Sabol, "Prisoners in 2010."

33. Ibid.

34. Natasha A. Frost, *The Punitive State: Crime, Punishment, and Imprisonment across the United States* (New York: LFB Scholarly Publications, 2006).

35. Guerino, Harrison, and Sabol, "Prisoners in 2010."

36. Stephanie Bontrager, William Bales, and Ted Chiricos, "Race, Ethnicity, Threat, and the Labeling of Convicted Felons," *Criminology*, 43/3 (2005), 589–622.

37. Paige M. Harrison and Allen J. Beck, "Prisoners in 2005" (Washington, DC: U.S. Department of Justice, Bureau of Justice Statistics, 2006).

38. Ibid., 10.

39. Bruce Western, *Punishment and Inequality in America* (New York: Russell Sage Foundation, 2006), 25-27.

40. Michael Tonry, *Punishing Race: A Continuing American Dilemma* (New York: Oxford University Press, 2011).

41. Samuel Walker, Cassia Spohn, and Miriam Delone, *The Color of Justice: Race, Ethnicity, and Crime in America* (4th edition Belmont, CA: Wadsworth, 2008).

42. Alfred Blumstein and Jacqueline Cohen, "A Theory of the Stability of Punishment," *Journal of Criminal Law, Criminology, and Police Science,* 63 (1973), 198–207, Alfred Blumstein, Jacqueline Cohen, and Daniel Nagin, "The Dynamics of a Homeostatic Punishment Process," *Journal of Criminal Law and Criminology,* 67 (1977), 317–34, Alfred Blumstein and S. Moitra, "An Analysis of the Time-Series of the Imprisonment Rate in the States of the United States: A Further Test of the Stability of Punishment Hypothesis," *Journal of Criminal Law and Criminology,* 70 (1979), 376–90.

43. Hermann Mannheim, "American Criminology and Penology in War Time," *Sociological Review,* 34 (1942), 222–34, at 222, cited in Michael Tonry, "Has the Prison a Future?" in Michael Tonry (ed.), *The Future of Imprisonment* (New York: Oxford University Press, 2004), 3–24, at 3.

44. Norval Morris, "Prison in Evolution," in Tadeusz Grygier, Howard Jones, and John C. Spencer (eds.), *Criminology in Transition: Essays in Honour of Hermann Mannheim* (London: Tavistock, 1965), 268, cited in Tonry, "Has the Prison a Future?" 3.

45. David J. Rothman, *The Discovery of the Asylum: Social Order and Disorder in the New Republic* (revised edition Boston: Little, Brown, 1990/1971), at 295.

46. Franklin E. Zimring, *The Great American Crime Decline* (Studies in Crime and Public Policy) (New York: Oxford University Press, 2007), xiv, 258.

47. Franklin E. Zimring, "Imprisonment Rates and the New Politics of Criminal Punishment," *Punishment & Society,* 3 (2001), 161–66.

48. James Q. Wilson, "Thinking about Crime: The Debate over Deterrence," *Atlantic Monthly,* 252/3 (1983), 72–88.

49. Zimring, "Imprisonment Rates and the New Politics of Criminal Punishment," 162.

50. Alfred Blumstein and Allen J. Beck, "Population Growth in U.S. Prisons, 1980–1996," in Michael Tonry and Joan Petersilia (eds.), *Prisons* (Chicago: University of Chicago Press, 1999), 17–61, Alfred Blumstein and Allen J. Beck, "Reentry as a Transient State between Liberty and Recommitment," in Jeremy Travis and Christy Visher (eds.), *Prisoner Reentry and Crime in America* (New York: Cambridge University Press, 2005), 50–79.

51. David Garland, *The Culture of Control: Crime and Social Order in Contemporary Society* (Chicago: University of Chicago Press, 2001) , xiii, 307.

52. Bert Useem, Raymond V. Liedka, and Anne Morrison Piehl, "Popular Support for the Prison Build-Up," *Punishment & Society*, 5/1 (2003), 5–32.
53. Clear and Austin, "Reducing Mass Incarceration: Implications of the Iron Law of Prison Populations."
54. Blumstein and Beck, "Population Growth in U.S. Prisons, 1980–1996."
55. Blumstein and Beck, "Reentry as a Transient State between Liberty and Recommitment."
56. Steven Raphael and Michael A. Stoll, "Why Are So Many Americans in Prison?" in Steven Raphael and Michael A. Stoll (eds.), *Do Prisons Make Us Safer? The Benefits and Costs of the Prison Boom* (Washington, DC: Russell Sage Foundation, 2009), 27–72.
57. Ibid.
58. Ibid., 65.
59. Zimring, *The Great American Crime Decline*.
60. Although most people incarcerated in prisons have been convicted, those incarcerated in jails and other detention facilities have often not. See Sharon Dolovich, "Confronting the Costs of Incarceration. Foreward: Incarceration American-Style," *Harvard Law and Policy Review*, 3 (2009), 237–59.
61. David H. Greenberg and Valerie West, "State Prison Populations and Their Growth, 1971–1991," *Criminology* 39/3 (2001), 615–54.
62. Ibid., 638.
63. See Todd R. Clear, "Backfire: When Incarceration Increases Crime," *Journal of the Oklahoma Criminal Justice Research Consortium*, 3 (1996), 1–10, Todd R. Clear, "The Problem with 'Addition by Subtraction': The Prison-Crime Relationship in Low-Income Communities," in Marc Mauer and Meda Chesney-Lind (eds.), *Invisible Punishment: The Collateral Consequences of Mass Imprisonment* (New York: New Press, 2002), 181–93, Todd R. Clear et al., "Coercive Mobility and Crime: A Preliminary Examination of Concentrated Incarceration and Social Disorganization," *Justice Quarterly*, 20/1 (2003), 33–64, Jeffrey Fagan, "Crime, Law, and the Community: Dynamics of Incarceration in New York City," in Michael Tonry (ed.), *The Future of Imprisonment* (New York: Oxford University Press, 2004), 27–59, James P. Lynch and William J. Sabol, "Assessing the Effects of Mass Incarceration on Informal Social Control in Communities," *Criminology & Public Policy*, 3/2 (2004), 267–94, James P. Lynch and William J. Sabol, "Effects of Incarceration on Informal Social Control in Communities ," in Mary Patillo, David F. Weiman, and Bruce Western (eds.), *Imprisoning America: The Social Effects of Mass Incarceration* (New York: Russell Sage Foundation, 2004), 135–64, Dina Rose and Todd R. Clear, "Incarceration, Social Capital, and Crime: Implications for Social Disorganization Theory," *Criminology*, 36 (1998), 441–80.
64. Tomislav Kovandzic and Lynne Vieraitis, "The Effect of County-Level Prison Population Growth on Crime Rates," *Criminology & Public Policy*, 5/2 (2006), 213–44, Steven Levitt, "The Effect of Prison Population Size on Crime Rates: Evidence

from Prison Over-Crowding Litigation," *Quarterly Journal of Economics*, 111 (1996), 319–51, Raymond V. Liedka, Anne Morrison Piehl, and Bert Useem, "The Crime Control Effects of Incarceration: Does Scale Matter?" *Criminology & Public Policy*, 5/2 (2006), 245–76, Thomas B. Marvell and Carlisle E. Moody, "Prison Population Growth and Crime Reduction," *Journal of Quantitative Criminology*, 10/2 (1994), 109–40, Thomas B. Marvell and Carlisle E. Moody, "The Impact of Prison Growth on Homicide," *Homicide Studies*, 1 (1997), 205–33, Lynne Vieraitis, Tomislav Kovandzic, and Thomas B. Marvell, "The Criminogenic Effects of Imprisonment: Evidence from State Panel Data, 1974–2002," *Criminology & Public Policy*, 6/3 (2007), 589–622.

65. Edwin Zedlewski, "Making Confinement Decisions: Research in Brief" (Washington, DC: U.S. Department of Justice, 1987).

66. Western, *Punishment and Inequality in America*.

67. For a review, Don Stemen, "Reconsidering Incarceration: New Directions for Reducing Crime" (New York: VERA Institute of Justice, 2007).

68. Robert DeFina and Lance Hannon, "For Incapacitation, There Is No Time Like the Present: The Lagged Effects of Prisoner Reentry on Property and Violent Crime Rates," *Social Science Research*, 39 (2010), 1004–1014.

69. Donald Braman, *Doing Time on the Outside: Incarceration and Family Life in America* (Ann Arbor: University of Michigan Press, 2004), Rose and Clear, "Incarceration, Social Capital, and Crime: Implications for Social Disorganization Theory," Robert J. Sampson and Charles Loeffler, "Punishment's Place: The Local Concentration of Mass Incarceration," *Daedalus*, 139/3 (2010), 20–31.

70. Natasha A. Frost and Todd R. Clear, "Coercive Mobility," in Francis T. Cullen and Pamela Wilcox (eds.), *Oxford Handbook of Criminological Theory* (New York: Oxford University Press, 2012), 691–708.

71. See Todd R. Clear, "The Impacts of Incarceration on Public Safety," *Social Research: An International Quarterly of the Social Sciences*, 74/2 (2007), 613–30, Marc Mauer and Meda Chesney-Lind (eds.), *Invisible Punishment: The Collateral Consequences of Mass Imprisonment* (New York: New Press, 2003), x, 355.

72. See Clear 1996 for one of the earliest expressions of this idea and Rose and Clear 1998 for a more fully articulated theory.

73. David Garland, *Punishment and Modern Society: A Study in Social Theory* (Studies in Crime and Justice) (Chicago: University of Chicago Press, 1990), 312.

74. It should be noted that each of these findings needs qualification as research rarely demonstrates that imprisonment reduces all types of crime. Levitt (1996), for example, found that imprisonment overall reduced both violent and property crimes, but that in an analysis of individual crime types only robbery and burglary were significantly reduced.

75. Garland, *The Culture of Control: Crime and Social Order in Contemporary Society*. James Q. Whitman, *Harsh Justice: Criminal Punishment and the Widening Divide between America and Europe* (New York: Oxford University Press, 2003), viii, 311, [10] of plates. John Hagan, *Who Are the Criminals? The Politics of Crime Policy*

from the Age of Roosevelt to the Age of Reagan (Princeton, NJ: Princeton University Press, 2010).

76. Michelle Alexander, *The New Jim Crow: Mass Incarceration in the Age of Colorblindness* (New York: New Press, 2010), Katherine Beckett, *Making Crime Pay: Law and Order in Contemporary American Politics* (New York: Oxford University Press, 1997), vi, 158, Christian Parenti, *Lockdown America: Police and Prisons in the Age of Crisis* (New York: Verso, 1999), xiii, 290.

77. President's Commission on Law Enforcement and Administration of Justice, "The Challege of Crime in a Free Society," ed. President's Commission on Law Enforcement and Administration of Justice (Washington, DC: United States Government Printing Office, 1967).

78. Ibid., vi.

79. Thomas E. Feucht and Edwin Zedlewski, "The 40th Anniversary of the Crime Report," *NIJ Journal,* 257 (2007), 20–23.

80. See Ted Gest, *Crime and Politics: Big Government's Erratic Campaign for Law and Order* (New York: Oxford University Press, 2001), chapter 6, for a lengthy discussion.

81. Peter Reuter, "Assessing U.S. Drug Policy and Providing a Base for Future Decisions: Statement to the U.S. Congress, Joint Economic Committee, Hearing, June 18, 2008," *Illegal Drugs: Economic Impact, Societal Costs, Policy Responses* (Washington, DC: U.S. Congress, Joint Economic Committee, 2008).

82. Ibid.

83. Guerino, Harrison, and Sabol, "Prisoners in 2010."

84. Clear and Austin, "Reducing Mass Incarceration: Implications of the Iron Law of Prison Populations."

85. Marc Mauer, "Incarceration Nation," http://www.tompaine.com/articles/2006/12/11/incarceration_nation.php, accessed March 7, 2007.

86. Natasha A. Frost and Todd R. Clear, "Understanding Mass Incarceration as a Grand Social Experiment," *Studies in Law, Politics, and Society,* 47 (2009), 159–91.

87. This phrase is borrowed from the title of Travis Pratt's recent book on the use of incarceration across the United States. Travis C. Pratt, *Addicted to Incarceration: Corrections Policy and the Politics of Misinformation in the United States* (Thousand Oaks, CA: Sage, 2009).

88. Natasha A. Frost, Judy Greene, and Kevin Pranis, *Hard Hit: Growth in the Imprisonment of Women, 1977–2004* (New York: Women's Prison Association, 2006).

89. Michelle Brown, *The Culture of Punishment: Prison, Society, and Spectacle* (New York: New York University Press, 2009).

90. Pew Center on the States, "1 in 100: Behind Bars in America 2008."

91. Bonczar, "Prevalence of Imprisonment in the U.S. Population, 1974–2001."

92. Fagan, "Crime, Law, and the Community: Dynamics of Incarceration in New York City."

NOTES TO CHAPTER 3

1. Christopher Shea, "Life Sentence," *Boston Globe,* September 23, 2007, E1.
2. Alexis De Tocqueville, *Democracy in America,* Volume 1 (New York: Vintage, 1990).
3. We feel it is important to distinguish "grand social experiments" from "social experiments" in the traditional sense. We use the phrase "social experiment" in a higher-order way than it is frequently used in the social sciences; we mean to talk about "grand" social experiments. In a series of works, David Greenberg and colleagues have chronicled literal social experiments in public policy programs. They describe the design and effects of programmatic experiments in the traditional sense—those that include random assignment to treatment and control groups; the application of the "treatment condition" (whether that might be economic incentives, work opportunities, etc.) to the treatment group; measurement of outcomes of interest; and the careful analysis of those outcomes across the treatment and control groups. Greenberg et al. identify Heather Ross's 1960s New Jersey Income Maintenance Experiment as the very first example of the kind of experiment in which they are interested. The vast majority of social experiments that Greenberg et al. then chronicle occur in the realms of health care and welfare—some have provided support for a particular policy, others have demonstrated the failure of a policy to succeed on its own terms. This type of controlled social experiment—though important—is not the type of social experiment that we are referring to here. (David H. Greenberg, Donna Kinksz, and Marvin Mandell, *Social Experimentation and Public Policymaking* (Washington, DC: Urban Institute Press, 2003), David H. Greenberg and Mark Shroder, *The Digest of Social Experiments* (third edition Washington, DC: Urban Institute Press, 2004), xx, 498.)
4. Although it is possible to find plenty of instances of the use of the idea of a grand social experiment in scholarly work, we are not aware of any instance in which this phrase is carefully defined. We, therefore, articulate what we mean by grand social experiment—explaining the term and identifying the criteria against which to judge shifts in social policy. Norman Daniels, "Toward Ethical Review of Health System Transformations," *American Journal of Public Health,* 96/3 (2006), 447–51.
5. Michael Tonry, "Criminology, Mandatory Minimums, and Public Policy," *Criminology & Public Policy,* 5/1 (2006), 45–56.
6. Katherine Beckett and Bruce Western, "Governing Social Marginality: Welfare, Incarceration, and the Transformation of State Policy," *Punishment & Society,* 3/1 (2001), 43–59, David Garland, *Punishment and Welfare: A History of Penal Strategies* (Brookfield, VT: Gower, 1985), x, 297, Michael Tonry, "Explanations of American Punishment Policies," *Punishment & Society,* 11/3 (2009), 377–94, Loïc Wacquant, "Class, Race, and Hyperincarceration in Revanchist America," *Daedalus,* 139/3 (Summer 2010), 74–90.

7. Mimi Abramovitz, "Neither Accidental, nor Simply Mean-Spirited: The Context for Welfare Reform," in Keith M. Kilty and Elizabeth A. Segal (eds.), *The Promise of Welfare Reform: Political Rhetoric and the Reality of Poverty in the Twenty-First Century* (Binghamton, NY: Haworth, 2006), 23–37.
8. Keith M. Kilty and Elizabeth A. Segal (eds.), *The Promise of Welfare Reform: Political Rhetoric and the Reality of Poverty in the Twenty-First Century* (Binghamton, NY: Haworth, 2006), xxi, 329.
9. Abramovitz, "Neither Accidental, nor Simply Mean-Spirited: The Context for Welfare Reform," 24.
10. Frances Fox Piven and Richard A. Cloward, *Regulating the Poor: The Functions of Public Welfare* (second edition New York: Vintage Books, 1993).
11. Jeff Manza, "Political Sociological Models of the U.S. New Deal," *Annual Review of Sociology,* 26 (2000), 297–322.
12. Eric Rauchway, *The Great Depression and the New Deal: A Very Short Introduction* (New York: Oxford University Press, 2008).
13. Abramovitz, "Neither Accidental, nor Simply Mean-Spirited: The Context for Welfare Reform," Manza, "Political Sociological Models of the U.S. New Deal."
14. Frances Fox Piven, "Remarks. Transcript from Conference Proceedings, New York City and the New Deal" (New York: Gotham Center for New York City History, 2002).
15. Manza, "Political Sociological Models of the U.S. New Deal."
16. Lyndon B. Johnson, "Remarks at the University of Michigan," http://www.lbjlib.utexas.edu/johnson/archives.hom/speeches.hom/640522.asp, accessed March 11, 2007.
17. Eli Ginzberg and Robert M. Solow (eds.), *The Great Society: Lessons for the Future* (New York: Basic Books, 1974).
18. Ibid., 9.
19. Harvard Sitkoff, *A New Deal for Blacks: Thirtieth Anniversary Edition* (New York: Oxford University Press, 2009), 44.
20. *Brown v. Board of Education of Topeka, Kansas,* 347 U.S. 483 (1954).
21. Taylor Branch, *Parting the Waters: America in the King Years, 1954–63* (New York: Simon & Schuster, 1989), Michael Harrington, *The Other America* (New York: Macmillan, 1962).
22. Abramovitz, "Neither Accidental, nor Simply Mean-Spirited: The Context for Welfare Reform."
23. Katherine Beckett, *Making Crime Pay: Law and Order in Contemporary American Politics* (New York: Oxford University Press, 1997), vi, 158.
24. Beckett and Western, "Governing Social Marginality: Welfare, Incarceration, and the Transformation of State Policy." See also Garland, *Punishment and Welfare: A History of Penal Strategies.*
25. See also Jock Young, *The Exclusive Society: Social Exclusion, Crime, and Difference in Late Modernity* (Thousand Oaks, CA: Sage, 1999), vii, 216.

26. Cited in Michael Tonry (ed.), *The Future of Imprisonment* (New York: Oxford University Press, 2004), viii, 263.

27. David J. Rothman, *The Discovery of the Asylum: Social Order and Disorder in the New Republic* (revised edition Boston: Little, Brown, 1990/1971), 273.

28. Alfred Blumstein and Jacqueline Cohen, "A Theory of the Stability of Punishment," *Journal of Criminal Law, Criminology, and Police Science*, 63 (1973), 198–207, Alfred Blumstein, Jacqueline Cohen, and Daniel Nagin, "The Dynamics of a Homeostatic Punishment Process," *Journal of Criminal Law and Criminology*, 67 (1977), 317–34, Alfred Blumstein and S. Moitra, "An Analysis of the Time-Series of the Imprisonment Rate in the States of the United States: A Further Test of the Stability of Punishment Hypothesis," *Journal of Criminal Law and Criminology*, 70 (1979), 376–90.

29. Marc Mauer, "The Causes and Consequences of Prison Growth in the USA," *Punishment & Society*, 3/1 (2001), 9–20.

30. Todd R. Clear, *Imprisoning Communities: How Mass Incarceration Makes Disadvantaged Neighborhoods Worse* (New York: Oxford University Press, 2007).

31. Kevin Reitz, "Don't Blame Determinacy: U.S. Incarceration Growth Has Been Driven by Other Forces," *Texas Law Review*, 84 (2006), 1784–802, at 1793.

32. David Garland, *The Culture of Control: Crime and Social Order in Contemporary Society* (Chicago: University of Chicago Press, 2001), xiii, 307. (See also Jonathan Simon, *Governing through Crime: How the War on Crime Transformed American Democracy and Created a Culture of Fear* (Studies in Crime and Public Policy) (New York: Oxford University Press, 2007), viii, 330.)

33. See especially chapter 5 in Michael Tonry, *Thinking about Crime: Sense and Sensibility in American Penal Culture* (New York: Oxford University Press, 2004), x, 260.

34. President's Commission on Law Enforcement and Administration of Justice, "The Challenge of Crime in a Free Society" (Washington, DC: United States Government Printing Office, 1967).

35. Garland, *The Culture of Control: Crime and Social Order in Contemporary Society*. Tonry, *Thinking about Crime: Sense and Sensibility in American Penal Culture*. John Hagan has recently argued that we should think about criminal justice in terms of two eras that he has called the Age of Roosevelt (1933–1973) and the Age of Reagan (1974–2008). John Hagan, *Who Are the Criminals? The Politics of Crime Policy from the Age of Roosevelt to the Age of Reagan* (Princeton, NJ: Princeton University Press, 2010).

36. James Q. Wilson, *Thinking about Crime* (New York: Random House, 1975).

37. Young, *The Exclusive Society: Social Exclusion, Crime, and Difference in Late Modernity*.

38. Ted Gest, *Crime and Politics: Big Government's Erratic Campaign for Law and Order* (New York: Oxford University Press, 2001).

39. Bill Clinton's political success in the early 1990s was due partly to his ability to neutralize the Republicans on the crime issue. Clinton famously returned to

Arkansas at the height of the election season to watch an execution in his home state (Alexander Nguyen, "Bill Clinton's death penalty waffle," *American Prospect* (December 19, 2001), http://prospect.org/article/bill-clintons-death-penalty-waffle, accessed March 6, 2013).

40. See also Beckett, *Making Crime Pay: Law and Order in Contemporary American Politics*.

41. Pew Center on the States, "1 in 100: Behind Bars in America 2008" (Washington, DC: Pew Charitable Trusts, 2008).

42. Pew Center on the States, "One in 31: The Long Reach of Corrections" (Washington, DC: Pew Charitable Trusts, 2009).

43. Pew Center on the States, "1 in 100: Behind Bars in America 2008."

44. Robert Martinson, "What Works? Questions and Answers about Prison Reform," *Public Interest*, 35 (1974), 22–54.

45. Wilson, *Thinking about Crime*.

46. Malcolm M. Feeley, "Crime, Social Order, and the Rise of Neo-Conservative Politics," *Theoretical Criminology*, 7/1 (2003), 111–30, at 120–21 (emphasis added).

47. See for example Francis T. Cullen and Karen E. Gilbert, *Reaffirming Rehabilitation* (Cincinnati, OH: Anderson, 1982).

48. John J. DiIulio Jr., "Prisons Are a Bargain, by Any Measure," *New York Times*, January 16, 1996, A17.

49. Ibid.

50. John A. Andrew II, *Lyndon Johnson and the Great Society* (Blue Ridge, PA: Dee, 1968).

51. *Brown v. Board of Education of Topeka, Kansas*.

52. Franklin E. Zimring and Gordon Hawkins, *The Scale of Imprisonment* (Studies in Crime and Justice) (Chicago: University of Chicago Press, 1991), xiv, 244.

NOTES TO CHAPTER 4

1. Francis T. Cullen, Bonnie S. Fisher, and Brandon K. Applegate, "Public Opinion about Punishment and Corrections," *Crime and Justice*, 27 (2000), 1–79, at 2.

2. President's Commission on Law Enforcement and Administration of Justice, "The Challege of Crime in a Free Society," ed. President's Commission on Law Enforcement and Administration of Justice (Washington, DC. United States Government Printing Office, 1967), 15.

3. It is important to note that when the Crime Commission published its report in 1967, it was very hard to determine exactly how big the crime program actually was. As Feucht and Zedlewski (2007) have noted, at the time "the Nation lacked even the most basic information about crime and crime trends." Indeed, today, scholars caution against making pre- and post-1960s crime rate comparisons because the FBI's Uniform Crime Reporting Program underwent substantial changes in that decade (see Useem et al., 2003).

4. James Vorenberg, "The War on Crime: The First Five Years," *Atlantic Monthly*, http://www.theatlantic.com/politics/crime/crimewar.htm, accessed July 2, 2009.

5. See Ernest Van Den Haag, *Punishing Criminals: Concerning a Very Old and Painful Question* (New York: Basic Books, 1975), James Q. Wilson, *Thinking about Crime* (New York: Random House, 1975).

6. See Statistical Analysis Center, "Impact of the New Drug Trafficking Law on the Delaware Criminal Justice System" (Washington, DC : National Criminal Justice Reference Service, 1991).

7. See Bruce Western, *Punishment and Inequality in America* (New York: Russell Sage Foundation, 2006), table 2.3.

8. New York State Department of Correctional Services, "Under Custody Report: Profile of Inmate Population under Custody on January 1, 2010" (Albany: New York State Department of Corrections and Community Services, 2010).

9. John J. DiIulio Jr., "My Black Crime Problem, and Ours," *City Journal,* September 1996.

10. William J. Bennett, John J. DiIulio Jr., and John P. Walters, *Body Count: Moral Poverty . . .and How to Win America's War against Crime and Drugs* (New York: Simon & Schuster, 1996).

11. James Alan Fox, "Crime: The Young and the Ruthless," *Chicago Tribune,* January 10, 1992.

12. Although some states have abolished discretionary parole release, parole as a release mechanism still exists in every state. The difference is in the mechanism by which offenders are released. Under discretionary parole systems, a paroling authority (the parole board) would determine when individual offenders were ready for release. In states that have abolished discretionary parole release, offenders are still "paroled"— their release date is simply determined by deducting earned good time from their sentence, rather than human judgments about their suitability for release.

13. Beginning with California and Maine in 1976, states began to abandon the indeterminate sentencing structure and replace it with the determinate sentencing structure. By 2002, seventeen states had adopted a determinate sentencing scheme. Don Stemen, Andres Rengifo, and James Wilson, "Of Fragmentation and Ferment: The Impact of State Sentencing Policies on Incarceration Rates, 1975–2002" (Washington, DC: Final Report to the U.S. Department of Justice, 2006).

14. It would be disingenuous, however, to attribute the collapse of a sentencing structure that had been in place for almost one hundred years to the publication of one article—and indeed, our intention here is to complicate that notion. Moreover, the force with which Martinson made the now infamous "nothing works" declaration is contested. Some suggest that he declared nothing worked and then back-tracked (Malcolm M. Feeley, "Crime, Social Order, and the Rise of Neo-Conservative Politics," *Theoretical Criminology,* 7/1 (2003), 111–30), and others note that he never unequivocally argued that *nothing* worked (see Francis T. Cullen, "Assessing the Penal Harm Movement," *Journal of Research in Crime and Delinquency,* 32 (1995), 338–58).

15. Wilson, *Thinking about Crime.*

16. David J. Rothman, *Conscience and Convenience: The Asylum and Its Alternatives in Progressive America* (New Lines in Criminology) (revised edition New York: Gruyter, 2002), xvi, 482.

17. See, for example, Franklin E. Zimring and Gordon Hawkins, *The Scale of Imprisonment* (Studies in Crime and Justice) (Chicago: University of Chicago Press, 1991), xiv, 244.

18. According to Zimring, Hawkins, and Kamin (2001), this tendency for sentences to bark louder than they bite has always been integral to the effective functioning of the criminal justice system. It is only in recent years that we have begun to see sentences that not only bite as hard as their bark is loud, but in some cases, bite harder (see the discussion of three-strikes legislation that follows).

19. Stemen, Rengifo, and Wilson, "Of Fragmentation and Ferment: The Impact of State Sentencing Policies on Incarceration Rates, 1975–2002."

20. Thomas B. Marvell and Carlisle E. Moody, "Determinate Sentencing and Abolishing Parole: The Long-Term Impacts on Prisons and Crime," *Criminology,* 34/1 (1996), 107–28, Kevin R. Reitz, "The Disassembly and Reassembly of U.S. Sentencing Practices," in Michael Tonry and Richard S. Frase (eds.), *Sentencing and Sanctions in Western Countries* (New York: Oxford University Press, 2001), 222–58.

21. Marvell and Moody, "Determinate Sentencing and Abolishing Parole: The Long-Term Impacts on Prisons and Crime."

22. Reitz, "The Disassembly and Reassembly of U.S. Sentencing Practices," 231.

23. Bureau of Justice Assistance, "1996 National Survey of State Sentencing Structures" (Washington DC: Government Printing Office, 1998).

24. Reitz, "The Disassembly and Reassembly of U.S. Sentencing Practices."

25. Stemen, Rengifo, and Wilson, "Of Fragmentation and Ferment: The Impact of State Sentencing Policies on Incarceration Rates, 1975–2002."

26. Richard Frase, "State Sentencing Guidelines: Still Going Strong," *Judicature,* 78 (1995), 173–79.

27. See Thomas B. Marvell, "Sentencing Guidelines and Prison Population Growth," *Journal of Criminal Law and Criminology,* 85 (1995), 696–708, Sean Nicholson-Crotty, "The Impact of Sentencing Guidelines on State-Level Sanctions: An Analysis over Time," *Crime & Delinquency,* 50/3 (2004), 395–411.

28. Michael Tonry, "The Success of Judge Frankel's Sentencing Commission," *University of Colorado Law Review,* 64 (1993), 713–22.

29. Michael Tonry, *Sentencing Matters* (New York: Oxford University Press, 1996), 64 and 71, respectively.

30. See Albert W. Altschuler, "The Failure of Sentencing Guidelines: A Plea for Less Aggregation," *University of Chicago Law Review,* 58 (1991), 901–51, Joachim Savelsberg, "Law That Does Not Fit Society: Sentencing Guidelines as Neoclassical Reaction to the Dilemmas of Substantivized Law," *American Journal of Sociology,* 97 (1992), 1346–81.

31. Although the federal guidelines are frequently described as too harsh, again it is important to consider the intentions of those charged with developing law. In the case of the federal guidelines, increased harshness in sentencing *was the object* and so, on their own terms, they could actually be described as quite successful. See Tonry, *Sentencing Matters*.

32. Richard S. Frase, "Is Guided Discretion Sufficient? Overview of State Sentencing Guidelines," *St. Louis University Law Journal*, 44 (2000), 425–46, at 426.

33. Ibid., 426.

34. James Austin et al., *Unlocking America: Why and How to Reduce America's Prison Population* (Washington, DC: JFA Institute, 2007).

35. Michael Jacobson, *Downsizing Prisons: How to Reduce Crime and End Mass Incarceration* (New York: New York University Press, 2005).

36. Reitz, "The Disassembly and Reassembly of U.S. Sentencing Practices."

37. Tonry, *Sentencing Matters*.

38. Ashley Nellis, "Throwing Away the Key: The Expansion of Life without Parole Sentences in the United States," *Federal Sentencing Reporter*, 23/1 (2010), 27–32.

39. Reitz, "The Disassembly and Reassembly of U.S. Sentencing Practices," 229.

40. Families Against Mandatory Minimums, "Federal Mandatory Minimums" (Washington, DC: Families Against Mandatory Minimums, 2009).

41. Bureau of Justice Assistance, "1996 National Survey of State Sentencing Structures."

42. The Bureau of Justice Assistance (1998) reports that the number of states reporting a mandatory minimum for an offense other than the primary five offenses targeted by this type of legislation tripled between 1994 and 1996. In 1994, only eleven states reported a mandatory minimum for some "other" offense; by 1996, thirty-two states reported these additional mandatory minimums. Ibid.

43. Franklin E. Zimring, Gordon Hawkins, and Sam Kamin, *Punishment and Democracy: Three-Strikes and You're Out in California* (Studies in Crime and Public Policy) (New York: Oxford University Press, 2001), 164.

44. The full text of Justice Kennedy's address to the American Bar Association can be found at http://www.november.org/stayinfo/breaking/Kennedyspeech.html, accessed December 29, 2011.

45. Tonry, *Sentencing Matters*.

46. Paula M. Ditton and Doris James Wilson, "Truth in Sentencing in State Prisons" (Washington, DC: Bureau of Justice Statistics, 1999).

47. For a detailed discussion of the development of VOI-TIS and an evaluation of its impact, see Susan Turner et al., "An Evaluation of the Federal Government's Violent Offender Incarceration and Truth-in-Sentencing Incentive Grants," *Prison Journal*, 86/3 (2006), 364-85.

48. Franklin E. Zimring, "Imprisonment Rates and the New Politics of Criminal Punishment," *Punishment & Society*, 3 (2001), 161–66.

49. Depending upon the source consulted, between five and nine states enacted 85 percent TIS laws before 1994, with Washington enacting the first TIS law in 1984.

According to Ditton and Wilson (1999), the five states with 85 percent TIS laws before 1993 are Delaware, Minnesota, Tennessee, Utah, and Washington. According to Sabol et al. (2002), there were nine states with 85 percent requirements prior to 1994, including Arizona, California, Georgia, Minnesota, Missouri, North Carolina, Oregon, Virginia, and Washington. There is also discrepancy between sources as to whether Delaware, Pennsylvania, and Michigan actually meet the requirement, with Ditton and Wilson (1999) reporting that they do, and Sabol et al. (2002) reporting that they do not. Ditton and Wilson, "Truth in Sentencing in State Prisons." William J. Sabol et al., "The Influences of Truth-in-Sentencing Reforms on Changes in States' Sentencing Practices and Prison Populations" (Washington, DC: Urban Institute, 2002).

50. According to Turner and her colleagues who conducted the funded evaluation of VOI-TIS grants, only 2.7 billion of the $10 billion appropriated was actually disbursed to the states before the grant program was discontinued in 2002. Turner et al., "An Evaluation of the Federal Government's Violent Offender Incarceration and Truth-in-Sentencing Incentive Grants."

51. According to Sabol et al., "The Influences of Truth-in-Sentencing Reforms on Changes in States' Sentencing Practices and Prison Populations," under this standard all states received some VOI/TIS funding, though they note that in 1996, the law was amended to require that the 85 percent standard be implemented within three years to qualify for the grants. The effect of the VOI/TIS grant program on the adoption of TIS laws is debated. Sabol et al. (v), for example, report that thirty states left existing standards intact and only twenty adopted or altered their TIS laws in response to the grant program, with twelve states "[increasing] the severity of their existing truth-in-sentencing laws" and eight states drafting new TIS laws.

52. Sabol et al., "The Influences of Truth-in-Sentencing Reforms on Changes in States' Sentencing Practices and Prison Populations," vii.

53. Ditton and Wilson, "Truth in Sentencing in State Prisons." In their evaluation of the VOI/TIS grant program, Turner and her colleagues also note that it will be some time before we can actually assess the impact of TIS on the time served by offenders subject to the requirements. Turner et al., "An Evaluation of the Federal Government's Violent Offender Incarceration and Truth-in-Sentencing Incentive Grants."

54. Ditton and Wilson, "Truth in Sentencing in State Prisons."

55. It should be noted that Massachusetts very recently passed its own version of a three-strikes law, Melissa's bill, named for murder victim Melissa Gosule. The bill gained momentum following the previously described shooting of a Woburn police officer by the parolee Dominic Cinelli. Glenn Johnson and Brian R. Ballou, "Deval Patrick Signs Repeat Offender Crime Bill in Private State House Ceremony," *Boston Globe,* August 2, 2012.

56. In a series of publications, James Austin and colleagues (Clark, Austin, and Henry 1997; Austin, Clark, Hardyman, and Henry 2000) provide a concise summary of

the variation in three strikes laws across states that we rely on here to describe some of the variations across states.

57. States with two-strike provisions include Arkansas, California, Connecticut, Georgia, Kansas, Montana, North Dakota, Pennsylvania, South Carolina, and Tennessee (Clark, Austin, and Henry 1997). Georgia has two- and four-strike provisions and Louisiana three- and four-strike provisions (both stipulate that upon the fourth felony conviction of any type, the offender is sentenced to the maximum term for the fourth offense in Georgia and life without parole in Louisiana—Louisiana requires that one of the four felonies be one of the three-strike offenses). Maryland has only a four-strike provision requiring that the offender serve life in prison without parole upon the fourth conviction for one of the statutorily listed offenses provided that the offender served prison terms for the first three offenses separately.

58. Indiana, Louisiana, and California include various drug offenses while North Dakota and Utah allow the enhanced penalties for the commission of a broad range of felonies (see Clark, Austin, and Henry 1997 for a concise description of variations in state laws).

59. This phrase is borrowed from Zimring, Hawkins, and Kamin (2001), who document the history of, and critique, the adoption of California's exceptional three-strike law in the book *Punishment and Democracy*.

60. John Clark, James Austin, and D. Alan Henry, "'Three Strikes and You're Out': A Review of State Legislation," *National Institute of Justice, Research in Brief* (1997), Zimring, "Imprisonment Rates and the New Politics of Criminal Punishment."

61. See Clark, Austin, and Henry, "'Three Strikes and You're Out': A Review of State Legislation," for an extended discussion.

62. Zimring, "Imprisonment Rates and the New Politics of Criminal Punishment," Zimring, Hawkins, and Kamin, *Punishment and Democracy: Three-Strikes and You're Out in California.*

63. Zimring, "Imprisonment Rates and the New Politics of Criminal Punishment." (It is also worth noting that three-strikes-type legislation was not the only punitive legislation passed in the 1990s to bear a catchy sound-bite name. Other legislation, such as Florida's "10-20-Life" legislation, imposes increasingly harsh sentences for the use of a weapon during the commission of a crime. Zimring, Hawkins, and Kamin, *Punishment and Democracy: Three-Strikes and You're Out in California.*

64. Robert Martinson, "California Research at the Crossroads," *Crime and Delinquency,* 22/2 (1976), 180–91, at 191.

65. For a history, see Joan Petersilia and Susan Turner, "Intensive Probation and Parole," *Crime and Justice: A Review of Research,* 17 (1993).

66. Todd R. Clear and Vincent O'Leary, *Controlling the Offender in the Community: Reforming the Community Supervision Function* (Lexington, MA: Lexington, 1983).

67. Joan Petersilia, "When Probation Becomes More Dreaded Than Prison," *Federal Probation*, 54/1 (1990), 23–27. See also Joan Petersilia and Susan Turner, "Intensive Probation and Parole."

68. Joan Petersilia and Susan Turner, "Intensive Supervision for High-Risk Probationers: Findings from Three California Experiments" (Santa Monica, CA: RAND, 1990).

69. Petersilia and Turner, "Intensive Probation and Parole."

70. Pew Center on the States, "When Offenders Break the Rules: Smart Responses to Parole and Probation Violations" (Washington, DC: Pew Charitable Trusts, November 2007).

71. Ryken Grattet, Joan Petersilia, and Jeffrey Lin, "Parole Violations and Revocations in California" (Washington, DC: U.S. Department of Justice, 2008).

72. A number of critics have noted that it seems somewhat dubious that community notification laws pertain only to sex offenders. Sex offender notification has been described as "yet another example of treating sex offenders differently from other criminals" (Berliner 1996, at 294). Critics of sex offender notification argue that it might be equally useful for communities to be notified and aware of other classes of violent criminals moving into the neighborhood. Lucy Berliner, "Community Notification of Sex Offenders: A New Tool or a False Promise? " *Journal of Interpersonal Violence*, 11/2 (1996), 294–300.

73. Harvard Law Review, "Prevention vs. Punishment: Toward a Principled Distinction in the Restraint of Released Sex Offenders," *Harvard Law Review*, 109/7 (1996), 1711–28.

74. Michelle Ruess, "Megan's Law Signed by Governor," *Record*, November 1, 1994, A1.

75. Although no state copied Washington's notification statute (Wash. Rev. Code Ann. § 4.24.550) verbatim, it has served as a model for other states.

76. Ralph Siegel, "Suspect Admits Killing Girl," *Record*, 1994, A1, A4.

77. Timmendequas has two previous convictions for sexual offenses: one for attempted sexual contract in 1981 and the other for attempted sexual assault in 1982. Ibid.

78. While notification laws have become generically referred to as "Megan's Laws," within each state, community notification laws are frequently named after a local child victim of a sexual predator (Indiana's community notification law, for example, is referred to as "Zachary's Law"). B. Telpner, "Constructing Safe Communities: Megan's Law and the Purposes of Punishment," *Georgetown Law Journal*, 85(6): 2039–68.

79. The 1994 federal crime bill, also known as the Violent Crime Control and Law Enforcement Act of 1994, required that states enact provisions for the registration and notification of sex offenders by 1997. Failure to comply would result in the loss of 10 percent of federal law enforcement funding. Perhaps not surprisingly, all states have complied. The bill did not provide for any additional federal support in implementing the programs. Brian Telpner, "Constructing Safe Communities: Megan's Law and the Purposes of Punishment," *Georgetown Law Journal*, 85/6 (1997), 2039–68.

80. Ibid.
81. *Doe v. Pataki*, 940 F. Supp. 603 (1996) at 624 (referring to New York Corrections Law § 168-a(2)(a)).
82. Roxanne Lieb, Vernon Quinsey, and Lucy Berliner, "Sexual Predators and Social Policy," *Crime & Justice: A Review of Research*, 23 (1998), 43–114.
83. See Jenny A. Montana, "An Ineffective Weapon in the Fight against Child Sexual Abuse: New Jersey's Megan's Law," *Journal of Law and Policy*, 3 (1995), 569–604, Lois Presser and Elaine Gunnison, "Strange Bedfellows: Is Sex Offender Notification a Form of Community Justice?" *Crime & Delinquency*, 45/3 (1999), 299–315, Telpner, "Constructing Safe Communities: Megan's Law and the Purposes of Punishment."
84. Robert A. Prentky, "Community Notification and Constructive Risk Reduction," *Journal of Interpersonal Violence*, 11/2 (1997), 295–98.
85. Amy L. Anderson and Lisa L. Sample, "Public Awareness and Action Resulting from Sex Offender Community Notification Laws," *Criminal Justice Policy Review*, 19/4 (2008), 371–96.
86. Telpner, "Constructing Safe Communities: Megan's Law and the Purposes of Punishment."
87. Richard Tewksbury, "Validity and Utility of the Kentucky Sex Offender Registry," *Federal Probation*, 66/1 (2002), 21–26.
88. Presser and Gunnison, "Strange Bedfellows: Is Sex Offender Notification a Form of Community Justice?"
89. Telpner, "Constructing Safe Communities: Megan's Law and the Purposes of Punishment," 2059, citing Tracy Dell'Angela, "Sex Offenders' New Lives Can Include Old Behavior," *Chicago Tribune*, August 22, 1996, 1.
90. Mary Zahn, "Notification Law on Sex Offenders Puts Strains on Residents," *Milwaukee Journal Sentinel*, March 29 1998, sec. Watching the Offenders, p. 1.
91. Roger N. Lancaster, "Sex Offenders: The Last Pariahs," *New York Times*, August 21, 2011, SR6.
92. John Zarrella and Patrick Oppmann, "Florida Housing Sex Offenders under Bridge," http://articles.cnn.com/2007-04-05/justice/bridge.sex.offenders_1_sexual-offenders-parks-and-other-places-fewer-places?_s=PM:LAW, accessed December 29, 2011.
93. Austin et al., *Unlocking America: Why and How to Reduce America's Prison Population*.
94. Todd R. Clear, Dina Rose, and Judith Ryder, "Incarceration and the Community: The Problem of Removing and Returning Offenders," *Crime & Delinquency*, 47/3 (2001), 335–51.
95. See Anthony C. Thompson, *Releasing Prisoners, Redeeming Communities: Reentry, Race, and Politics* (New York: New York University Press, 2008).
96. Much of the material in this section on prisoner reentry and legislative barriers first appeared in Natasha A. Frost, "Reentry as a Process Rather Than a Moment,"

in Karim Ismaili (ed.), *U.S. Criminal Justice Policy: A Contemporary Reader* (Sudbury, MA: Jones and Bartlett Learning, 2011), 159–82.

97. Jeremy Travis, *But They All Come Back: Facing the Challenges of Prisoner Reentry* (Washington, DC: Urban Institute Press, 2005), xxvii, 391.

98. Ashley Nellis and Ryan S. King, "No Exit: The Expanding Use of Life Sentences in America" (Washington, DC: Sentencing Project, 2009).

99. Travis, *But They All Come Back: Facing the Challenges of Prisoner Reentry.*

100. James P. Lynch and William J. Sabol, "Prisoner Reentry in Perspective" (Washington, DC: Urban Institute, 2001).

101. Michael Tonry, *Malign Neglect: Race, Crime, and Punishment in America* (New York: Oxford University Press, 1995), 4.

102. Devah Pager, *Marked: Race, Crime, and Finding Work in an Era of Mass Incarceration* (Chicago: University of Chicago Press, 2007).

103. Jeremy Travis and Christy Ann Visher (eds.), *Prisoner Reentry and Crime in America* (New York: Cambridge University Press, 2005), ix, 264.

104. Joshua Page, "Eliminating the Enemy: The Import of Denying Prisoners Access to Higher Education in Clinton's America," *Punishment & Society,* 6/4 (2004), 357–78.

105. The most recent reauthorization occurred in 2008 and the next reauthorization is scheduled to take place in 2013.

106. Page, "Eliminating the Enemy: The Import of Denying Prisoners Access to Higher Education in Clinton's America."

107. Donna Leinwand, "Drug Convictions Costing Students Their Financial Aid," *USA Today Online,* April 17, 2006.

108. Legal Action Center, "After Prison: Roadblocks to Reentry; A Report on State Legal Barriers Facing People with Criminal Records" (New York: Legal Action Center, 2004).

109. Coalition for Higher Education Act Reform, "Falling through the Cracks: Loss of State-Based Financial Aid Eligibility for Students Affected by the Federal Higher Education Act Drug Provision" (Washington, DC: Coalition for Higher Education Act Reform, 2006).

110. Gwen Rubinstein and Debbie Mukamal, "Welfare and Housing: Denial of Benefits to Drug Offenders," in Marc Mauer and Meda Chesney-Lind (eds.), *Invisible Punishment: The Collateral Consequences of Mass Imprisonment* (New York: New Press, 2002), 37–49.2002

111. Anti-Drug Abuse Act of 1986, P.L. 99-570, 100 Stat. 3207.

112. Deborah J. Vagins and Jesselyn Mccurdy, "Cracks in the System: Twenty Years of Unjust Federal Crack Cocaine Law" (New York: American Civil Liberties Union, 2006).

113. *Anti-Drug Abuse Act of 1988,* 42 U.S.C. 1437d(1)(5) (1990).

114. Ibid.

115. *Housing Opportunity Program Extensions (Hope) Act*, P.L. 104-130, 110 Stat. 834 (1996).

116. *Quality Housing and Work Responsibility Act*, P.L. 105-276, Title V (1998).

117. William J. Clinton, "Address before a Joint Session of the Congress on the State of the Union," http://www.presidency.ucsb.edu/ws/?pid=53091#axzz1iiQrVHuF, accessed December 29, 2011.

118. John F. Harris, "Clinton Links Housing Aid to Eviction of Crime Suspects," *Washington Post,* March 29, 1996, A14.

119. *Rucker v. Davis*, 237 F.3d 1113 (2001).

120. Ibid. It is estimated that at least 10 percent of those leaving prison end up homeless. See Caterina Gouvis Roman and Jeremy Travis, "Taking Stock: Housing, Homelessness, and Prisoner Reentry" (Washington, DC: Urban Institute, 2004).

121. Anonymous, *Department of Housing and Urban Development v. Rucker*, 535 U.S. 125 (2002).

122. Ibid.

123. Rubinstein and Mukamal, "Welfare and Housing: Denial of Benefits to Drug Offenders."

124. Ibid., 48.

125. Martin Carcasson, "Ending Welfare as We Know It: President Clinton and the Rhetorical Transformation of the Anti-Welfare Culture," *Rhetoric & Public Affairs,* 9/4 (2006), 655–92.

126. Rubinstein and Mukamal, "Welfare and Housing: Denial of Benefits to Drug Offenders."

127. Legal Action Center, "After Prison: Roadblocks to Reentry; A Report on State Legal Barriers Facing People with Criminal Records."

128. For an excellent review of the early impact of the welfare ban on women (including those who are mothers with dependent children) see Patricia Allard, "Life Sentences: Denying Welfare Benefits to Women Convicted of Drug Offenses" (Washington, DC: Sentencing Project, 2002).

129. Joan Petersilia, "From Cell to Society," in Jeremy Travis and Christy Visher (eds.), *Prisoner Reentry and Crime in America* (New York: Cambridge University Press, 2005), 15–49.

130. *Adoption and Safe Families Act*, P.L. 105-89 (1997).

131. Sarah Schirmer, Ashley Nellis, and Marc Mauer, "Incarcerated Parents and Their Children: Trends, 1991–2007" (Washington, DC: Sentencing Project, 2009).

132. Christopher J. Mumola, "Incarcerated Parents and Their Children" (Washington, DC: Bureau of Justice Statistics, 2000).

133. Ibid.

134. Schirmer, Nellis, and Mauer, "Incarcerated Parents and Their Children: Trends, 1991–2007," at 1.

135. For a comprehensive review of other policies affecting parental rights, see Thompson, *Releasing Prisoners, Redeeming Communities: Reentry, Race, and Politics.*.

136. Jeremy Travis, "Invisible Punishment: An Instrument of Social Exclusion," in Marc Mauer and Meda Chesney-Lind (eds.), *Invisible Punishment: The Collateral Consequences of Mass Imprisonment* (New York: New Press, 2002), 15–362002, at 32.

137. Schirmer, Nellis, and Mauer, "Incarcerated Parents and Their Children: Trends, 1991–2007."

138. See Thompson, *Releasing Prisoners, Redeeming Communities: Reentry, Race, and Politics*, 49.

NOTES TO CHAPTER 5

1. In the introduction to their edited collection examining the costs and benefits of mass imprisonment, Raphael and Stoll (2009) recently noted that "the increase in the imprisoned as well as the growth in ex-offenders represents a policy experiment of sorts, in that it reflects both a break with the past as well as a consequence of public choice" (11). Steven Raphael and Michael A. Stoll (eds.), *Do Prisons Make Us Safer? The Benefits and Costs of the Prison Boom* (Washington, DC: Russell Sage Foundation, 2009). See also Kevin Reitz, "Don't Blame Determinacy: U.S. Incarceration Growth Has Been Driven by Other Forces," *Texas Law Review*, 84 (2006), 1784–802. Marie Gottschalk, *The Prison and the Gallows: The Politics of Mass Incarceration in America* (New York: Cambridge University Press, 2006), xiii, 451, Glenn C. Loury, *Race, Incarceration, and American Values* (Cambridge, MA: MIT Press, 2008), Glenn C. Loury, "Crime, Inequality, and Social Justice," *Daedalus*, 139/3 (2010), 134–40.

2. As leading conservative criminologist and political scientist James Q. Wilson noted in a widely read article published in *Atlantic Monthly* in the early 1980s,

    The average citizen hardly needs to be persuaded that crimes will be committed more frequently if, other things being equal, crime becomes more profitable than other ways of spending one's time. Accordingly, the average citizen thinks it obvious that one major reason why crime has increased is that people have discovered they can get away with it. By the same token, a good way to reduce crime is to make its consequences to the would-be offender more costly (by making penalties swifter, more certain, or more severe), or to make alternatives to crime more attractive (by increasing the availability and pay of legitimate jobs), or both. These citizens may be surprised to learn that social scientists who study crime are deeply divided over the correctness of such views.

    James Q. Wilson, "Thinking about Crime: The Debate over Deterrence," *Atlantic Monthly*, 252/3 (1983): 72–88.

3. See also Vanessa Barker, *The Politics of Imprisonment: How the Democratic Process Shapes the Way America Punishes Offenders* (New York: Oxford University Press, 2009).

4. Jonathan Simon, *Governing through Crime: How the War on Crime Transformed American Democracy and Created a Culture of Fear* (Studies in Crime and Public Policy) (New York: Oxford University Press, 2007), viii, 330.

5. Marvin Frankl, *Criminal Sentences: Law without Order* (New York: Hill and Wang, 1974).

6. American Friends Service Committee, *Struggle for Justice: A Report on Crime and Punishment in America* (New York: Farrar, Straus & Giroux, 1971).

7. It is important to note that there is no single felony sentencing authority in the United States; each state has its own laws, as does the federal government—a total of fifty-one different statutory practices. To discuss them all as fitting a single storyline can be inherently misleading. Even so—and with considerable differences in the structure of sentencing codes—the story line in the United States is a consistent pattern of change within these widely different sentencing structures.

8. Michael Tonry, *Sentencing Matters* (New York: Oxford University Press, 1996).

9. Nancy Merritt, Terry Fain, and Susan Turner, "Oregon's Get-Tough Sentencing Reform: A Lesson in Justice System Adaptation," *Criminology & Public Policy,* 5/1 (2006), 5–36.

10. United States Sentencing Commission, "Special Report to the Congress: Mandatory Minimum Penalties in the Federal Criminal Justice System" (Washington, DC: United States Sentencing Commission, 1991).

11. Tonry, *Sentencing Matters.*

12. Michael Tonry, "Punishment Policies and Patterns in Western Countries," in Michael Tonry and Richard S. Frase (eds.), *Sentencing and Sanctions in Western Countries* (New York: Oxford University Press, 2001), 3–28, at 21.

13. Deborah J. Vagins and Jesselyn Mccurdy, "Cracks in the System: Twenty Years of Unjust Federal Crack Cocaine Law" (New York: American Civil Liberties Union, 2006).

14. Steven Donziger (ed.), *The Real War on Crime: The Report of the National Criminal Justice Commission* (New York: Harper Perrenial, 1996).

15. Kara Gotsch, "Breakthrough in U.S. Drug Sentencing Reform: The Fair Sentencing Act and the Unfinished Reform Agenda" (Washington, DC: Washington Office on Latin America, 2011).

16. Tonry, "Punishment Policies and Patterns in Western Countries," at 6.

17. In Massachusetts, mandatory minimum sentences for drug offenses have resulted in an increasing number of max-outs (where offenders serve every day of their sentence and leave with no further supervision). As reported by the Urban Institute in its report on prisoner reentry in Massachusetts,

    in conjunction with the imposition of mandatory minimum terms for specific (largely drug) offenses, judges increasingly imposed sentences with a one-day difference between the minimum and maximum terms (i.e., 5 years to 5 years and one day). As a result, a greater proportion of offenders are virtually ineligible for parole consideration and "wrapping up" their sentences. In 2003, more than 43 percent of prison sentences had a one-day difference between the minimum and maximum terms.

See page 16 in Lisa E. Brooks et al., "Prisoner Reentry in Massachusetts" (Washington, DC: Urban Institute, 2005).

18. See chapter 21 in Todd R. Clear, George F. Cole, and Michael D. Reisig, *American Corrections* (9th edition Belmont, CA: Wadsworth, 2010).

19. Edwin Zedlewski, "Making Confinement Decisions: Research in Brief" (Washington, DC: U.S. Department of Justice, 1987).

20. Peter Greenwood and Allan Abrahamse, "Selective Incapacitation" (Santa Monica, CA: RAND, 1982).

21. Kathleen Auerhahn, *Selective Incapacitation and Public Policy: Evaluating California's Imprisonment Crisis* (Albany: State University of New York Press, 2003), Franklin E. Zimring and Gordon Hawkins, "The New Mathematics of Imprisonment," *Crime & Delinquency,* 34/4 (1988), 425–36.

22. Franklin E. Zimring and Gordon Hawkins, *Incapacitation: Penal Confinement and the Restraint of Crime* (Studies in Crime and Public Policy) (New York: Oxford University Press, 1995), ix, 188.

23. Robert DeFina and Lance Hannon, "For Incapacitation, There Is No Time Like the Present: The Lagged Effects of Prisoner Reentry on Property and Violent Crime Rates," *Social Science Research,* 39 (2010), 1004–1014.

24. Franklin E. Zimring, Gordon Hawkins, and Sam Kamin, *Punishment and Democracy: Three-Strikes and You're Out in California* (Studies in Crime and Public Policy) (New York: Oxford University Press, 2001), xi, 244.

25. Morgan O. Reynolds, "Punishment Up, Crime Down," http://heartland.org/policy-documents/punishment-crime-down, accessed December 28, 2011.

26. Daniel S. Nagin, "Criminal Deterrence Research at the Outset of the Twenty-First Century," *Crime and Justice,* 23 (1998), 1–42, Daniel S. Nagin and Greg Pogarsky, "Integrating Celerity, Impulsivity, and Extralegal Sanction Threats into a Model of General Deterrence: Theory and Evidence," *Criminology,* 39/4 (2001), 865–91.

27. Gary Kleck et al., "The Missing Link in General Deterrence Research," *Criminology,* 43/3 (2005), 623–60, Thomas A. Loughran et al., "On Ambiguity in Perceptions of Risk: Implications for Criminal Decision Making and Deterrence," *Criminology,* 49/4 (2011), 1029–61, Raymond Paternoster, "Decisions to Participate in and Desist from Four Types of Common Delinquency: Deterrence and the Rational Choice Perspective," *Law & Society Review,* 23/1 (1989), 7–40.

28. Alfred Blumstein, Jacqueline Cohen, and Daniel S. Nagin (eds.), *Deterrence and Incapacitation: Estimating the Effects of Criminal Sanctions on Crime Rates.* (Washington, DC: National Academy of Sciences, 1978).

29. Albert J. Reiss and Jeffrey A. Roth (eds.), *Understanding and Preventing Violence: Panel on the Understanding and Control of Violent Behavior* (Washington, DC: National Academy of Sciences, 1993).

30. Angela Hawken and Mark A. R. Kleiman, "Managing-Drug Involved Probation-
ers with Swift and Certain Sanctions: Evaluating Hawaii's Hope" (Washington,
DC: National Institute of Justice, 2009), Mark A. R. Kleiman, *When Brute Force
Fails: How to Have Less Crime and Less Punishment* (Princeton, NJ: Princeton
University Press, 2009).

31. Hawken and Kleiman, "Managing Drug-Involved Probationers with Swift and
Certain Sanctions: Evaluating Hawaii's Hope."

32. Francis T. Cullen et al., "Nothing Works Revisited: Deconstructing Farabee's
Rethinking Rehabilitation," *Victims & Offenders*, 4/2 (2009), 101–23.

33. Mark A. R. Kleiman, "Toward Fewer Prisoners and Less Crime," *Daedalus*, 139/3
(2010), 115–23.

34. Mark A. R. Kleiman, "Justice Reinvestment in Community Supervision," *Criminology & Public Policy*, 10/3 (2011), 651–59.

35. Edward J. Latessa, "The Challenge of Change: Correctional Programs and
Evidence-Based Practices," *Criminology and Public Policy*, 3/4 (2004), 547–60.

36. Though see David Farabee's critique of rehabilitation and the treatment camp's
response to that critique. David Farabee, *Rethinking Rehabilitation: Why Can't We
Reform Our Criminals* (Washington, DC: AEI Press, 2005). Cullen et al., "Nothing
Works Revisited: Deconstructing Farabee's *Rethinking Rehabilitation*."

37. John Hagan and Ronit Dinovitzer, "Collateral Consequences of Imprisonment
for Children, Communities, and Prisoners," in Michael Tonry and Joan Petersilia
(eds.), *Prisons* (Chicago: University of Chicago Press, 1999), 121–62, Marc Mauer
and Meda Chesney-Lind (eds.), *Invisible Punishment: The Collateral Consequences
of Mass Imprisonment* (New York: New Press, 2003), x, 355.

38. Gwen Rubinstein and Debbie Mukamal, "Welfare and Housing: Denial of Benefits
to Drug Offenders," in Marc Mauer and Meda Chesney-Lind (eds.), *Invisible
Punishment: The Collateral Consequences of Mass Imprisonment* (New York: New
Press, 2003).2003

39. Michael Pinard, "Reflections and Perspectives on Reentry and Collateral
Consequences," *Journal of Criminal Law & Criminology*, 100/3 (Summer 2010),
1213–24, Kelly M. Socia, "The Policy Implications of Residence Restrictions on
Sex Offender Housing in Upstate NY," *Criminology & Public Policy*, 10/2 (2011),
351–89.

40. New York State Bar Association, "Reentry and Reintegration: The Road to Public
Safety" (Albany, NY, 2006).

41. Susan Herman, *Parallel Justice for Victims of Crime* (Washington, DC: National
Center for Victims of Crime, 2010).

42. For a comprehensive review of arguments for and against a restorative justice
framework, see John Braithwaite, "Restorative Justice: Assessing Optimistic and
Pessimistic Accounts," *Crime and Justice*, 25 (1999), 1–127.

43. Nagin and Pogarsky, "Integrating Celerity, Impulsivity, and Extralegal Sanction
Threats into a Model of General Deterrence: Theory and Evidence," Daniel S.

Nagin and Greg Pogarsky, "An Experimental Investigation of Deterrence: Cheating, Self-Servicing Bias, and Impulsivity," *Criminology,* 41/1 (2003), 167–93.

44. Kathleen Auerhahn, "Selective Incapacitation and the Problem of Prediction," *Criminology,* 37/4 (1999), 703–34, Auerhahn, *Selective Incapacitation and Public Policy: Evaluating California's Imprisonment Crisis,* D. Gottfredson Stephen and M. Don Gottfredson, *Classification, Prediction, and Criminal Justice Policy: Final Report to the National Institute of Justice* (Washington, DC: National Institute of Justice, 1990).

45. Ralph B. Taylor, *Breaking Away from Broken Windows: Baltimore Neighborhoods and the Nationwide Fight against Crime, Grime, Fear, and Decline* (Boulder, CO: Westview, 2000).

46. Susan Turner, Joan Petersilia, and Elizabeth Piper Deschenes, "Evaluating Intensive Supervision Probation/Parole (ISP) for Drug Offenders," *Crime & Delinquency,* 38/4 (October 1, 1992), 539–56.

47. Loic Wacquant, "The Great Penal Leap Backward: Incaceration in America from Nixon to Clinton," in John Pratt et al. (eds.), *The New Punitiveness: Trends, Theories, Perspectives* (Portland, OR: Willan, 2005), 3–26, Loic Wacquant, *Prisons of Poverty* (Minneapolis: University of Minnesota Press, 2009), Loic Wacquant, *Punishing the Poor: The Neoliberal Government of Social Insecurity* (Durham, NC: Duke University Press, 2009).

48. Katherine Beckett and Bruce Western, "Governing Social Marginality: Welfare, Incarceration, and the Transformation of State Policy," *Punishment & Society,* 3/1 (2001), 43–59, Katherine Beckett and Steve Herbert, *Banished: The New Social Control in Urban America* (New York: Oxford University Press, 2010), David Garland, *Punishment and Welfare: A History of Penal Strategies* (Brookfield, VT: Gower, 1985), x, 297, Gottschalk, *The Prison and the Gallows: The Politics of Mass Incarceration in America,* Jonathan Simon, *Poor Discipline: Parole and the Social Control of the Underclass, 1890–1990* (Studies in Crime and Justice) (Chicago: University of Chicago Press, 1993), x, 286, Jonathan Simon, "Clearing the 'Troubled Assets' of America's Punishment Bubble," *Daedalus,* 139/3 (2010), 91–101, Bruce Western and Becky Pettit, "Black-White Wage Inequality, Employment Rates, and Incarceration," *American Journal of Sociology,* 111/2 (2005), 553–78, Bruce Western, *Punishment and Inequality in America* (New York: Russell Sage Foundation, 2006), Bruce Western, "Mass Imprisonment and Economic Inequality," *Social Research: An International Quarterly of the Social Sciences,* 74/2 (2007), 509–32, Bruce Western and Becky Pettit, "Incarceration and Social Inequality," *Daedalus,* 139/3 (2010), 8–19.

49. Wacquant, *Punishing the Poor: The Neoliberal Government of Social Insecurity.*

50. Lisa Miller, *The Perils of Federalism: Race, Poverty, and the Politics of Crime Control.* (New York: Oxford University Press, 2008), Wacquant, *Prisons of Poverty.*

51. Loic Wacquant, *Urban Outcasts: A Comparative Sociology of Advanced Marginality* (Malden, MA: Polity, 2007).

52. Wacquant, *Prisons of Poverty.*

53. Simon, *Poor Discipline: Parole and the Social Control of the Underclass, 1890–1990.*

54. Ted Gest, *Crime and Politics: Big Government's Erratic Campaign for Law and Order* (New York: Oxford University Press, 2001).

55. Loïc Wacquant, "Class, Race, and Hyperincarceration in Revanchist America," *Daedalus,* 139/3 (Summer 2010), 74–90, at 74.

56. Simon, *Governing through Crime: How the War on Crime Transformed American Democracy and Created a Culture of Fear.*

57. William Julius Wilson, *When Work Disappears: The World of the New Urban Poor* (New York: Random House, 1996).

58. Jonathan P. Caulkins and Peter Reuter, "Illicit Drug Markets and Economic Irregularities," *Socio-Economic Planning Sciences,* 40/1 (2006), 1–14, Mark A. R. Kleiman, "The Problem of Replacement and the Logic of Drug Law Enforcement," *Drug Policy Analysis Bulletin* (1997), Mark A. R. Kleiman, "Toward Practical Drug Control Policies," *Social Research,* 68/3 (Fall 2001), 884–90.

59. Michael Tonry, *Malign Neglect: Race, Crime, and Punishment in America* (New York: Oxford University Press, 1995), xii, 233.

60. Bruce Western and Katherine Beckett, "How Unregulated Is the U.S. Labor Market? The Penal System as a Labor Market Institution," *American Journal of Sociology,* 104/4 (1999), 1030–60.

61. Ibid., table 4, p. 1041.

62. Richard Freeman, "Is the New Income Inequality the Achilles Heel of the American Economy?" in James A. Auerbach and Richard S. Belous (eds.), *The Inequality Paradox: Growth of Income Disparity* (Washington, DC: National Policy Association, 1998), 219–29.

63. Michael Tonry, *Thinking about Crime: Sense and Sensibility in American Penal Culture* (Studies in Crime and Public Policy) (New York: Oxford University Press, 2004), x, 260.

64. Alfred Blumstein and Joel Wallman (eds.), *The Crime Drop in America* (New York: Cambridge University Press, 2000), Franklin E. Zimring, *The Great American Crime Decline* (Studies in Crime and Public Policy) (New York: Oxford University Press, 2007), xiv, 258.

65. John Irwin, *The Warehouse Prison: Disposal of the New Dangerous Class* (Los Angeles: Roxbury, 2005), xii, 318.

NOTES TO CHAPTER 6

1. "Social Experiments," *Saturday Evening Post,* August 10, 1935, 22.

2. Michael Tonry, *Thinking about Crime: Sense and Sensibility in American Penal Culture* (Studies in Crime and Public Policy) (New York: Oxford University Press, 2004), x, 260.

3. Alfred Blumstein and Allen J. Beck, "Population Growth in U.S. Prisons, 1980–1996," in Michael Tonry and Joan Petersilia (eds.), *Prisons* (Chicago: University of Chicago Press, 1999), 17–61, David H. Greenberg and Valerie West, "State Prison

Populations and Their Growth, 1971–1991," *Criminology,* 39/3 (2001), 615–54, Marc Mauer, "The Causes and Consequences of Prison Growth in the USA," *Punishment & Society,* 3/1 (2001), 9–20.

4. Todd R. Clear, *Imprisoning Communities: How Mass Incarceration Makes Disadvantaged Neighborhoods Worse* (New York: Oxford University Press, 2007).

5. Franklin E. Zimring, The Great American Crime Decline (Studies in Crime and Public Policy) (New York: Oxford University Press, 2007), xiv, 258.

6. "Social Experiments."

7. Don Stemen, "Reconsidering Incarceration: New Directions for Reducing Crime" (New York: VERA Institute of Justice, 2007).

8. Steven Levitt, "The Effect of Prison Population Size on Crime Rates: Evidence from Prison Over-Crowding Litigation," *Quarterly Journal of Economics,* 111 (1996), 319–51, William Spelman, "The Limited Importance of Prison Expansion," in Alfred Blumstein and Joel Wallman (eds.), *The Crime Drop in America* (New York: Cambridge University Press, 2000), 97–129, William Spelman, "What Recent Studies Do (and Don't) Tell Us about Imprisonment and Crime," in Michael Tonry (ed.), *Crime and Justice: A Review of Research,* vol. 27 (Chicago: University of Chicago Press, 2000), 419–94.

9. Stemen, "Reconsidering Incarceration: New Directions for Reducing Crime."

10. Bruce Western, *Punishment and Inequality in America* (New York: Russell Sage Foundation, 2006), 191.

11. Shawn D. Bushway and Raymond Paternoster, "The Impact of Prison on Crime," in Steven Raphael and Michael A. Stoll (eds.), *Do Prisons Make Us Safer? The Benefits and Costs of the Prison Boom* (New York: Russell Sage Foundation, 2009), 119–50, John J. Donohue III, "Assessing the Relative Benefits of Incarceration: Overall Changes and the Benefits on the Margin," in Steven Raphael and Michael A. Stoll (eds.), *Do Prisons Make Us Safer? The Benefits and Costs of the Prison Boom* (New York: Russell Sage Foundation, 2009), 269–341.

12. Robert DeFina and Thomas M. Arvanites, "The Weak Effect of Imprisonment on Crime: 1971–1998," *Social Science Quarterly,* 83/3 (2002), 635–53, Spelman, "The Limited Importance of Prison Expansion," Western, *Punishment and Inequality in America.*

13. John J. DiIulio Jr. and Anne Morrison Piehl, "Does Prison Pay? The Stormy National Debate over the Cost-Effectiveness of Imprisonment," *Brookings Review* (1991), 28–35, John J. DiIulio, Jr. and Anne Morrison Piehl, "Does Prison Pay? Revisited," *Brookings Review,* 13/1 (1995), 20–26, Anne Morrison Piehl, Bert Useem, and John J. DiIulio Jr., *Right-Sizing Justice: A Cost-Benefit Analysis of Imprisonment in Three States* (New York: Manhattan Institute, 1999).

14. Raymond V. Liedka, Anne Morrison Piehl, and Bert Useem, "The Crime Control Effects of Incarceration: Does Scale Matter?" *Criminology & Public Policy,* 5/2 (2006), 245–76. Diminishing returns means that as incarceration increases beyond a certain point, adding additional prisoners to the incarcerated

population will have less and less of a crime-reducing effect. See Spelman, "The Limited Importance of Prison Expansion," Spelman, "What Recent Studies Do (and Don't) Tell Us about Imprisonment and Crime."

15. Liedka, Piehl, and Useem, "The Crime Control Effects of Incarceration: Does Scale Matter?" 272.

16. Todd R. Clear, "Backfire: When Incarceration Increases Crime," *Journal of the Oklahoma Criminal Justice Research Consortium*, 3 (1996), 1–10, Todd R. Clear et al., "Coercive Mobility and Crime: A Preliminary Examination of Concentrated Incarceration and Social Disorganization," *Justice Quarterly*, 20/1 (2003), 33–64, Robert DeFina and Lance Hannon, "For Incapacitation, There Is No Time Like the Present: The Lagged Effects of Prisoner Reentry on Property and Violent Crime Rates," *Social Science Research*, 39 (2010), 1004–14, Natasha A. Frost and Todd R. Clear, "Coercive Mobility," in Francis T. Cullen and Pamela Wilcox (eds.), *Oxford Handbook of Criminological Theory* (New York: Oxford University Press, 2012), 691–708, Natasha A. Frost and Laura A. Gross, "Coercive Mobility and the Impact of Prison Cycling on Crime," *Crime, Law, and Social Change*, 57/5 (2012), 459–74, Dina Rose and Todd R. Clear, "Incarceration, Social Capital, and Crime: Implications for Social Disorganization Theory," *Criminology*, 36 (1998), 441–80.

17. Tom Smith, "Trends in National Spending Priorities, 1973–2006" (Chicago: University of Chicago, National Opinion Research Center, 2007).

18. Ibid.

19. Ibid.

20. Paul Guerino, Paige M. Harrison, and William J. Sabol, "Prisoners in 2010" (Washington, DC: Bureau of Justice Statistics, 2011).

21. Alex Lichtenstein, "The Private and the Public in Penal History," *Punishment & Society*, 3/1 (2001), 189–96.

22. Kevin Reitz, "Don't Blame Determinacy: U.S. Incarceration Growth Has Been Driven by Other Forces," *Texas Law Review*, 84 (2006), 1784–802. See figure 2 at p. 1791.

23. Steven Donziger (ed.), *The Real War on Crime: The Report of the National Criminal Justice Commission* (New York: Harper Perennial, 1996), Marc Mauer, *Race to Incarcerate* (revised and updated second edition New York: New Press, 2006), xv, 240, Michael Tonry, *Malign Neglect: Race, Crime, and Punishment in America* (New York: Oxford University Press, 1995), xii, 233.

24. Alfred Blumstein, "On the Racial Disproportionality of United States' Prison Populations," *Journal of Criminal Law and Criminology*, 73 (1982), 1259–81, Alfred Blumstein, "Racial Disproportionality of U.S. Prison Populations Revisited," *University of Colorado Law Review*, 64 (1993), 743–60, Patrick A. Langan, "Racism on Trial: New Evidence to Explain the Racial Composition of Prisons in the United States," *Journal of Criminal Law and Criminology*, 76 (1985), 666–83.

25. Tonry, *Malign Neglect: Race, Crime, and Punishment in America*, 4.

26. Western, *Punishment and Inequality in America*.

27. Clear, *Imprisoning Communities: How Mass Incarceration Makes Disadvantaged Neighborhoods Worse.*
28. Stemen, "Reconsidering Incarceration: New Directions for Reducing Crime."
29. Michael Jacobson, *Downsizing Prisons: How to Reduce Crime and End Mass Incarceration* (New York: New York University Press, 2005).
30. Ibid.
31. M. Douglas Anglin et al., "Criminal Justice Treatment Admissions for Methamphetamine Use in California: A Focus on Proposition 36," *Journal of Psychoactive Drugs*, Supplement 4 (2007), 367–81, Douglas Longshore, Angela Hawken, and Darren Urada, "Sacpa Cost-Analysis Report" (Los Angeles: UCLA Integrated Substance Abuse Programs, 2006).
32. Michael Tonry, "Criminology, Mandatory Minimums, and Public Policy," *Criminology & Public Policy*, 5/1 (2006), 45–56.
33. Franklin E. Zimring, Gordon Hawkins, and Sam Kamin, *Punishment and Democracy: Three-Strikes and You're Out in California* (Studies in Crime and Public Policy) (New York: Oxford University Press, 2001), xi, 244.
34. Peter Greenwood et al., "Estimated Benefits and Costs of California's New Mandatory-Sentencing Law," in David Schicor and Dale K. Sechrest (eds.), *Three Strikes and You're Out: Vengeance as Public Policy* (Thousand Oaks, CA: Sage, 1996), 53–90, Public Safety Performance Project, "Public Safety, Public Spending: Forecasting America's Prison Population, 2007–2011" (Washington, DC: Pew Charitable Trusts, 2007).
35. Nancy Merritt, Terry Fain, and Susan Turner, "Oregon's Get-Tough Sentencing Reform: A Lesson in Justice System Adaptation," *Criminology & Public Policy*, 5/1 (2006), 5–36, Tonry, "Criminology, Mandatory Minimums, and Public Policy."
36. Zimring, Hawkins, and Kamin, *Punishment and Democracy: Three-Strikes and You're Out in California.*
37. Natasha A. Frost, "Mandatory Minimum Sentencing," *Criminology & Public Policy*, 5/1 (2006), 1–4.
38. Mary Patillo, David F. Weiman, and Bruce Western (eds.), *Imprisoning America: The Social Effects of Mass Incarceration* (New York: Russell Sage Foundation, 2004).
39. Donald Braman, *Doing Time on the Outside: Incarceration and Family Life in America* (Ann Arbor: University of Michigan Press, 2004). Clear, *Imprisoning Communities: How Mass Incarceration Makes Disadvantaged Neighborhoods Worse.*
40. William J. Sabol and James P. Lynch, "Assessing the Longer-Run Effects of Incarceration: Impact on Families and Employment," in Darnell Hawkins, Samuel Myers Jr., and Randolph Stine (eds.), *Crime Control and Social Justice: The Delicate Balance* (Westport, CT: Greenwood, 2003).
41. Eric Cadora, "Structural Racism and Neighborhood Incarceration," Presentation to the Aspen Roundtable on Mass Incarceration (Aspen, Colorado, 2007).

42. See for example Paul Gendreau, Claire Goggin, and Francis T. Cullen, "The Effects of Prison Sentences on Recidivism" (Ottawa: Public Works and Services of Canada, 1999), Alison Liebling and Shadd Maruna (eds.), *The Effects of Imprisonment* (Cullumpton, UK: Willan, 2006).

43. Devah Pager, *Marked: Race, Crime, and Finding Work in an Era of Mass Incarceration* (Chicago: University of Chicago Press, 2007).

44. Western, *Punishment and Inequality in America*, 120. See also Bruce Western, Jeffrey R. Kling, and David F. Weiman, "The Labor Market Consequences of Incarceration," *Crime & Delinquency*, 47/3 (2001), 410–27. See also, Harry J. Holzer, "Collateral Costs: Effects of Incarceration on Employment and Earnings among Young Workers," in Steven Raphael and Michael A. Stoll (eds.), *Do Prisons Make Us Safer? The Benefits and Costs of the Prison Boom* (New York: Russell Sage Foundation, 2009), 239–65.

45. Adam Thomas, "The Old Ball and Chain: Unlocking the Correlation between Incarceration and Marriage," unpublished manuscript (Cambridge, MA: Harvard University, 2005), Bruce Western, Leonard M. Lopoo, and Sara Mclanahan, "Incarceration and the Bonds between Parents in Fragile Families," in Mary Pattillo, David F. Weiman, and Bruce Western (eds.), *Imprisoning America: The Social Effects of Mass Incarceration* (New York: Russell Sage Foundation, 2004), 21–45.

46. Kathryn Edin, Timothy Nelson, and Rechelle Paranal, "Fatherhood and Incarceration as Potential Turning Points in the Criminal Careers of Unskilled Men," in Mary Patillo, David F. Weiman, and Bruce Western (eds.), *Imprisoning America: The Social Effects of Mass Incarceration* (New York: Russell Sage Foundation, 2004), 46–75.

47. James P. Lynch and William J. Sabol, "Assessing the Effects of Mass Incarceration on Informal Social Control in Communities," *Criminology & Public Policy*, 3/2 (2004), 267–94.

48. Joseph Murray, "The Effects of Imprisonment on the Families and Children of Prisoners," in Alison Liebling and Shadd Maruna (eds.), *The Effects of Imprisonment* (Cullompton, UK: Willan, 2005), 466.

49. Todd R. Clear, Dina Rose, and Judith Ryder, "Incarceration and the Community:The Problem of Removing and Returning Offenders," *Crime & Delinquency*, 47/3 (2001), 335–51.

50. David P. Farrington, Jeremy W. Coid, and Joseph Murray, "Family Factors in the Intergenerational Transmission of Offending," *Criminal Behaviour & Mental Health*, 19/2 (2009), 109–24, Joseph Murray and David Farrington, "The Effects of Parental Imprisonment on Children," *Crime and Justice*, 37 (2008), 133–206.

51. Dina Rose, Todd R. Clear, and Judith Ryder, "Drugs, Incarceration, and Neighborhood Life: The Impact of Reintegrating Offenders into the Community" (Washington, DC: National Institute of Justice, 2000), Dina R. Rose and Todd R. Clear, "Who Doesn't Know Someone in Jail? The Impact of Exposure to Prison

on Attitudes toward Informal and Formal Controls," *Prison Journal*, 84/2 (2004), 228–47.

52. Braman, *Doing Time on the Outside: Incarceration and Family Life in America*, Adrian Nicole Leblanc, *Random Family: Love, Drugs, Trouble, and Coming of Age in the Bronx* (New York: Scribners, 2004), Sudhir Alladi Venkatesh, *Off the Books: The Underground Economy of the Urban Poor* (Cambridge, MA: Harvard University Press, 2006).

53. For marriage: William A. Darity et al., *The Black Underclass: Critical Essays on Race and Unwantedness* (New York: Garland, 1994), Beth M. Huebner, "The Effect of Incarceration on Marriage and Work over the Life-Course," *Justice Quarterly*, 22/3 (2005), 281–303, Beth M. Huebner, "Racial and Ethnic Differences in the Likelihood of Marriage: The Effect of Incarceration," *Justice Quarterly*, 24/1 (2007), 156–83. For effects on children and families: Murray, "The Effects of Imprisonment on the Families and Children of Prisoners," Murray and Farrington, "The Effects of Parental Imprisonment on Children," Joseph Murray et al., "Parental Incarceration: Effects on Children's Antisocial Behaviour and Mental Health: A Systematic Review," *Campbell Systematic Reviews*, 4 (2009), Western, Lopoo, and Mclanahan, "Incarceration and the Bonds between Parents in Fragile Families."

54. Clifford Robe Shaw and Henry D. Mckay, *Juvenile Delinquency and Urban Areas* (Chicago: University of Chicago Press, 1942).

55. Jeffrey D. Morenoff, Robert J. Sampson, and Stephen W. Raudenbush, "Neighborhood Inequality, Collective Efficacy, and the Spatial Dynamics of Urban Violence," *Criminology*, 39/3 (2001), 517–58, Robert J. Sampson, Jeffrey D. Morenoff, and Thomas Gannon-Rowley, "Assessing Neighborhood Effects: Social Processes and New Directions in Research," *Annual Review of Sociology*, 28/1 (2002), 443–78, Robert J. Sampson and Charles Loeffler, "Punishment's Place: The Local Concentration of Mass Incarceration," *Daedalus*, 139/3 (2010), 20–31.

56. Lance Hannon and Robert DeFina, "Sowing the Seeds: How Adult Incarceration Promotes Juvenile Delinquency," *Law, Crime, and Social Change*, 57 (2012), 475–91, Ralph B. Taylor et al., "Short-Term Changes in Adult Arrest Rates Influence Later Short-Term Changes in Serious Male Delinquency Prevalence: A Time-Dependent Relationship," *Criminology*, 47/3 (2009), 657–97.

57. Andres F. Rengifo, "Neighborhood Effects and Informal Social Control: Examining the Role of Social Networks on the South Bronx" (City University of New York, 2007).

58. James C. Thomas and Lynne A. Sampson, "High Rates of Incarceration as a Social Force Associated with Community Rates of Sexually Transmitted Infection," *Journal of Infectious Diseases*, 191 (2005), S55–S60, James C. Thomas and Elizabeth Torrone, "Incarceration as Forced Migration: Effects on Selected Community Health Outcomes," *American Journal of Public Health*, 96/10 (2006), 1–5.

59. Robert DeFina and Lance Hannon, "The Impact of Mass Incarceration on Poverty," *Crime & Delinquency* (Online First), Feb. 12, 2009, http://cad.sagepub.com/

content/early/recent, Robert DeFina and Lance Hannon, "The Impact of Adult Incarceration on Child Poverty: A County-Level Analysis, 1995–2007," *Prison Journal*, 90/4 (2010), 377–96.

60. Todd R. Clear, "The Impacts of Incarceration on Public Safety," *Social Research: An International Quarterly of the Social Sciences*, 74/2 (2007), 613–30, Todd R. Clear, "The Effects of High Imprisonment Rates on Communities," *Crime and Justice*, 37 (2008), 97–132.

61. Jeffrey Fagan and Tracey L. Meares, "Punishment, Deterrence, and Social Control: The Paradox of Punishment in Minority Communities," *Ohio State Journal of Criminal Law*, 6 (2008), 173–229, James P. Lynch and William J. Sabol, "Assessing the Effects of Mass Incarceration on Informal Social Control in Communities," *Criminology & Public Policy*, 3/2 (2004), 267–94, James P. Lynch and William J. Sabol, "Effects of Incarceration on Informal Social Control in Communities," in *Imprisoning America: The Social Effects of Mass Incarceration*, ed. Mary Patillo, David F. Weiman, and Bruce Western (New York: Russell Sage Foundation, 2004), 135–64, Jeremy Travis, *But They All Come Back: Facing the Challenges of Prisoner Reentry* (Washington, DC: Urban Institute Press, 2005), xxvii, 391.

62. Analyzing data from Tallahassee, Florida, Todd Clear and colleagues found evidence of a "coercive mobility" effect, in which the reentry of people from prison had a positive linear effect on crime at the neighborhood level in the year they returned, while rates of removal (in the preceding year) had a curvilinear impact, driving up crime at the higher levels after a certain "tipping point." Clear et al., "Coercive Mobility and Crime: A Preliminary Examination of Concentrated Incarceration and Social Disorganization."

63. Western, *Punishment and Inequality in America*, 190.

64. Tonry, *Malign Neglect: Race, Crime, and Punishment in America*, Michael Tonry, *Punishing Race: A Continuing American Dilemma* (New York: Oxford University Press, 2011).

65. Michelle Alexander, *The New Jim Crow: Mass Incarceration in the Age of Colorblindness* (New York: New Press, 2010).

66. Ibid., 4.

67. Ibid., 180–81.

NOTES TO CHAPTER 7

1. Todd R. Clear and James Austin, "Reducing Mass Incarceration: Implications of the Iron Law of Prison Populations," *Harvard Law and Policy Review*, 3 (2009), 307–24.

2. Natasha A. Frost, "The Mismeasure of Punishment: Alternative Measures of Punitiveness and Their (Substantial) Consequences," *Punishment & Society*, 10/3 (2008), 277–300.

3. James Austin et al., *Unlocking America: Why and How to Reduce America's Prison Population* (Washington, DC: JFA Institute, 2007).

4. David Farabee, *Rethinking Rehabilitation: Why Can't We Reform Our Criminals* (Washington, DC: AEI Press, 2005), Douglas Marlowe, "When 'What Works' Never Did: Dodging the 'Scarlet M' in Correctional Rehabilitation," *Criminology & Public Policy*, 5/2 (2006), 339–46, James A. Wilson and Robert C. Davis, "Good Intentions Meet Hard Realities: An Evaluation of the Project Greenlight Reentry Program," *Criminology & Public Policy*, 5/2 (2006), 303–38.

5. Francis T. Cullen et al., "Nothing Works Revisited: Deconstructing Farabee's *Rethinking Rehabilitation*," *Victims & Offenders*, 4/2 (2009), 101–23, Christopher T. Lowenkamp and Edward J. Latessa, "Developing Successful Reentry Programs: Lessons Learned from the 'What Works' Research," *Corrections Today*, 67/2 (2005), 72–77, Christopher T. Lowenkamp, Edward J. Latessa, and Paula Smith, "Does Correctional Program Quality Really Matter? The Impact of Adhering to the Principles of Effective Intervention," *Criminology & Public Policy*, 5/3 (2006), 575–94, Christopher T. Lowenkamp, Edward J. Latessa, and Alexander M. Holsinger, "The Risk Principle in Action: What Have We Learned from 13,676 Offenders and 97 Correctional Programs?" *Crime & Delinquency*, 52/1 (2006), 77–93.

6. Joan Petersilia, "California's Correctional Paradox of Excess and Deprivation," *Crime and Justice*, 37 (2008), 207–78.

7. Faye S. Taxman, Matthew L. Perdoni, and Lana D. Harrison, "Drug Treatment Services for Adult Offenders: The State of the State," *Journal of Substance Abuse and Treatment*, 32/3 (2007), 239–54.

8. Todd R. Clear, *Imprisoning Communities: How Mass Incarceration Makes Disadvantaged Neighborhoods Worse* (New York: Oxford University Press, 2007).

9. James Austin and his colleagues have estimated that three policy changes (reducing length of stay, not returning parole violators to prison for technical violations, and keeping those who commit victimless crimes out of prison) would reduce incarceration rates by more than 50 percent. Austin et al., *Unlocking America: Why and How to Reduce America's Prison Population*. See also James Austin, "Making Imprisonment Unprofitable," *Criminology & Public Policy*, 10/3 (2011), 629–35, Alfred Blumstein, "Approaches to Reducing Both Imprisonment and Crime," *Criminology & Public Policy*, 10/1 (2011), 93–102, Alfred Blumstein, "Bringing Down the U.S. Prison Population," *Prison Journal*, 91/3 suppl. (September 1, 2011), 12S–26S, Todd R. Clear and Dennis Schrantz, "Strategies for Reducing Prison Populations," *Prison Journal*, 91/3 suppl. (September 1, 2011), 138S–59S, Steven N. Durlauf and Daniel S. Nagin, "Imprisonment and Crime: Can Both Be Reduced?" *Criminology & Public Policy*, 10/1 (2011), 13–54, Marie Gottschalk, "Money and Mass Incarceration: The Bad, the Mad, and Penal Reform," *Criminology & Public Policy*, 8/1 (2009), 97–109, Judith Greene and Marc Mauer, "Downscaling Prisons: Lessons from Four States" (Washington, DC: Sentencing Project, 2010), Karol Lucken, "Leaving Mass Incarceration," *Criminology & Public Policy*, 10/3 (2011), 707–14.

10. For a summary table, see table 1.3 on page 27–28, Natasha A. Frost, *The Punitive State: Crime, Punishment, and Imprisonment across the United States* (New York: LFB Scholarly Publications, 2006).

11. Don Stemen, Andres Rengifo, and James Wilson, "Of Fragmentation and Ferment: The Impact of State Sentencing Policies on Incarceration Rates, 1975–2002" (Washington, DC: Final Report to the U.S. Department of Justice, 2006).

12. Nancy Merritt, Terry Fain, and Susan Turner, "Oregon's Get-Tough Sentencing Reform: A Lesson in Justice System Adaptation," *Criminology & Public Policy*, 5/1 (2006), 5–36.

13. Michael Tonry, "Criminology, Mandatory Minimums, and Public Policy," *Criminology & Public Policy*, 5/1 (2006), 45–56.

14. United States Sentencing Commission, "Special Report to the Congress: Mandatory Minimum Penalties in the Federal Criminal Justice System" (Washington, DC: United States Sentencing Commission, 1991).

15. Ibid.

16. Joint Committee on New York Drug Law Evaluation, "The Nation's Toughest Drug Law: Evaluating the New York Experience" (Washington, DC: U.S. Department of Justice, LEAA, 1978).

17. James A. Beha II, "'And Nobody Can Get You Out': The Impact of a Mandatory Prison Sentence for the Illegal Carrying of a Firearm on the Use of Firearms and on the Administration of Criminal Justice in Boston," *Boston University Law Review*, 57 (1977), 96–146 and 289–333, Glenn L. Pierce and William J. Bowers, "The Bartley-Fox Gun Law's Short-Term Impact on Crime in Massachusetts," *Annals of the American Academy of Political and Social Science*, 455 (1981), 120–37.

18. Timothy Bynum, "Prosecutorial Discretion and the Implementation of a Legislative Mandate," in Merry Morash (ed.), *Implementing Criminal Justice Policies* (Beverly Hills, CA: Sage, 1982).

19. Merritt, Fain, and Turner, "Oregon's Get-Tough Sentencing Reform: A Lesson in Justice System Adaptation."

20. Michael Tonry, "Punishment Policies and Patterns in Western Countries," in Michael Tonry and Richard S. Frase (eds.), *Sentencing and Sanctions in Western Countries* (New York: Oxford University Press, 2001), 3–28, at 6.

21. Kevin R. Reitz, "The Disassembly and Reassembly of U.S. Sentencing Practices," in Michael Tonry and Richard S. Frase (eds.), *Sentencing and Sanctions in Western Countries* (New York: Oxford University Press, 2001), 222–58, Michael Tonry, *Sentencing Matters* (New York: Oxford University Press, 1996).

22. Tonry, "Punishment Policies and Patterns in Western Countries," 21.

23. Kara Gotsch, "Breakthrough in U.S. Drug Sentencing Reform: The Fair Sentencing Act and the Unfinished Reform Agenda" (Washington, DC: Washington Office on Latin America, 2011), Deborah J. Vagins and Jesselyn Mccurdy, "Cracks in the System: Twenty Years of Unjust Federal Crack Cocaine Law" (New York: American Civil Liberties Union, 2006).

24. John J. DiIulio Jr., "Against Mandatory Minimums: Drug Sentencing Run Amok," *National Review,* 51/9 (1999): 46–51, at 48.

25. Franklin E. Zimring, "Imprisonment Rates and the New Politics of Criminal Punishment," *Punishment & Society,* 3 (2001), 161–66, at 164.

26. Anthony M. Kennedy, "Speech at the American Bar Association Annual Meeting," August 9, 2003, available at http://www.americanbar.org/content/dam/aba/migrated/leadership/initiative/kennedyspeech.authcheckdam.pdf. The full text of Justice Kennedy's address can also be found online at www.november.org/stayinfo/breaking/Kennedyspeech.html, accessed December 29, 2011.

27. American Bar Association Justice Kennedy Commission, "Reports with Recommendations to the ABA House of Delegates" (Washington, DC: American Bar Association, 2004).

28. Ibid., iii.

29. Quoted in David P. Kopel, "Prison Blues: How America's Foolish Sentencing Policies Endanger Public Safety," *CATO Policy Analysis No. 208* (Washington, DC: Cato Institute, 1994).

30. Judith Greene, "Smart on Crime: Positive Trends in State-Level Sentencing and Correctional Policy" (Washington, DC: Families Against Mandatory Minimums, 2003).

31. Ibid.

32. Families Against Mandatory Minimums, "State Responses to Mandatory Minimum Laws" (Washington, DC: Families Against Mandatory Minumums, 2011).

33. American Bar Association Justice Kennedy Commission, "Reports with Recommendations to the ABA House of Delegates," Stemen, Rengifo, and Wilson, "Of Fragmentation and Ferment: The Impact of State Sentencing Policies on Incarceration Rates, 1975–2002."

34. "COMPAS" is the common acronym for Correctional Offender Management Profiling for Alternative Sanctions; "VASOR" is an acronym for the Vermont Assessment of Sex Offender Risk.

35. Pew Center on the States, "State of Recidivism: The Revolving Door of America's Prisons" (Washington, DC: Pew Charitable Trusts, 2011).

36. As a result of this downward trend, the accompanying reduction of new court commits coming into prison, and a reconfiguration of the way prisoners were housed, Michigan closed twenty-one prison facilities from 2002 to 2011. The estimated savings of these prison closings is about $333 million. Nicole D. Porter, "On the Chopping Block: State Prison Closings" (Washington, DC: Sentencing Project, 2011).

37. Angela Hawken and Mark A. R. Kleiman, "Managing Drug-Involved Probationers with Swift and Certain Sanctions: Evaluating Hawaii's Hope" (Washington, DC: National Institute of Justice, 2009).

38. Mark A. R. Kleiman, *When Brute Force Fails: How to Have Less Crime and Less Punishment* (Princeton, NJ: Princeton University Press, 2009).

39. Council of State Governments, "Justice Reinvestment: Connecticut," http://www. justicereinvestment.org/states/connecticut, accessed December 29, 2011.

40. Marshall Clement, Matthew Schwarzfeld, and Michael Thompson, "The National Summit on National Reinvestment and Public Safety: Addressing Recidivism, Crime, and Corrections Spending" (New York: Council of State Governments Justice Center, 2011).

41. Urban Institute, "Justice Reinvestment at the Local Level," http://www.urban.org/ center/jpc/justice-reinvestment, accessed December 9, 2011.

42. Clement, Schwarzfeld, and Thompson, "The National Summit on National Reinvestment and Public Safety: Addressing Recidivism, Crime, and Corrections Spending," Greene and Mauer, "Downscaling Prisons: Lessons from Four States."

43. Joan Petersilia, *When Prisoners Come Home: Parole and Prisoner Reentry* (New York: Oxford University Press, 2003), Anthony C. Thompson, *Releasing Prisoners, Redeeming Communities: Reentry, Race, and Politics* (New York: New York University Press, 2008), Jeremy Travis, *But They All Come Back: Facing the Challenges of Prisoner Reentry* (Washington, DC: Urban Institute Press, 2005), xxvii, 391. For a state-by-state report on collateral consequences, see Legal Action Center, "After Prison: Roadblocks to Reentry; A Report on State Legal Barriers Facing People with Criminal Records" (New York: Legal Action Center, 2004).

44. Susan Tucker and Eric Cadora, "Justice Reinvestment," *Ideas for an Open Society,* 13/3 (2003), 3.

45. Greene and Mauer, "Downscaling Prisons: Lessons from Four States," John Schmitt, Kris Warner, and Sarika Gupta, "The High Budgetary Cost of Incarceration" (Washington, DC: Center for Economic and Policy Research, 2010).

46. Roland V. Anglin, *Building the Organizations That Build Communities* (Washington, DC: Department of Housing and Urban Development, 2004).

47. Todd R. Clear, John R. Hamilton Jr., and Eric Cadora, *Community Justice* (second edition New York: Routledge, 2011), Clement, Schwarzfeld, and Thompson, "The National Summit on National Reinvestment and Public Safety: Addressing Recidivism, Crime, and Corrections Spending," Tucker and Cadora, "Justice Reinvestment," Urban Institute, "Justice Reinvestment at the Local Level."

48. Nancy G. La Vigne et al., "Justice Reinvestment at the Local Level: Planning and Implementation Guide" (Washington, DC: Urban Institute, 2010).

49. Nancy G. La Vigne, "Housing DC Code Felons Far Away from Home: Effects on Crime, Recidivism, and Reentry," *Testimony Before the House of Representatives Oversight and Government Reform Subcommittee on Federal Workforce, Postal Service, and the District of Columbia* (Washington, DC: Urban Institute, 2010).

50. Taxman, Perdoni, and Harrison, "Drug Treatment Services for Adult Offenders: The State of the State."

51. Tucker and Cadora, "Justice Reinvestment," 5.

52. Albert Hunter, "Private, Parochial, and Public Social Orders: The Problem of Crime and Incivility in Urban Communities," in Gerald Suttles and Mayer Zald

(eds.), *The Challenge of Social Control: Citizenship and Institution Building in Modern Society* (Norwood, NJ: Ablex, 1985), 230–42.

53. Edwin M. Lemert and Forrest Dill, *The Offender in the Community* (Lexington, MA: Lexington Books, 1978).

54. Todd R. Clear, George F. Cole, and Michael D. Reisig, *American Corrections* (ninth edition Belmont, CA: Wadsworth, 2010).

55. In severely overcrowded states such as California, the prospects for saving money on prison through justice reinvestment are meager. What justice reinvestment really means, in this context, is using community strategies to control the explosive growth in correctional costs. But experience shows that in every setting, calculations of "actual savings" are extremely difficult to nail down.

56. James Austin, Eric Cadora, Todd Clear, Vanita Gupta, Judith Greene, and Malcolm Young. (2013) Ending Mass Incarceration: Charting a New Justice Reinvestment. Washington, D.C.: JFA Institute.

57. Ram Subramanian and Rebecca Tublitz, "Realigning Justice Resources: A Review of Population and Spending Shifts in Prison and Community Corrections" (New York: VERA Institute of Justice, 2012).

58. Alaska, California, Connecticut, Delaware, Georgia, Hawaii, Illinois, Kansas, Maryland, Massachusetts, Michigan, Nevada, New Jersey, New York, Oklahoma, South Carolina, Texas, Utah, and Wisconsin have all reduced both prison populations and crime. See page 5 of Pew Center on the States, "State of Recidivism: The Revolving Door of America's Prisons."

59. We see concerns about the impacts of reducing prison populations voiced long before we actually see any of those potential impacts come to fruition. When a divided U.S. Supreme Court affirmed a lower federal court ruling mandating the reduction of prison populations in California earlier this year, Samuel Alito noted in his dissent that reducing prison populations to alleviate overcrowding was "gambling with the safety of the people of California." Bill Mears, "High Court Orders Drastic Prison Population Reduction in California," *CNN.com,* May 23, 2011.

60. Charles A. Murray, *Does Prison Work?* (London: Institute of Economic Affairs, 1997).

61. Michael Tonry, *Malign Neglect: Race, Crime, and Punishment in America* (New York: Oxford University Press, 1995), xii, 233, Tonry, *Sentencing Matters.*

62. William J. Bennett, John J. DiIulio Jr., and John P. Walters, *Body Count: Moral Poverty . . . and How to Win America's War against Crime and Drugs* (New York: Simon & Schuster, 1996), Peter Greenwood and Allan Abrahamse, "Selective Incapacitation" (Santa Monica, CA: RAND, 1982), Steven Levitt, "The Effect of Prison Population Size on Crime Rates: Evidence from Prison Over-Crowding Litigation," *Quarterly Journal of Economics,* 111 (1996), 319–51, James Q. Wilson, *Thinking about Crime* (New York: Random House, 1975), James Q. Wilson, "Thinking about Crime: The Debate over Deterrence," *Atlantic Monthly,* 252/3 (1983), 72–88.

63. Public Safety Performance Project, "Public Safety, Public Spending: Forecast-ing America's Prison Population, 2007–2011" (Washington, DC: Pew Charitable Trusts, 2007). The latest Bureau of Justice Statistics figures suggest that the prison population grew by just short of seventy thousand prisoners between 2005 and 2010. Lauren Glaze, "Correctional Populations in the United States, 2010" (Wash-ington, DC: Bureau of Justice Statistics, 2011).

64. Malcolm Young points out that the prison population decrease of just over nine thousand prisoners, while important symbolically, represents just "six tenths of one percent of the more than 1.6 million in state and federal custody. Malcolm C. Young, "Getting Prison Numbers Down—for Good," http://www.thecrimereport. org/news/inside-criminal-justice/2012-01-getting-prison-numbers-downfor-good, accessed January 6, 2012.

65. Thomas P. Bonczar, "Prevalence of Imprisonment in the U.S. Population, 1974–2001" (Washington, DC: Bureau of Justice Statistics, 2003).

REFERENCES

Abramovitz, Mimi. 2006. "Neither accidental, nor simply mean-spirited: The context for welfare reform." Pp. 23–37 in *The Promise of Welfare Reform: Political Rhetoric and the Reality of Poverty in the Twenty-First Century*, edited by Keith M. Kilty and Elizabeth A. Segal. Binghamton, NY: Haworth.

Adoption and Safe Families Act. 1997. Public Law 105-89.

Alexander, Michelle. 2010. *The New Jim Crow: Mass Incarceration in the Age of Colorblindness*. New York: New Press.

Allard, Patricia. 2002. "Life Sentences: Denying Welfare Benefits to Women Convicted of Drug Offenses." Washington, DC: Sentencing Project.

Altschuler, Albert W. 1991. "The failure of sentencing guidelines: A plea for less aggregation." *University of Chicago Law Review* 58:901–51.

American Bar Association Justice Kennedy Commission. 2004. "Reports with Recommendations to the ABA House of Delegates." Washington, DC: American Bar Association.

American Friends Service Committee. 1971. *Struggle for Justice: A Report on Crime and Punishment in America*. New York: Farrar, Straus & Giroux.

Anderson, Amy L., and Lisa L. Sample. 2008. "Public awareness and action resulting from sex offender community notification laws." *Criminal Justice Policy Review* 19(4):371–96.

Andrew, John A., II. 1968. *Lyndon Johnson and the Great Society*. Blue Ridge, PA: Dee.

Anglin, M. Douglas, Darren Urada, Mary-Lynn Brecht, Angela Hawken, Richard Rawson, and Douglas Longshore. 2007. "Criminal justice treatment admissions for methamphetamine use in California: A focus on Proposition 36." *Journal of Psychoactive Drugs* (Supplement 4):367–81.

Anglin, Roland V. 2004. *Building the Organizations That Build Communities*. Washington, DC: Department of Housing and Urban Development.

Anti-Drug Abuse Act of 1988. 1990. 42 U.S.C. 1437d(1)(5).

Audi, Tamara, and Gary Fields. 2010. "L.A. is latest city to see crime drop." *Wall Street Journal*, Jan. 8, A9.

Auerhahn, Kathleen. 1999. "Selective incapacitation and the problem of prediction." *Criminology* 37(4):703–34.

———. 2003. *Selective Incapacitation and Public Policy: Evaluating California's Imprisonment Crisis.* Albany: State University of New York Press.

Austin, James. 2011. "Making imprisonment unprofitable." *Criminology & Public Policy* 10(3):629–35.

James Austin, Eric Cadora, Todd Clear, Vanita Gupta, Judith Greene, and Malcolm Young. (2013) *Ending Mass Incarceration: Charting a New Justice Reinvestment.* Washington, D.C.: JFA Institute.

Austin, James, John Clark, Patricia Hardyman, and D. Alan Henry. The impact "Three Strikes and You're Out." *Punishment & Society* 1(2):131–62.

Austin, James, Todd R. Clear, Troy Duster, David F. Greenberg, John Irwin, Candace McCoy, Alan Mobley, Barbara Owen, and Joshua Page. 2007. *Unlocking America: Why and How to Reduce America's Prison Population.* Washington, DC: JFA Institute.

Barker, Vanessa. 2009. *The Politics of Imprisonment: How the Democratic Process Shapes the Way America Punishes Offenders.* New York: Oxford University Press.

Beckett, Katherine. 1997. *Making Crime Pay: Law and Order in Contemporary American Politics.* New York: Oxford University Press.

Beckett, Katherine, and Steve Herbert. 2010. *Banished: The New Social Control in Urban America.* New York: Oxford University Press.

Beckett, Katherine, and Bruce Western. 2001. "Governing social marginality: Welfare, incarceration, and the transformation of state policy." *Punishment & Society* 3(1):43–59.

Beha, James A., II. 1977. "'And nobody can get you out': The impact of a mandatory prison sentence for the illegal carrying of a firearm on the use of firearms and on the administration of criminal justice in Boston." *Boston University Law Review* 57:96–146 and 289–333.

Bennett, Brian. 2012. "Fact check: Romney says it's illegal to have automatic weapons." *Los Angeles Times,* Oct. 16.

Bennett, William J., John J. DiIulio Jr., and John P. Walters. 1996. *Body Count: Moral Poverty . . . and How to Win America's War against Crime and Drugs.* New York: Simon & Schuster.

Berliner, Lucy. 1996. "Community notification of sex offenders: A new tool or a false promise?" *Journal of Interpersonal Violence* 11(2):294–300.

Blumstein, Alfred. 1982. "On the racial disproportionality of United States' prison populations." *Journal of Criminal Law and Criminology* 73:1259–81.

———. 1993. "Racial disproportionality of U.S. prison populations revisited." *University of Colorado Law Review* 64:743–60.

———. 2011a. "Approaches to reducing both imprisonment and crime." *Criminology & Public Policy* 10(1):93–102.

———. 2011b. "Bringing down the U.S. prison population." *Prison Journal* 91(3 suppl):12S–26S.

Blumstein, Alfred, and Allen J. Beck. 1999. "Population growth in U.S. prisons, 1980–1996." Pp. 17–61 in *Prisons*, edited by Michael Tonry and Joan Petersilia. Chicago: University of Chicago Press.

———. 2005. "Reentry as a transient state between liberty and recommitment." Pp. 50–79 in *Prisoner Reentry and Crime in America*, edited by Jeremy Travis and Christy Visher. New York: Cambridge University Press.

Blumstein, Alfred, and Jacqueline Cohen. 1973. "A theory of the stability of punishment." *Journal of Criminal Law, Criminology, and Police Science* 63:198–207.

Blumstein, Alfred, Jacqueline Cohen, and Daniel Nagin. 1977. "The dynamics of a homeostatic punishment process." *Journal of Criminal Law and Criminology* 67:317–34.

Blumstein, Alfred, Jacqueline Cohen, and Daniel S. Nagin (Eds.). 1978. *Deterrence and Incapacitation: Estimating the Effects of Criminal Sanctions on Crime Rates*. Washington, DC: National Academy of Sciences.

Blumstein, Alfred, and S. Moitra. 1979. "An analysis of the time-series of the imprisonment rate in the states of the United States: A further test of the stability of punishment hypothesis." *Journal of Criminal Law and Criminology* 70:376–90.

Blumstein, Alfred, and Kiminori Nakamura. 2009. "Redemption in the presence of widespread criminal background checks." *Criminology* 47(2):327–60.

Blumstein, Alfred, and Joel Wallman (Eds.). 2000. *The Crime Drop in America*. New York: Cambridge University Press.

Bonczar, Thomas P. 2003. "Prevalence of Imprisonment in the U.S. Population, 1974–2001." Washington, DC: Bureau of Justice Statistics.

———. 2007a. "Table 1. State prison admissions, 2003: Offense, by type of admission." Washington, DC: Bureau of Justice Statistics.

———. 2007b. "Table 8. State prison releases, 2003: Time served in prison, by offense and release type." Washington, DC: Bureau of Justice Statistics.

Bontrager, Stephanie, William Bales, and Ted Chiricos. 2005. "Race, ethnicity, threat, and the labeling of convicted felons." *Criminology* 43(3):589–622.

Braithwaite, John. 1999. "Restorative justice: Assessing optimistic and pessimistic accounts." *Crime and Justice* 25:1–127.

Braman, Donald. 2004. *Doing Time on the Outside: Incarceration and Family Life in America*. Ann Arbor: University of Michigan Press.

Branch, Taylor. 1989. *Parting the Waters: America in the King Years, 1954–63*. New York: Simon & Schuster.

Brooks, Lisa E., Amy L. Solomon, Sinead Keegan, Rhianna Kohl, and Lori Lahue. 2005. "Prisoner Reentry in Massachusetts." Washington, DC: Urban Institute.

Brown v. Board of Education of Topeka, Kansas. 347 U.S. 483 (1954).

Brown, Michelle. 2009. *The Culture of Punishment: Prison, Society, and Spectacle*. New York: New York University Press.

Bureau of Justice Assistance. 1998. "1996 National Survey of State Sentencing Structures." Washington, DC: Government Printing Office.

Bureau of Justice Statistics. 2008. "Justice Expenditure and Employment Extracts."
    Washington, DC: U.S. Department of Justice.

Bushway, Shawn D., and Raymond Paternoster. 2009. "The impact of prison on crime."
    Pp. 119–50 in *Do Prisons Make Us Safer? The Benefits and Costs of the Prison Boom*,
    edited by Steven Raphael and Michael A. Stoll. New York: Russell Sage Foundation.

Bynum, Timothy. 1982. "Prosecutorial discretion and the implementation of a legisla-
    tive mandate." In *Implementing Criminal Justice Policies*, edited by Merry Morash.
    Beverly Hills, CA: Sage.

Cadora, Eric. 2007. "Structural racism and neighborhood incarceration." Presentation
    to the Aspen Roundtable on Mass Incarceration. Aspen, Colorado.

Caplan, Thomas. 2011. "Cuomo administration is closing 7 prisons: 2 are in the city."
    New York Times, July 1.

Carcasson, Martin. 2006. "Ending welfare as we know it: President Clinton and the rhetor-
    ical transformation of the anti-welfare culture." *Rhetoric & Public Affairs* 9(4):655–92.

Carter, Terry. 2012. "Prison break: Budget crises drive reform, but private jails press
    on." *ABA Journal* (October):44–51.

Caulkins, Jonathan P., and Peter Reuter. 2006. "Illicit drug markets and economic
    irregularities." *Socio-Economic Planning Sciences* 40(1):1–14.

Chambliss, William J. 2001. *Power, Politics, and Crime*. Boulder, CO: Westview.

Clark, John, James Austin, and D. Alan Henry. 1997. ""Three strikes and you're out":
    A review of state legislation." *National Institute of Justice, Research in Brief*, Sept.,
    https://www.ncjrs.gov/pdffiles/165369.pdf.

Clear, Todd R. 1996. "Backfire: When incarceration increases crime." *Journal of the
    Oklahoma Criminal Justice Research Consortium* 3:1–10.

———. 2002. "The problem with 'addition by subtraction': The prison-crime relation-
    ship in low-income communities." Pp. 181–93 in *Invisible Punishment: The Collateral
    Consequences of Mass Imprisonment*, edited by Marc Mauer and Meda Chesney-
    Lind. New York: New Press.

———. 2007a. "The impacts of incarceration on public safety." *Social Research: An
    International Quarterly of the Social Sciences* 74(2):613–30.

———. 2007b. *Imprisoning Communities: How Mass Incarceration Makes Disadvantaged
    Neighborhoods Worse*. New York: Oxford University Press.

———. 2008. "The effects of high imprisonment rates on communities." *Crime and
    Justice* 37:97–132.

Clear, Todd R., and James Austin. 2009. "Reducing mass incarceration: Implications of
    the iron law of prison populations." *Harvard Law and Policy Review* 3:307–24.

Clear, Todd R., George F. Cole, and Michael D. Reisig. 2010. *American Corrections*.
    Belmont, CA: Wadsworth.

Clear, Todd R., John R. Hamilton Jr., and Eric Cadora. 2011. *Community Justice*. New
    York: Routledge.

Clear, Todd R., and Vincent O'Leary. 1983. *Controlling the Offender in the Community:
    Reforming the Community Supervision Function*. Lexington, MA: Lexington Books.

Clear, Todd R., Dina Rose, and Judith Ryder. 2001. "Incarceration and the community: The problem of removing and returning offenders." *Crime & Delinquency* 47(3):335–51.

Clear, Todd R., Dina Rose, Elin Waring, and Kristen Scully. 2003. "Coercive mobility and crime: A preliminary examination of concentrated incarceration and social disorganization." *Justice Quarterly* 20(1):33–64.

Clear, Todd R., and Dennis Schrantz. 2011. "Strategies for reducing prison populations." *Prison Journal* 91(3 suppl):138S–59S.

Clement, Marshall, Matthew Schwarzfeld, and Michael Thompson. 2011. "The National Summit on National Reinvestment and Public Safety: Addressing Recidivism, Crime, and Corrections Spending." New York: Council of State Governments Justice Center.

Clinton, William J. 1996. "Address before a Joint Session of the Congress on the State of the Union." *The American Presidency Project*, http://www.presidency.ucsb.edu/ws/index.php?pid=53091 , accessed 3/6/2013.

Coalition for Higher Education Act Reform. 2006. "Falling through the Cracks: Loss of State-Based Financial Aid Eligibility for Students Affected by the Federal Higher Education Act Drug Provision." Washington, DC: Coalition for Higher Education Act Reform.

Cohen, Stanley. 1985. *Visions of Social Control: Crime, Punishment, and Classification.* New York: Polity.

Council of State Governments. 2010. "Justice Reinvestment: Connecticut." Washington, DC: Council of State Governments.

Cullen, Francis T. 1995. "Assessing the penal harm movement." *Journal of Research in Crime and Delinquency* 32:338–58.

Cullen, Francis T., Bonnie S. Fisher, and Brandon K. Applegate. 2000. "Public opinion about punishment and corrections." *Crime and Justice* 27:1–79.

Cullen, Francis T., and Karen E. Gilbert. 1982. *Reaffirming Rehabilitation.* Cincinnati, OH: Anderson.

Cullen, Francis T., Paula Smith, Christopher T. Lowenkamp, and Edward J. Latessa. 2009. "Nothing works revisited: Deconstructing Farabee's *Rethinking Rehabilitation.*" *Victims & Offenders* 4(2):101–23.

Daniels, Norman. 2006. "Toward ethical review of health system transformations." *American Journal of Public Health* 96(3):447–51.

Darity, William A., Samuel Myers Jr., Emmitt Carson, and William J. Sabol. 1994. *The Black Underclass: Critical Essays on Race and Unwantedness.* New York: Garland.

DeFina, Robert, and Thomas M. Arvanites. 2002. "The weak effect of imprisonment on crime: 1971–1998." *Social Science Quarterly* 83(3):635–53.

DeFina, Robert, and Lance Hannon. 2009. "The impact of mass incarceration on poverty." *Crime & Delinquency* (Online First), Feb. 12, http://cad.sagepub.com/content/early/recent.

———. 2010a. "For incapacitation, there is no time like the present: The lagged effects of prisoner reentry on property and violent crime rates." *Social Science Research* 39:1004–1014.

———. 2010b. "The impact of adult incarceration on child poverty: A county-level analysis, 1995–2007." *Prison Journal* 90(4):377–96.

Department of Housing and Urban Development v. Rucker. 535 U.S. 125 (2001).

DiIulio, John J. Jr. 1996a. "My black crime problem, and ours." *City Journal,* Spring. http://www.city-journal.org/html/6_2_my_black.html.

———. 1996b. "Prisons are a bargain, by any measure." *New York Times,* Jan. 16, A17.

———. 1999. "Against mandatory minimums: Drug sentencing run amok." *National Review,* May 17, 46–51.

DiIulio, John J. Jr., and Anne Morrison Piehl. 1991. "Does prison pay? The stormy national debate over the cost-effectiveness of imprisonment." *Brookings Review* (Fall): 28–35.

———. 1995. "Does prison pay? Revisited." *Brookings Review* (Winter):20–26.

Ditton, Paula M., and Doris James Wilson. 1999. "Truth in Sentencing in State Prisons." Washington, DC: Bureau of Justice Statistics.

Dolovich, Sharon. 2009. "Confronting the costs of incarceration. Foreword: Incarceration American-style." *Harvard Law and Policy Review* 3:237–59.

Donohue, John J. III. 2009. "Assessing the relative benefits of incarceration: Overall changes and the benefits on the margin." Pp. 269–341 in *Do Prisons Make Us Safer? The Benefits and Costs of the Prison Boom,* edited by Steven Raphael and Michael A. Stoll. New York: Russell Sage Foundation.

Donziger, Steven (Ed.). 1996. *The Real War on Crime: The Report of the National Criminal Justice Commission.* New York: HarperPerennial.

Durlauf, Steven N., and Daniel S. Nagin. 2011. "Imprisonment and crime: Can both be reduced?" *Criminology & Public Policy* 10(1):13–54.

Edin, Kathryn, Timothy Nelson, and Rechelle Paranal. 2004. "Fatherhood and incarceration as potential turning points in the criminal careers of unskilled men." In *Imprisoning America: The Social Effects of Mass Incarceration,* edited by Mary Patillo, David F. Weiman, and Bruce Western. New York: Russell Sage Foundation.

Fagan, Jeffrey. 2004. "Crime, law, and the community: Dynamics of incarceration in New York City." Pp. 27–59 in *The Future of Imprisonment,* edited by Michael Tonry. New York: Oxford University Press.

Fagan, Jeffrey, and Tracey L. Meares. 2008. "Punishment, deterrence, and social control: The paradox of punishment in minority communities." *Ohio State Journal of Criminal Law* 6:173–229.

Families Against Mandatory Minimums. 2009. "Federal Mandatory Minimums." Washington, DC: Families Against Mandatory Minimums.

———. 2011. "State Responses to Mandatory Minimum Laws." Washington, DC: Families Against Mandatory Minimums.

Farabee, David. 2005. *Rethinking Rehabilitation: Why Can't We Reform Our Criminals.* Washington, DC: AEI Press.

Farrington, David P., Jeremy W. Coid, and Joseph Murray. 2009. "Family factors in the intergenerational transmission of offending." *Criminal Behaviour & Mental Health* 19(2):109–24.

Feeley, Malcolm M. 2003. "Crime, social order, and the rise of neo-conservative politics." *Theoretical Criminology* 7(1):111–30.

Feucht, Thomas E., and Edwin Zedlewski. 2007. "The 40th anniversary of the crime report." *NIJ Journal* 257:20–23.

Fox, James Alan. 1992. "Crime: The young and the ruthless." *Chicago Tribune*, Jan. 10.

Frankl, Marvin. 1974. *Criminal Sentences: Law without Order*. New York: Hill and Wang.

Frase, Richard. 1995. "State sentencing guidelines: Still going strong." *Judicature* 78:173–79.

———. 2000. "Is guided discretion sufficient? Overview of state sentencing guidelines." *St. Louis University Law Journal* 44:425–46.

Freeman, Richard. 1998. "Is the new income inequality the Achilles heel of the American economy?" Pp. 219–29 in *The Inequality Paradox: Growth of Income Disparity*, edited by James A. Auerbach and Richard S. Belous. Washington, DC: National Policy Association.

Frost, Natasha A. 2006a. "Mandatory minimum sentencing." *Criminology & Public Policy* 5(1):1–4.

———. 2006b. *The Punitive State: Crime, Punishment, and Imprisonment across the United States*. New York: LFB Scholarly Publications.

———. 2008. "The mismeasure of punishment: Alternative measures of punitiveness and their (substantial) consequences." *Punishment & Society* 10(3):277–300.

———. 2011. "Reentry as a process rather than a moment." Pp. 159–82 in *U.S. Criminal Justice Policy: A Contemporary Reader*, edited by Karim Ismaili. Sudbury, MA: Jones and Bartlett Learning.

Frost, Natasha A., and Todd R. Clear. 2009. "Understanding mass incarceration as a grand social experiment." *Studies in Law, Politics, and Society* 47:159–91.

———. 2012a. "Coercive mobility." Pp. 691–708 in *Oxford Handbook of Criminological Theory*, edited by Francis T. Cullen and Pamela Wilcox. New York: Oxford University Press.

———. 2012b. "New directions in correctional research." *Justice Quarterly* 29(5):619–49.

Frost, Natasha A., Judy Greene, and Kevin Pranis. 2006. *Hard Hit: Growth in the Imprisonment of Women, 1977–2004*. New York: Women's Prison Association.

Frost, Natasha A., and Laura A. Gross. 2012. "Coercive mobility and the impact of prison cycling on crime." *Crime, Law, and Social Change* 57(5):459–74.

Gallup Inc. 2012. "Most Important Problem." Gallup Inc.

Garland, David. 1985. *Punishment and Welfare: A History of Penal Strategies*. Brookfield, VT: Gower.

———. 1990. *Punishment and Modern Society: A Study in Social Theory*. Chicago: University of Chicago Press.

———. 2001. *The Culture of Control: Crime and Social Order in Contemporary Society*. Chicago: University of Chicago Press.

———. 2007. "The peculiar forms of American capital punishment." *Social Research: An International Quarterly of the Social Sciences* 74(2):435–64.

———. 2010. *Peculiar Institution: America's Death Penalty in an Age of Abolition*: Cambridge, MA: Harvard University Press.

Gendreau, Paul, Claire Goggin, and Francis T. Cullen. 1999. "The Effects of Prison Sentences on Recidivism." Ottawa, Canada: Public Works and Services of Canada.

Gest, Ted. 2001. *Crime and Politics: Big Government's Erratic Campaign for Law and Order*. New York: Oxford University Press.

Ginzberg, Eli, and Robert M. Solow (Eds.). 1974. *The Great Society: Lessons for the Future*. New York: Basic Books.

Glaze, Lauren. 2011. "Correctional Populations in the United States, 2010." Washington, DC: Bureau of Justice Statistics.

Glaze, Lauren E., and Thomas P. Bonczar. 2009. "Probation and Parole in the United States: 2007 Statistical Tables." Washington, DC: Bureau of Justice Statistics.

———. 2011. "Probation and Parole in the United States, 2010." Washington, DC: Bureau of Justice Statistics.

Gordon, Diana. 1990. *The Justice Juggernaut: Fighting Street Crime, Controlling Citizens*. New Brunswick, NJ: Rutgers University Press.

Gotsch, Kara. 2011. "Breakthrough in U.S. Drug Sentencing Reform: The Fair Sentencing Act and the Unfinished Reform Agenda." Washington, DC: Washington Office on Latin America.

Gottfredson, Stephen D., and Don M. Gottfredson. 1990. "Classification, Prediction, and Criminal Justice Policy: Final Report to the National Institute of Justice." Washington, DC: National Institute of Justice.

Gottschalk, Marie. 2006. *The Prison and the Gallows: The Politics of Mass Incarceration in America*. New York: Cambridge University Press.

———. 2007. "Dollars, sense, and penal reform: Social movements and the future of the carceral state." *Social Research: An International Quarterly of the Social Sciences* 74(2):669–94.

———. 2009. "Money and mass incarceration: The bad, the mad, and penal reform." *Criminology & Public Policy* 8(1):97–109.

———. 2010. "Cell blocks and red ink: Mass incarceration, the great recession, and penal reform." *Daedalus* 139(3):62–73.

Grattet, Ryken, Joan Petersilia, and Jeffrey Lin. 2008. "Parole Violations and Revocations in California." Washington, DC: U.S. Department of Justice.

Gray, Steven. 2011. "Why Mississippi is reversing its prison policy." *Time*, June 10.

Greenberg, David H., Donna Kinksz, and Marvin Mandell. 2003. *Social Experimentation and Public Policymaking*. Washington, DC: Urban Institute Press.

Greenberg, David H., and Mark Shroder. 2004. *The Digest of Social Experiments*. Washington, DC: Urban Institute Press.

Greenberg, David H., and Valerie West. 2001. "State prison populations and their growth, 1971–1991." *Criminology* 39(3):615–54.

Greene, Judith. 2003. "Smart on Crime: Positive Trends in State-Level Sentencing and Correctional Policy." Washington, DC: Families Against Mandatory Minimums.

Greene, Judith, and Marc Mauer. 2010. "Downscaling Prisons: Lessons from Four States." Washington, DC: Sentencing Project.

Greenwood, Peter, and Allan Abrahamse. 1982. *Selective Incapacitation*. Santa Monica, CA: RAND.

Greenwood, Peter, C. Peter Rydell, Allan F. Abrahamse, Jonathan P. Caulkins, James Chiesa, Karyn E. Model, and Stephen P. Klein. 1996. "Estimated benefits and costs of California's new mandatory-sentencing law." Pp. 53–90 in *Three Strikes and You're Out: Vengeance as Public Policy*, edited by David Schicor and Dale K. Sechrest. Thousand Oaks, CA: Sage.

Guerino, Paul, Paige M. Harrison, and William J. Sabol. 2011. "Prisoners in 2010." Washington, DC: Bureau of Justice Statistics.

Hagan, John. 2010. *Who Are the Criminals? The Politics of Crime Policy from the Age of Roosevelt to the Age of Reagan*. Princeton, NJ: Princeton University Press.

Hagan, John, and Ronit Dinovitzer. 1999. "Collateral consequences of imprisonment for children, communities, and prisoners." Pp. 121–62 in *Prisons*, edited by Michael Tonry and Joan Petersilia. Chicago: University of Chicago Press.

Hagan, John, Carla Shedd, and Monique R. Payne. 2005. "Race, ethnicity, and youth perceptions of criminal injustice." *American Sociological Review* 70:381–407.

Hannon, Lance, and Robert DeFina. 2012. "Sowing the seeds: How adult incarceration promotes juvenile delinquency." *Law, Crime, and Social Change* 57:475–91.

Harrington, Michael. 1962. *The Other America*. New York: Macmillan.

Harris, John F. 1996. "Clinton links housing aid to eviction of crime suspects." *Washington Post*, March 29, A14.

Harrison, Paige M., and Allen J. Beck. 2006. "Prisoners in 2005." Washington, DC: Bureau of Justice Statistics.

Harrison, Paige M., and Jennifer C. Karberg. 2003. "Prison and Jail Inmates at Midyear 2002." Washington, DC: Bureau of Justice Statistics.

Harvard Law Review. 1996. "Prevention vs. punishment: Toward a principled distinction in the restraint of released sex offenders." *Harvard Law Review* 109(7):1711–28.

Hawken, Angela, and Mark A. R. Kleiman. 2009. "Managing Drug-Involved Probationers with Swift and Certain Sanctions: Evaluating Hawaii's HOPE." Washington, DC: National Institute of Justice.

Herman, Susan. 2010. *Parallel Justice for Victims of Crime*. Washington, DC: National Center for Victims of Crime.

Holzer, Harry J. 2009. "Collateral costs: Effects of incarceration on employment and earnings among young workers." Pp. 239–65 in *Do Prisons Make Us Safer? The Benefits and Costs of the Prison Boom*, edited by Steven Raphael and Michael A. Stoll. New York: Russell Sage Foundation.

Housing Opportunity Program Extensions (HOPE) Act. 1996. Public Law 104–130, 110 Stat. 834.

Huebner, Beth M. 2005. "The effect of incarceration on marriage and work over the life-course." *Justice Quarterly* 22(3):281–303.

———. 2007. "Racial and ethnic differences in the likelihood of marriage: The effect of incarceration." *Justice Quarterly* 24(1):156–83.

Hunter, Albert. 1985. "Private, parochial, and public social orders: The problem of crime and incivility in urban communities." Pp. 230–42 in *The Challenge of Social Control: Citizenship and Institution Building in Modern Society*, edited by Gerald Suttles and Mayer Zald. Norwood, NJ: Ablex.

Irwin, John. 2005. *The Warehouse Prison: Disposal of the New Dangerous Class*. Los Angeles: Roxbury.

Jacobson, Michael. 2005. *Downsizing Prisons: How to Reduce Crime and End Mass Incarceration*. New York: New York University Press.

Johnson, Glenn, and Brian R. Ballou. 2012. "Deval Patrick signs repeat offender crime bill in private State House ceremony." *Boston Globe*, Aug. 2.

Johnson, Lyndon B. 1964. "Remarks at the University of Michigan." Lyndon Baines Johnson Library and Museum; National Archives and Records Administration.

Joint Committee on New York Drug Law Evaluation. 1978. "The Nation's Toughest Drug Law: Evaluating the New York Experience." Washington, DC: U.S. Department of Justice, LEAA.

Kandel, Jason. 2012. "LA continues 9-year crime drop." NBC Southern California, Jan. 5.

Kilty, Keith M., and Elizabeth A. Segal (Eds.). 2006. *The Promise of Welfare Reform: Political Rhetoric and the Reality of Poverty in the Twenty-First Century*. Binghamton, NY: Haworth.

Kleck, Gary, Brion Sever, Spencer Li, and Marc Gertz. 2005. "The missing link in general deterrence research." *Criminology* 43(3):623–60.

Kleiman, Mark A. R. 1997. "The problem of replacement and the logic of drug law enforcement." *Drug Policy Analysis Bulletin*.

———. 2001. "Toward practical drug control policies." *Social Research* 68(3):884–90.

———. 2009. *When Brute Force Fails: How to Have Less Crime and Less Punishment*. Princeton, NJ: Princeton University Press.

———. 2010. "Toward fewer prisoners and less crime." *Daedalus* 139(3):115–23.

———. 2011. "Justice reinvestment in community supervision." *Criminology & Public Policy* 10(3):651–59.

Kopel, David P. 1994. "Prison blues: How America's foolish sentencing policies endanger public safety." In *CATO Policy Analysis* no. 208. Washington, DC: Cato Institute.

Kovandzic, Tomislav, and Lynne Vieraitis. 2006. "The effect of county-level prison population growth on crime rates." *Criminology & Public Policy* 5(2):213–44.

La Vigne, Nancy G. 2010. "Housing D.C. Code Felons Far Away from Home: Effects on Crime, Recidivism, and Reentry." In *Testimony before the House of Representatives Oversight and Government Reform Subcommittee on Federal Workforce, Postal Service, and the District of Columbia*. Washington, DC: Urban Institute.

La Vigne, Nancy G., S. Rebecca Neusteter, Pamela Lachman, Allison Dwyer, and Carey Anne Nadeau. 2010. "Justice Reinvestment at the Local Level: Planning and Implementation Guide." Washington, DC: Urban Institute.

Lancaster, Roger N. 2011. "Sex offenders: The last pariahs." *New York Times,* Aug. 21, SR6.

Langan, Patrick A. 1985. "Racism on trial: New evidence to explain the racial composition of prisons in the United States." *Journal of Criminal Law and Criminology* 76:666–83.

Latessa, Edward J. 2004. "The challenge of change: Correctional programs and evidence-based practices." *Criminology & Public Policy* 3(4):547–60.

LeBlanc, Adrian Nicole. 2004. *Random Family: Love, Drugs, Trouble, and Coming of Age in the Bronx.* New York: Scribners.

Legal Action Center. 2004. "After Prison: Roadblocks to Reentry; A Report on State Legal Barriers Facing People with Criminal Records." New York: Legal Action Center.

Leinwand, Donna. 2006. "Drug convictions costing students their financial aid." *USA Today Online,* April 17.

Lemert, Edwin M., and Forrest Dill. 1978. *The Offender in the Community.* Lexington, MA: Lexington Books.

Levitt, Steven. 1996. "The effect of prison population size on crime rates: Evidence from prison over-crowding litigation." *Quarterly Journal of Economics* 111:319–51.

Lichtenstein, Alex. 2001. "The private and the public in penal history." *Punishment & Society* 3(1):189–96.

Lieb, Roxanne, Vernon Quinsey, and Lucy Berliner. 1998. "Sexual predators and social policy." *Crime and Justice: A Review of Research* 23:43–114.

Liebling, Alison, and Shadd Maruna (Eds.). 2006. *The Effects of Imprisonment.* Cullumpton, UK: Willan.

Liedka, Raymond V., Anne Morrison Piehl, and Bert Useem. 2006. "The crime control effects of incarceration: Does scale matter?" *Criminology & Public Policy* 5(2):245–76.

Liptak, Adam. 2008. "Inmate count in U.S. dwarfs other nations." *New York Times,* April 23, A1.

Longshore, Douglas, Angela Hawken, and Darren Urada. 2006. "SACPA Cost-Analysis Report." Los Angeles: UCLA Integrated Substance Abuse Programs.

Loughran, Thomas A., Raymond Paternoster, Alex R. Piquero, and Greg Pogarsky. 2011. "On ambiguity in perceptions of risk: Implications for criminal decision making and deterrence." *Criminology* 49(4):1029–61.

Loury, Glenn C. 2008. *Race, Incarceration, and American Values.* Cambridge, MA: MIT Press.

———. 2010. "Crime, inequality, and social justice." *Daedalus* 139(3):134–40.

Lowenkamp, Christopher T., and Edward J. Latessa. 2005. "Developing successful reentry programs: Lessons learned from the 'what works' research." *Corrections Today* 67(2):72–77.

Lowenkamp, Christopher T., Edward J. Latessa, and Alexander M. Holsinger. 2006. "The risk principle in action: What have we learned from 13,676 offenders and 97 correctional programs?" *Crime & Delinquency* 52(1):77–93.

Lowenkamp, Christopher T., Edward J. Latessa, and Paula Smith. 2006. "Does correctional program quality really matter? The impact of adhering to the principles of effective intervention." *Criminology & Public Policy* 5(3):575–94.

Lucken, Karol. 2011. "Leaving mass incarceration." *Criminology & Public Policy* 10(3):707–14.

Lynch, James P., and William J. Sabol. 2001. "Prisoner Reentry in Perspective." Washington, DC: Urban Institute.

———. 2004a. "Assessing the effects of mass incarceration on informal social control in communities." *Criminology & Public Policy* 3(2):267–94.

———. 2004b. "Effects of incarceration on informal social control in communities." Pp. 135–64 in *Imprisoning America: The Social Effects of Mass Incarceration*, edited by Mary Patillo, David F. Weiman, and Bruce Western. New York: Russell-Sage.

Mannheim, Hermann. 1942. "American criminology and penology in war time." *Sociological Review* 34:222–34.

Manza, Jeff. 2000. "Political sociological models of the U.S. New Deal." *Annual Review of Sociology* 26:297–322.

Marlowe, Douglas. 2006. "When 'what works' never did: Dodging the "Scarlet M" in correctional rehabilitation." *Criminology & Public Policy* 5(2):339–46.

Martinson, Robert. 1974. "What works? Questions and answers about prison reform." *Public Interest* 35:22–54.

———. 1976. "California research at the crossroads." *Crime and Delinquency* 22(2):180–91.

Maruna, Shadd. 2011. "Reentry as a rite of passage." *Punishment & Society* 13(1):3–27.

Maruna, Shadd, and Anna King. 2009. "Once a criminal, always a criminal? 'Redeemability' and the psychology of punitive public attitudes." *European Journal of Criminal Policy and Research* 15:7–24.

Marvell, Thomas B. 1995. "Sentencing guidelines and prison population growth." *Journal of Criminal Law and Criminology* 85:696–708.

Marvell, Thomas B., and Carlisle E. Moody. 1994. "Prison population growth and crime reduction." *Journal of Quantitative Criminology* 10(2):109–40.

———. 1996. "Determinate sentencing and abolishing parole: The long-term impacts on prisons and crime." *Criminology* 34(1):107–28.

———. 1997. "The impact of prison growth on homicide." *Homicide Studies* 1:205–33.

Matthews, Roger. 2005. "The myth of punitiveness." *Theoretical Criminology* 9(2):175–201.

Mauer, Marc. 2001. "The causes and consequences of prison growth in the USA." *Punishment & Society* 3(1):9–20.

———. 2006a. "Incarceration Nation." *Tom Paine.com* (December 11), http://www.tompaine.com/articles/2006/12/11/incarceration_nation.php.

———. 2006b. *Race to Incarcerate*. New York: New Press.

Mauer, Marc, and Meda Chesney-Lind (Eds.). 2003. *Invisible Punishment: The Collateral Consequences of Mass Imprisonment*. New York: New Press.

Mears, Bill. 2011. "High court orders drastic prison population reduction in California." *CNN.com* (May 24), http://www.cnn.com/2011/CRIME/05/23/scotus.california. prisons/index.html.

Merritt, Nancy, Terry Fain, and Susan Turner. 2006. "Oregon's get-tough sentencing reform: A lesson in justice system adaptation." *Criminology & Public Policy* 5(1):5–36.

Miller, Lisa. 2008. *The Perils of Federalism: Race, Poverty, and the Politics of Crime Control.* New York: Oxford University Press.

Montana, Jenny A. 1995. "An ineffective weapon in the fight against child sexual abuse: New Jersey's Megan's Law." *Journal of Law and Policy* 3:569–604.

Morenoff, Jeffrey D., Robert J. Sampson, and Stephen W. Raudenbush. 2001. "Neighborhood inequality, collective efficacy, and the spatial dynamics of urban violence." *Criminology* 39(3):517–58.

Morris, Norval. 1965. "Prison in evolution." In *Criminology in Transition: Essays in Honour of Hermann Mannheim,* edited by Tadeusz Grygier, Howard Jones, and John C. Spencer. London: Tavistock.

Morris, Norval, and Michael H. Tonry. 1990. *Between Prison and Probation: Intermediate Punishments in a Rational Sentencing System.* New York: Oxford University Press.

Mumola, Christopher J. 2000. "Incarcerated Parents and Their Children." Washington, DC: Bureau of Justice Statistics.

Murray, Charles A. 1997. *Does Prison Work?* London: Institute of Economic Affairs.

Murray, Joseph. 2005. "The effects of imprisonment on the families and children of prisoners." In *The Effects of Imprisonment,* edited by Alison Liebling and Shadd Maruna. Cullompton, UK: Willan.

Murray, Joseph, and David Farrington. 2008. "The effects of parental imprisonment on children." *Crime and Justice* 37:133–206.

Murray, Joseph, David Farrington, Ivana Sekol, and Rikke F. Olsen. 2009. "Parental incarceration: Effects on children's antisocial behaviour and mental health; A systematic review." *Campbell Systematic Reviews* 4.

Nagin, Daniel S. 1998. "Criminal deterrence research at the outset of the twenty-first century." *Crime and Justice* 23:1–42.

Nagin, Daniel S., and Greg Pogarsky. 2001. "Integrating celerity, impulsivity, and extralegal sanction threats into a model of general deterrence: Theory and evidence." *Criminology* 39(4):865–91.

———. 2003. "An experimental investigation of deterrence: Cheating, self-servicing bias, and impulsivity." *Criminology* 41(1):167–93.

Nellis, Ashley. 2010. "Throwing away the key: The expansion of life without parole sentences in the United States." *Federal Sentencing Reporter* 23(1):27–32.

Nellis, Ashley, and Ryan S. King. 2009. "No Exit: The Expanding Use of Life Sentences in America." Washington, DC: Sentencing Project.

New York State Bar Association. 2006. "Reentry and Reintegration: The Road to Public Safety." Albany: New York State Bar Association.

New York State Department of Correctional Services. 2010. "Under Custody Report: Profile of Inmate Population under Custody on January 1, 2010." Albany: New York State Department of Corrections and Community Services.

NGA Center for Best Practices. 2011. "Issue Brief: State Efforts in Sentencing and Corrections Reform." Washington, DC: National Governors Association.

Nguyen, Alexander. 2001. "Bill Clinton's death penalty waffle." *American Prospect* (December 19), http://prospect.org/article/bill-clintons-death-penalty-waffle, accessed 3/6/2013.

Nicholson-Crotty, Sean. 2004. "The impact of sentencing guidelines on state-level sanctions: An analysis over time." *Crime & Delinquency* 50(3):395–411.

Oppel, Richard A. 2011. "Steady decline in major crime baffles experts." *New York Times,* May 24, A17.

Page, Joshua. 2004. "Eliminating the enemy: The import of denying prisoners access to higher education in Clinton's America." *Punishment & Society* 6(4):357–78.

Pager, Devah. 2007. *Marked: Race, Crime, and Finding Work in an Era of Mass Incarceration.* Chicago: University of Chicago Press.

Parenti, Christian. 1999. *Lockdown America: Police and Prisons in the Age of Crisis.* New York: Verso.

Paternoster, Raymond. 1989. "Decisions to participate in and desist from four types of common delinquency: Deterrence and the rational choice perspective." *Law & Society Review* 23(1):7–40.

Patillo, Mary, David F. Weiman, and Bruce Western (Eds.). 2004. *Imprisoning America: The Social Effects of Mass Incarceration.* New York: Russell Sage Foundation.

Petersilia, Joan. 1990. "When probation becomes more dreaded than prison." *Federal Probation* 54(1):23–27.

———. 2003. *When Prisoners Come Home: Parole and Prisoner Reentry.* New York: Oxford University Press.

———. 2005. "From cell to society." Pp. 15–49 in *Prisoner Reentry and Crime in America,* edited by Jeremy Travis and Christy Visher. New York: Cambridge University Press.

———. 2006. "Understanding California Corrections: A Policy Research Program Report." Berkeley: California Policy Research Center.

———. 2008. "California's correctional paradox of excess and deprivation." *Crime and Justice* 37:207–78.

Petersilia, Joan, and Susan Turner. 1990. "Intensive Supervision for High-Risk Probationers: Findings from Three California Experiments." Santa Monica, CA: RAND.

———. 1993. "Intensive probation and parole." *Crime and Justice: A Review of Research* 17:281–336.

Pew Center on the States. 2007. "When Offenders Break the Rules: Smart Responses to Parole and Probation Violations." Washington, DC: Pew Charitable Trusts.

———. 2008. "1 in 100: Behind Bars in America 2008." Washington, DC: Pew Charitable Trusts.

———. 2009. "One in 31: The Long Reach of Corrections." Washington, DC: Pew Charitable Trusts.

———. 2010. "State Population Declines for the First Time in 38 Years." Washington, DC: Pew Charitable Trusts.

———. 2011. "State of Recidivism: The Revolving Door of America's Prisons." Washington, DC: Pew Charitable Trusts.

———. 2012. "2012 Georgia Public Safety Reform: Legislation to Reduce Recidivism and Cut Corrections Costs." Washington, DC: Pew Charitable Trusts.

Piehl, Anne Morrison, Bert Useem, and John J. DiIulio Jr. 1999. *Right-Sizing Justice: A Cost-Benefit Analysis of Imprisonment in Three States*. New York: Manhattan Institute.

Pierce, Glenn L., and William J. Bowers. 1981. "The Bartley-Fox gun law's short-term impact on crime in Massachusetts." *Annals of the American Academy of Political and Social Science* 455:120–37.

Pinard, Michael. 2010. "Reflections and perspectives on reentry and collateral consequences." *Journal of Criminal Law & Criminology* 100(3):1213–24.

Piven, Frances Fox. 2002. "Remarks: Transcript from Conference Proceedings, New York City and the New Deal." New York: Gotham Center for New York City History.

Piven, Frances Fox, and Richard A. Cloward. 1993. *Regulating the Poor: The Functions of Public Welfare*. 2nd edition. New York: Vintage.

Porter, Nicole D. 2011. "On the Chopping Block: State Prison Closings." Washington, DC: Sentencing Project.

Pratt, Travis C. 2009. *Addicted to Incarceration: Corrections Policy and the Politics of Misinformation in the United States*. Thousand Oaks, CA: Sage.

Prentky, Robert A. 1997. "Community notification and constructive risk reduction." *Journal of Interpersonal Violence* 11(2):295–98.

President's Commission on Law Enforcement and Administration of Justice. 1967. "The Challenge of Crime in a Free Society." Edited by President's Commission on Law Enforcement and Administration of Justice. Washington, DC: United States Government Printing Office.

Presser, Lois, and Elaine Gunnison. 1999. "Strange bedfellows: Is sex offender notification a form of community justice?" *Crime & Delinquency* 45(3):299–315.

Public Safety Performance Project. 2007. "Public Safety, Public Spending: Forecasting America's Prison Population, 2007–2011." Washington, DC: Pew Charitable Trusts.

Quality Housing and Work Responsibility Act. 1998. Public Law 105-276, Title V.

Raphael, Steven, and Michael A. Stoll (Eds.). 2009a. *Do Prisons Make Us Safer? The Benefits and Costs of the Prison Boom*. Washington, DC: Russell Sage Foundation.

———. 2009b. "Why are so many Americans in prison?" Pp. 27–72 in *Do Prisons Make Us Safer? The Benefits and Costs of the Prison Boom*, edited by Steven Raphael and Michael A. Stoll. Washington, DC: Russell Sage Foundation.

Rauchway, Eric. 2008. *The Great Depression and the New Deal: A Very Short Introduction*. New York: Oxford University Press.

Reiss, Albert J., and Jeffrey A. Roth (Eds.). 1993. *Understanding and Preventing Violence: Panel on the Understanding and Control of Violent Behavior.* Washington, DC: National Academy of Sciences.

Reitz, Kevin R. 2001. "The disassembly and reassembly of U.S. sentencing practices." Pp. 222–58 in *Sentencing and Sanctions in Western Countries,* edited by Michael Tonry and Richard S. Frase. New York: Oxford University Press.

———. 2006. "Don't blame determinacy: U.S. incarceration growth has been driven by other forces." *Texas Law Review* 84:1784–802.

Rengifo, Andres F. 2007. "Neighborhood Effects and Informal Social Control: Examining the Role of Social Networks on the South Bronx." New York: City University of New York.

Reuter, Peter. 2008. "Assessing U.S. drug policy and providing a base for future decisions. Statement to the U.S. Congress, Joint Economic Committee, Hearing, June 18, 2008." In *Illegal Drugs: Economic Impact, Societal Costs, Policy Responses.* Washington, DC: U.S. Congress, Joint Economic Committee.

Reynolds, Morgan O. 1997. "Punishment Up, Crime Down." Chicago: Heartland Institute, http://heartland.org/policy-documents/punishment-crime-down.

Right on Crime. 2010. "Statement of Principles." Austin: Texas Public Policy Foundation.

Roman, Caterina Gouvis, and Jeremy Travis. 2004. "Taking Stock: Housing, Homelessness, and Prisoner Reentry." Washington, DC: Urban Institute.

Rose, Dina, and Todd R. Clear. 1998. "Incarceration, social capital, and crime: Implications for social disorganization theory." *Criminology* 36:441–80.

———. 2004. "Who doesn't know someone in jail? The impact of exposure to prison on attitudes toward informal and formal controls." *Prison Journal* 84(2):228–47.

Rose, Dina, Todd R. Clear, and Judith Ryder. 2000. "Drugs, Incarceration and Neighborhood Life: The Impact of Reintegrating Offenders into the Community." Washington, DC: National Institute of Justice.

Rothman, David J. 1990/1971. *The Discovery of the Asylum: Social Order and Disorder in the New Republic.* Boston: Little, Brown.

———. 2002. *Conscience and Convenience: The Asylum and Its Alternatives in Progressive America.* New York: de Gruyter.

Rucker v. Davis. 237 F.3d 1113 (2001).

Rubinstein, Gwen, and Debbie Mukamal. 2002. "Welfare and housing: Denial of benefits to drug offenders." Pp. 37–49 in *Invisible Punishment: The Collateral Consequences of Mass Imprisonment,* edited by Marc Mauer and Meda Chesney-Lind. New York: New Press.

Ruess, Michelle. 1994. "Megan's Law signed by governor." *The Record,* Nov. 1, A1.

Saad, Lydia. 2011, March 21. "Americans' Worries about Economy, Budget Top Other Issues: Worry about Energy Up since 2010, Flat for Other Issues." Washington, DC: Gallup.

Sabol, William J., and James P. Lynch. 2003. "Assessing the longer-run effects of incarceration: Impact on families and employment." In *Crime Control and Social Justice:*

The Delicate Balance, edited by Darnell Hawkins, Samuel Myers Jr., and Randolph Stine. Westport, CT: Greenwood.

Sabol, William J., Katherine Rosich, Kamala Mallik-Kane, David P. Kirk, and Glenn Dubin. 2002. "The Influences of Truth-in-Sentencing Reforms on Changes in States' Sentencing Practices and Prison Populations." Washington, DC: Urban Institute.

Sabol, William J., Heather C. West, and Matthew Cooper. 2009. "Prisoners in 2008." Washington, DC: Bureau of Justice Statistics.

Sampson, Robert J., and Charles Loeffler. 2010. "Punishment's place: The local concentration of mass incarceration." *Daedalus* 139(3):20–31.

Sampson, Robert J., Jeffrey D. Morenoff, and Thomas Gannon-Rowley. 2002. "Assessing neighborhood effects: Social processes and new directions in research." *Annual Review of Sociology* 28(1):443–78.

Savage, Charlie. 2011. "Trend to lighten sentences catches on in conservative states." *New York Times,* Aug. 13.

Savelsberg, Joachim. 1992. "Law that does not fit society: Sentencing guidelines as neoclassical reaction to the dilemmas of substantivized law." *American Journal of Sociology* 97:1346–81.

Schirmer, Sarah, Ashley Nellis, and Marc Mauer. 2009. "Incarcerated Parents and Their Children: Trends, 1991–2007." Washington, DC: Sentencing Project.

Schmitt, John, Kris Warner, and Sarika Gupta. 2010. "The High Budgetary Cost of Incarceration." Washington, DC: Center for Economic and Policy Research.

Shaw, Clifford Robe, and Henry D. McKay. 1942. *Juvenile Delinquency and Urban Areas.* Chicago: University of Chicago Press.

Shea, Christopher. 2007. "Life sentence." *Boston Globe,* Sept. 23, E1.

Sherman, Lawrence W., and Heather Strang. 2007. "Restorative Justice: The Evidence." London: Smith Institute.

Siegel, Ralph. 1994. "Suspect admits killing girl." Hackensack, NJ *Record,* Aug. 2, A1, A4.

Simon, Jonathan. 1993. *Poor Discipline: Parole and the Social Control of the Underclass, 1890–1990.* Chicago: University of Chicago Press.

———. 2007. *Governing through Crime: How the War on Crime Transformed American Democracy and Created a Culture of Fear.* New York: Oxford University Press.

———. 2010. "Clearing the 'troubled assets' of America's punishment bubble." *Daedalus* 139(3):91–101.

Sitkoff, Harvard. 2009. *A New Deal for Blacks: Thirtieth Anniversary Edition.* New York: Oxford University Press.

Smith, Tom. 2007. "Trends in National Spending Priorities, 1973–2006." Chicago: University of Chicago, National Opinion Research Center.

Socia, Kelly M. 2011. "The policy implications of residence restrictions on sex offender housing in Upstate NY." *Criminology & Public Policy* 10(2):351–89.

"Social experiments." 1935. *Saturday Evening Post,* Aug. 10, 22.

Special Council on Criminal Justice Reform for Georgians. 2011. "Report of the Special Council on Criminal Justice Reform for Georgians." Atlanta: Georgia General Assembly.

Spelman, William. 2000a. "The limited importance of prison expansion." Pp. 97–129 in *The Crime Drop in America*, edited by Alfred Blumstein and Joel Wallman. New York: Cambridge University Press.

———. 2000b. "What recent studies do (and don't) tell us about imprisonment and crime." Pp. 419–94 in *Crime and Justice: A Review of Research*, edited by Michael Tonry. Chicago: University of Chicago Press.

Statistical Analysis Center. 1991. "Impact of the New Drug Trafficking Law on the Delaware Criminal Justice System." Washington, DC: National Criminal Justice Reference Service.

Stemen, Don. 2007. "Reconsidering Incarceration: New Directions for Reducing Crime." New York: VERA Institute of Justice.

Stemen, Don, Andres Rengifo, and James Wilson. 2006. "Of Fragmentation and Ferment: The Impact of State Sentencing Policies on Incarceration Rates, 1975–2002." Washington, DC: Final Report to the U.S. Department of Justice.

Subramanian, Ram, and Rebecca Tublitz. 2012. "Realigning Justice Resources: A Review of Population and Spending Shifts in Prison and Community Corrections." New York: Vera Institute of Justice.

Taxman, Faye S., Matthew L. Perdoni, and Lana D. Harrison. 2007. "Drug treatment services for adult offenders: The state of the state." *Journal of Substance Abuse and Treatment* 32(3):239–54.

Taylor, Ralph B. 2000. *Breaking Away from Broken Windows: Baltimore Neighborhoods and the Nationwide Fight against Crime, Grime, Fear, and Decline*. Boulder, CO: Westview.

Taylor, Ralph B., Phillip W. Harris, Peter R. Jones, Doris Weiland, R. Marie Garcia, and Eric S. McCord. 2009. "Short-term changes in adult arrest rates influence later short-term changes in serious male delinquency prevalence: A time-dependent relationship." *Criminology* 47(3):657–97.

Telpner, Brian. 1997. "Constructing safe communities: Megan's law and the purposes of punishment." *Georgetown Law Journal* 85(6):2039–68.

Tewksbury, Richard. 2002. "Validity and utility of the Kentucky sex offender registry." *Federal Probation* 66(1):21–26.

The Commonwealth of Massachusetts Executive Office of Public Safety and Security. 2011, January 12. "Official Review of the Cinelli Case for the Office of the Governor." Boston, MA: Executive Office of Public Safety and Security.

Thomas, Adam. 2005. "The Old Ball and Chain: Unlocking the Correlation between Incarceration and Marriage." Unpublished manuscript. Cambridge, MA: Harvard University.

Thomas, James C., and Lynne A. Sampson. 2005. "High rates of incarceration as a social force associated with community rates of sexually transmitted infection." *Journal of Infectious Diseases* 191:S55–S60.

Thomas, James C., and Elizabeth Torrone. 2006. "Incarceration as forced migration: Effects on selected community health outcomes." *American Journal of Public Health* 96(10):1–5.

Thompson, Anthony C. 2008. *Releasing Prisoners, Redeeming Communities: Reentry, Race, and Politics*. New York: New York University Press.

Tocqueville, Alexis de. 1990. *Democracy in America, Volume 1*. New York: Vintage.

Tonry, Michael. 1993. "The success of Judge Frankel's sentencing commission." *University of Colorado Law Review* 64:713–22.

———. 1995. *Malign Neglect: Race, Crime, and Punishment in America*. New York: Oxford University Press.

———. 1996. *Sentencing Matters*. New York: Oxford University Press.

———. 2001. "Punishment policies and patterns in western countries." Pp. 3–28 in *Sentencing and Sanctions in Western Countries*, edited by Michael Tonry and Richard S. Frase. New York: Oxford University Press.

——— (Ed.). 2004a. *The Future of Imprisonment*. New York: Oxford University Press.

———. 2004b. "Has the prison a future?" Pp. 3–24 in *The Future of Imprisonment*, edited by Michael Tonry. New York: Oxford University Press.

———. 2004c. *Thinking about Crime: Sense and Sensibility in American Penal Culture*. New York: Oxford University Press.

———. 2006. "Criminology, mandatory minimums, and public policy." *Criminology & Public Policy* 5(1):45–56.

———. 2007. "Looking back to see the future of punishment in America." *Social Research: An International Quarterly of the Social Sciences* 74(2):353–78.

———. 2009. "Explanations of American punishment policies." *Punishment & Society* 11(3):377–94.

———. 2011. *Punishing Race: A Continuing American Dilemma*. New York: Oxford University Press.

Travis, Jeremy. 2002. "Invisible punishment: An instrument of social exclusion." Pp. 15–36 in *Invisible Punishment: The Collateral Consequences of Mass Imprisonment*, edited by Marc Mauer and Meda Chesney-Lind. New York: New Press.

———. 2005. *But They All Come Back: Facing the Challenges of Prisoner Reentry*. Washington, DC: Urban Institute Press.

Travis, Jeremy, and Christy Ann Visher (Eds.). 2005. *Prisoner Reentry and Crime in America*. New York: Cambridge University Press.

Tucker, Susan, and Eric Cadora. 2003. "Justice reinvestment." *Ideas for an Open Society* 13(3).

Turner, Susan, Peter Greenwood, Terry Fain, and James R. Chiesa. 2006. "An evaluation of the federal government's violent offender incarceration and truth-in-sentencing incentive grants." *The Prison Journal* 86(3):364–85.

Turner, Susan, Joan Petersilia, and Elizabeth Piper Deschenes. 1992. "Evaluating intensive supervision probation/parole (ISP) for drug offenders." *Crime & Delinquency* 38(4):539–56.

United States Sentencing Commission. 1991. "Special Report to the Congress: Mandatory Minimum Penalties in the Federal Criminal Justice System." Washington, DC: United States Sentencing Commission.

Urban Institute. 2011. "Justice Reinvestment at the Local Level." Washington, DC: Urban Institute.

Useem, Bert, Raymond V. Liedka, and Anne Morrison Piehl. 2003. "Popular support for the prison build-up." *Punishment & Society* 5(1):5–32.

Vagins, Deborah J., and Jesselyn McCurdy. 2006. "Cracks in the System: Twenty Years of Unjust Federal Crack Cocaine Law." New York: American Civil Liberties Union.

van den Haag, Ernest. 1975. *Punishing Criminals: Concerning a Very Old and Painful Question.* New York: Basic Books.

Venkatesh, Sudhir Alladi. 2006. *Off the Books: The Underground Economy of the Urban Poor.* Cambridge, MA: Harvard University Press.

Vieraitis, Lynne, Tomislav Kovandzic, and Thomas B. Marvell. 2007. "The criminogenic effects of imprisonment: Evidence from state panel data, 1974–2002." *Criminology & Public Policy* 6(3):589–622.

Vorenberg, James. 1972. "The war on crime: The first five years." *Atlantic Monthly*, May.

Wacquant, Loic. 2005. "The great penal leap backward: Incarceration in America from Nixon to Clinton." Pp. 3–26 in *The New Punitiveness: Trends, Theories, Perspectives*, edited by John Pratt, David Brown, Mark Brown, Simon Hallsworth, and Wayne Morrison. Portland, OR: Willan.

———. 2007. *Urban Outcasts: A Comparative Sociology of Advanced Marginality.* Malden, MA: Polity.

———. 2009a. *Prisons of Poverty.* Minneapolis: University of Minnesota Press.

———. 2009b. *Punishing the Poor: The Neoliberal Government of Social Insecurity.* Durham, NC: Duke University Press.

———. 2010. "Class, race, and hyperincarceration in revanchist America." *Daedalus* 139(3):74–90.

Walker, Samuel, Cassia Spohn, and Miriam DeLone. 2008. *The Color of Justice: Race, Ethnicity, and Crime in America.* Belmont, CA: Wadsworth.

Walmsley, Roy. 2009. "World Prison Population, 8th Edition." London, UK: International Centre for Prison Studies.

Webb, Jim. 2009. "Why we must fix our prisons." *Parade Magazine*, March.

West, Heather C., and William J. Sabol. 2008. "Prisoners in 2007." Washington, DC: Bureau of Justice Statistics.

Western, Bruce. 2006. *Punishment and Inequality in America.* New York: Russell Sage Foundation.

———. 2007. "Mass imprisonment and economic inequality." *Social Research: An International Quarterly of the Social Sciences* 74(2):509–32.

Western, Bruce, and Katherine Beckett. 1999. "How unregulated is the U.S. labor market? The penal system as a labor market institution." *American Journal of Sociology* 104(4):1030–60.

Western, Bruce, Jeffrey R. Kling, and David F. Weiman. 2001. "The labor market consequences of incarceration." *Crime & Delinquency* 47(3):410–27.

Western, Bruce, Leonard M. Lopoo, and Sara McLanahan. 2004. "Incarceration and the bonds between parents in fragile families." In *Imprisoning America: The Social Effects of Mass Incarceration*, edited by Mary Pattillo, David F. Weiman, and Bruce Western. New York: Russell Sage Foundation.

Western, Bruce, and Becky Pettit. 2005. "Black-white wage inequality, employment rates, and incarceration." *American Journal of Sociology* 111(2):553–78.

———. 2010. "Incarceration and social inequality." *Daedalus* 139(3):8–19.

Whitman, James Q. 2003. *Harsh Justice: Criminal Punishment and the Widening Divide between America and Europe*. New York: Oxford University Press.

———. 2007. "What happened to Tocqueville's America?" *Social Research: An International Quarterly of the Social Sciences* 74(2):251–68.

Wilson, James A., and Robert C. Davis. 2006. "Good intentions meet hard realities: An evaluation of the Project Greenlight reentry program." *Criminology & Public Policy* 5(2):303–38.

Wilson, James Q. 1975. *Thinking about Crime*. New York: Random House.

———. 1983. "Thinking about crime: The debate over deterrence." *Atlantic Monthly*, Sept., 72–88.

Wilson, William Julius. 1996. *When Work Disappears: The World of the New Urban Poor*. New York: Random House.

Young, Jock. 1999. *The Exclusive Society: Social Exclusion, Crime, and Difference in Late Modernity*. Thousand Oaks, CA: Sage.

Young, Malcolm C. 2012. "Getting prison numbers down—for good." *The Crime Report*.

Zahn, Mary. 1998. "Notification law on sex offenders puts strains on residents, police." *Milwaukee Journal Sentinel*, March 29, 1.

Zarrella, John, and Patrick Oppmann. 2007. "Florida housing sex offenders under bridge." *Detention Ministry News*, April 5.

Zedlewski, Edwin. 1987. "Making Confinement Decisions: Research in Brief." Washington, DC: U.S. Department of Justice.

Zimring, Franklin E. 2001. "Imprisonment rates and the new politics of criminal punishment." *Punishment & Society* 3:161–66.

———. 2007. *The Great American Crime Decline*. New York: Oxford University Press.

Zimring, Franklin E., and Gordon Hawkins. 1988. "The new mathematics of imprisonment." *Crime & Delinquency* 34(4):425–36.

———. 1991. *The Scale of Imprisonment*. Chicago: University of Chicago Press.

———. 1995. *Incapacitation: Penal Confinement and the Restraint of Crime*. New York: Oxford University Press.

Zimring, Franklin E., Gordon Hawkins, and Sam Kamin. 2001. *Punishment and Democracy: Three-Strikes and You're Out in California*. New York: Oxford University Press.

ABOUT THE AUTHORS

Todd R. Clear is Dean of the School of Criminal Justice at Rutgers University. He received his Ph.D. in Criminal Justice from the University at Albany, State University of New York.

Natasha A. Frost is Associate Dean and Associate Professor in the School of Criminology and Criminal Justice at Northeastern University. She holds a Ph.D. in Criminal Justice from the City University of New York.